FOR GODS, GHOSTS AND ANCESTORS

To my mother and father

FOR GODS, GHOSTS AND ANCESTORS
The Chinese Tradition of Paper Offerings

Janet Lee Scott

UNIVERSITY OF WASHINGTON PRESS
Seattle

University of Washington Press
PO Box 50096
Seattle, WA 98145-5096, U.S.A.
www.washington.edu/uwpress

This book is published under license from Hong Kong University Press,
the University of Hong Kong, Pok Fu Lam Road, Hong Kong, China.

ISBN-13: 978-0-295-98718-7
ISBN-10: 0-295-98718-9

The paper used in this publication is acid-free.

Contents

Introduction

Some months into the formal research on paper offerings, during a visit to a retail shop in my old Kowloon neighborhood of Phoenix New Village (鳳凰新邨), a woman shopkeeper jokingly asked me and my assistant, "Why are you spending so much time trying to understand the details of these items? You young people should be doing other things rather than working so hard to get this information." While we were flattered to be described as young and hard-working, the question did make us stop for a moment and consider the reasons for studying paper offerings; after all, weren't there other, more pressing, topics to explore in Hong Kong? The sheer physical beauty of the items described in this book was certainly the first reason then and now, but it has taken time to appreciate the thoughts and actions that underlying them. One thing is certain, that after years of research, the items have never lost their fascination, and there are always new items and new ideas to consider.

Within the last fifteen years or so an increasing number of local newspaper and magazine articles, as well as television programs and radio broadcasts, have been devoted to discussions of Hong Kong's cultural heritage. While the media has often focused on antiquities such as monuments, historic buildings, and archaeological sites and the need to protect them in an environment where real estate is at a premium, the survival of traditional lifeways, arts, and crafts has also been a matter for concern. There are many ways in which this interest in Hong Kong's heritage has been expressed: in the revival of old-style restaurants and teahouses, in the re-examination of traditional foods (see, for example, Cheng 1997; Wu and Cheung 2002), and in the numbers of visitors to the museums of history, restored historic buildings and other sites.[1] This continuing appreciation of traditional Chinese culture, and concern for its preservation, did not weaken with Hong Kong's 1997 transition to a Special Administrative Region of the People's Republic of China. If anything, the post-handover period has seen a growing realization that traditional Chinese culture is significant to modern life and to the creation of contemporary identity, and that an appreciation of local history and customs is a relevant part of this awareness.

Ritual paper offerings form a particularly fascinating part of the traditional material culture of everyday life. Paper offerings are objects made of paper, many of them handmade and one of a kind, which are offered to the beings residing beyond the world of the living: the gods, the ghosts, and the ancestors (for a classic depiction of these three otherworldly entities, see Wolf 1974). Nearly all these paper items are burned in order to reach their destination in the other world. This burning is a vital component of both public and private worship during religious holidays and during everyday life. As such, the paper offerings are distinguished from other strictly secular and popular paper handicrafts such as paper-cuts (剪紙), prints and paper folding. The study of this rich and living area of traditional material culture affords an enhanced appreciation of the power of belief and traditional mores often said to be uniquely Chinese, but whose integration into modern life is not always fully appreciated.

For visitors and residents alike, one of the most satisfying aspects of life in modern Hong Kong is the celebration of the religious holidays of the lunar calendar. As the lunar year advances, the ritual cycle is regularly punctuated by these special events dedicated to the worship of gods, the appeasing of ghosts, and the commemoration of ancestors. Every month of the calendar contains at least one religious occasion, and four very popular holidays are the Lunar New Year (usually in January or February of the solar calendar); Qing Ming (清明), the grave-cleaning festival to honor the ancestors (usually in April of the solar year); Chong Yang (重陽), for honoring the ancestors and avoiding plague by climbing to a high place; and the Yu Lan (盂蘭) Festival or, as it will be referred to in this book, the Festival of the Hungry Ghosts. In between are the numerous days devoted to the birthdays or to other special days of individual deities. On the twenty-seventh day of the eighth month of the lunar year, ceremonies are held at the Wong Tai Sin Temple of Kowloon to honor the birthday of its namesake, the Great Sage Huang Da Xian (黃大仙), who will be referred to by the Hong Kong's spelling of Wong Tai Sin. The birthday of Che Gong (車公), the deified general of the Song Dynasty, celebrated on the third day of the Lunar New Year, attracts tens of thousands of worshippers to his temple in Sha Tin (沙田), and many devotees of the great female deities Guan Yin (觀音), the Goddess of Mercy, and Tian Hou (天后), the Empress of Heaven, celebrate their birthdays and other special days in grand style.

Each of these festivals is accompanied by splendid examples of paper offerings. The most colorful event of the calendar, the Lunar New Year, brings forth a great variety of items. Not only do shops sell the everyday offerings for worshipping the gods, but shops and temples also sell huge quantities of the special items that secure blessings and protection for the coming year: the intricate Pinwheels and the magnificent Golden Flowers with their accompanying red silk banners. The New Year is considered the best time to purchase the Golden Flowers which will adorn the images of the deities on both domestic and temple altars, and many households believe that purchasing a new Pinwheel during the New Year worship at the temple will keep the family safe and secure. The birthdays of the gods also bring out beautiful examples of clothing and accessories (for it is right to honor deities with gifts of adornment), and very special creations such as the towering and brilliantly colored Flower Cannons. Ancestors are honored during Qing Ming with large packages of Gold and Silver Paper and clothing, as well as any special item the family wishes to send, and during the Festival of the Hungry Ghosts, the unhappy ghosts are succored with ever more complicated bundles of money and clothing.

Paper offerings are not restricted to the special events of the lunar calendar, for worship is a daily occurrence, and can be devoted to more private concerns. Difficult circumstances — such as illness, moving to a new home, or beginning a new business — can be eased with rituals accompanied by special-purpose paper offerings. Deities may be worshipped or the ghosts of strangers fed any day of the year, while ancestors are remembered by an ever-changing array of items to ease their lives in the next world. Sending offerings to deceased kin helps to maintain the relationships among kinsmen, and ensures that the deceased will continue to enjoy the same comforts of life enjoyed while on earth. One may see at the curbside or at street corners, tall metal containers full of ashes, charred sticks, and fluttering bits of colored paper. These remnants of burned materials are funeral offerings for a relative and speak to the strength of traditional responsibilities and practices in this modern metropolis.

Given the great variety of paper offerings, it seems that there are few events or situations to which they could not be applied, to ease concerns or to get help in securing a desired outcome. The use of paper offerings in worship is a meaningful component of popular religious expression in Hong Kong (Liu 2003), one that has endured and adapted to a thoroughly modern, sophisticated and rapidly changing urbanized environment. This book will introduce a selection of the paper offerings currently available in Hong Kong, examining their designs and meanings, and how they are crafted, sold, and used in the contexts of everyday life. Personal and professional concerns and knowledge about offerings will be explored through the results of numerous discussions with the paper masters who craft the offerings, the shopkeepers who sell them, and the ordinary people who burn them. Their thoughts about the purposes of offerings and why they are meaningful, and their explanations of the ways in which offerings are used, will help the outsider better understand the beauty and complexity of this world of paper.

Discovering the Offerings

I became fascinated by ritual paper offerings during my first field visit to Hong Kong in the late 1970s, while conducting doctoral dissertation research[2] on women's networks and participation in the Mutual Aid Committees (popularly known as MACs, 互助委員會) of Kowloon. As this research took me into many of the public housing estates and older neighborhoods, I soon became aware that in these places there was yet another very interesting entity, something called a paper shop (衣紙舖). These shops were easy to spot, for even at a distance one could see the array of brightly colored paper items, three-dimensional objects, red ribbons and all kinds of wonderful things, hanging from the awnings and out over the sidewalks. One only had to look down the length of any street and scan the upper doorways of the shops to locate them, and I soon became a skilled spotter. A number of paper shops were also operating in the public housing estates where I conducted research on the MACs, so it became a habit to stop in after an interview to see what was available. It was simply impossible to ignore the wonderful things inside, although at that time I had only a general conception about what they represented. To me, they were appealing primarily because of their beauty and so it was not long before I began to buy some, mostly Golden Flowers and Pinwheels, but other items as well. My acquisitiveness was further encouraged by the fact that my home, an apartment shared with another graduate student on the roof of a nine-story building in Phoenix New Village, was just up the hill from the Wong Tai Sin Temple, which in those days was packed with sellers of enticing paper creations during the Lunar New Year and other holidays. My habit could be satisfied even further because my office at the Universities Service Center on Argyle Street[3] was within easy walking distance of both the old streets of the Kowloon City Area and of Ma Tau Wai Road (馬頭圍道) in To Kwa Wan (土瓜環), where many great old shops were still doing business.

In no time my office began to fill with items. I could not resist showing off my latest finds to the other scholars in residence at the Center and to one of my office mates, who on one occasion needed little coaxing to model one very fine crown for Monkey (孫悟空, 齊天大聖). Alas, my camera was not at hand to record the moment for anthropology. Yet, these wonderful papers were not the subject of dissertation research, and when my research period came to an end, I packed up as much of the collection as I could, mostly small-sized Pinwheels, along with notes and tapes from the primary project and sent them back to the United States. There they remained in the background until some time later, when I was finally ready to consider another research direction and called upon earlier training in fine art and archaeology.

By 1980 I had returned to Hong Kong, was working as a university lecturer, and was also back at the shops. It did not take long for the materials to exert their usual hold over me, and I again began collecting the items — especially the Pinwheels — which once again filled my office and my flat. I spent many happy hours during the Lunar New Year holiday inching through the original old maze of hawker stalls at the Wong Tai Sin Temple on New Year's Eve or packed in with the families and worshippers at Che Gong Temple on the third day of the New Year, seeking the best Pinwheels along with the thousands of other worshippers. After a series of preliminary studies funded by the Chinese University and by Baptist University, in 1989 I was awarded funding for an extended investigation of the world of paper offerings in urban Hong Kong. The study included examinations of the history of the items (such as was known), the items themselves and their meaning and construction, and the everyday work of the shops and the shopkeepers. Additional studies were to be conducted, as possible, with worshippers and purchasers.

From the beginning, work progressed from the object outward; the focus of the study was neither the criticism nor support of any specific theoretical orientation or school of thought concerning popular or traditional Chinese religion, but the objects themselves. To do this, I collected a very large number of paper offerings and had probably the largest private collection in existence, or so it appeared from the condition of my offices, which resembled paper offerings warehouses. While the glorious Golden Flowers and the Pinwheels took pride of place among the thousands of pieces collected, I attempted to assemble a collection as representative as possible. However, it was clear from the beginning that there could not be such a thing as a totally comprehensive collection, namely, one composed of samples of every example of current paper offering.

There were many reasons for this. First, as will be explained further in this book, contemporary paper offerings show considerable variability due to region and ethnicity. Some items could not be collected in sufficient quantities because they were so rare that few paper shops stocked them. Other examples, even of relatively common items, were not collected because their sizes were prohibitive. My collecting ardor was limited by space; I refrained from acquiring Flower Cannons, which on average are ten to fifteen feet in height, or the actual-sized paper replicas of cars made for funerals (but I did have Pinwheels that were nearly five feet tall). Even more modest items might have many sizes or many colors. The temptation to collect still more (or every size and every variation of each item) had to be resisted. Some items, such as charms and old-style paper images of deities, were not studied or collected for this project (the latter have nearly disappeared from Hong Kong), and lanterns were collected at the beginning of the research but were soon eliminated from the study as they were not placed by most masters within the categories of offerings to other-worldly entities. Yet, shopkeepers also had the habit of bringing out rare items that even they knew little about, but which could not be resisted, so collecting became a never-ending quest despite all these practical constraints.

In addition to the material core of the project, a major source of data was the interviews conducted with shopkeepers and some of their customers, with paper masters, and wholesalers. My assistants (there were a number of them) and I conducted all interviews as a team, which is why the word "we" is often used in the chapters that follow. Teamwork was necessary due to the nature of the research, which required simultaneous recording by tape recorder and by hand, recording of characters, labeling each item (or labeling each sheet of an item of many parts), packing the items,[4] and sketching the atmosphere and arrangement of the shop itself. Each interview was fully translated into English and, for approximately one-third of the interviews, a second handwritten version was done in Chinese characters. All interviews were transcribed as literally as possible, restrained only by the requirements of English clarity, usually word for word, to avoid altering the order and the substance of respondents' explanations. All interviews translated into English contained characters for objects, for phrases, for technical terms and for concepts as used by the respondents themselves. These steps were taken to ensure that informants' explanations were recorded as carefully and comprehensively as possible, that the manner in which they explained the offerings was preserved, and that vital information was recorded consistently.

The interview sample was selected primarily from urban Kowloon and Hong Kong Island, with some interviews conducted in Sha Tin, Tai Wai (大圍) and Tsuen Wan (荃灣) in the New Territories, taking care to spread the locations as evenly as possible. We visited retail paper shops, street hawkers, wholesalers, and workshops making funeral offerings, lanterns, and Flower Cannons. The sample also included nearly all of the paper masters who still handcrafted Pinwheels and Golden Flowers in Hong Kong (fewer of the latter as most of these items are now imported from the Mainland). The shopkeepers were quite interested in our visits and supportive of the research, and many remain friends and sources of information to this day. I could not have met a group of individuals more generous, more courteous, and more helpful; it was really a great pleasure going to each and every interview. A very modest group overall, few would have identified themselves as experts about paper items, even when speaking about their own specialities, but in actuality many were true masters of form and meaning, creating wondrous items. All were working hard at their businesses and were always trying to improve their skills and expand their knowledge.

Interviews were conducted at the place of business, most often the retail shop itself, at the wholesale shop or warehouse, in the street next to the stall, in the factory flat, or at the homes of craftsmen, where handcrafted items such as the Pinwheels were made. These visits were made mostly in the afternoons, and when the shops or craftsmen were not too busy (during major public holidays shops were simply overwhelmed with customers). While interviewing was pleasant and interesting, conditions were sometimes trying — in the open fronted shops near busy roads, roaring traffic and exhaust fumes assaulted our ears and lungs, and sometimes obscured the voices on the tapes. Working in the summer meant hours (it was common for a visit to last nearly two hours) in shops equipped with little more than weak overhead or floor fans. We left satisfied and loaded with paper samples, but with the strength of steamed noodles. All this was more than made up for by the discussions we had, the stories exchanged with the shopkeepers, and the greetings of customers and children.

Paper Offerings in Literature

As Seaman earlier observed, "It would take a great more labor than the results would perhaps justify to glean from out of the mass of Chinese literature the casual notices of the use of spirit money and other offerings to the spirits . . ." (1982: 85). His remarks were directed to the very few and scattered references to paper offerings in classical Chinese sources. A review of English-language studies of Chinese religion and social life in the nineteenth and twentieth centuries also suggests that paper offerings have not figured so prominently in these classic discussions of ritual and belief, often appearing only as tantalizing tidbits or as names with little description or context. Authors of the time simply did not give these items the amount of attention they gave to other aspects of popular religion such as the conduct of rituals. A fair amount of attention was paid to material culture in other social contexts such as wedding ceremonies, for which the descriptions are often lavish and detailed (see for example, Doolittle's 1865a description of the events of betrothal and marriage). One exception was paper funeral offerings, for funeral practices were of particular interest to many scholars and missionaries keen to understand the content of such practices. Only if a non-funeral paper object was quite spectacular, or if the writer had a particular point to make regarding the ritual or practice where it was used, would it receive greater attention. When traditional paper-making was the topic, however, a few paper offerings were mentioned as examples of how the different varieties of paper were used; these examples are helpful in thinking about the earlier form of items. A further problem is the multiplicity of terms and the lack of Chinese characters in many publications. This makes identification of the items, and firm comparison with current examples, somewhat difficult. Nevertheless, the following sample of books and publications includes material sufficient for better understanding the historical setting and background of paper offerings.

The oft-quoted classic on Chinese religion, written by Henry Dore, S. J., and published in thirteen volumes between 1914 and 1938, is entitled *Researches into Chinese Superstitions.* Dore's massive investigation covered such topics as Chinese gods, incense, auspicious plants and animals, the heavenly bureaucracy, superstitious practices and many more. Illustrated with fine colored plates, it contained numerous scholarly references and a full inclusion of Chinese characters for easy reference. While he devoted most attention to religious rituals, and not to the paper material culture that accompanied them, Dore did include small references to the paper offerings accompanying some rites, and carefully drawn and colored examples of spirit money and funeral offerings were included in the illustrations. Like many scholars of his time, he was most attracted to funeral ceremonies and most of his references to paper dealt with the offerings burned at the funeral and during the subsequent commemoration ceremonies (see Volume One, 1914). Small notes in Volume Four (1917) mention mock money for the gods, and what he termed "superstitious prints," or paper images of the gods (1917: 425–7), a variety of ritual paper not included in this book as they have become nearly obsolete in their original form.[5]

In 1940, Clarence Day's marvelous comprehensive study of these "superstitious prints" mentions some of the ritual paper offerings discussed in this book, including selected funeral offerings (such as paper clothing in a box, chairs, water pails, and a bed) and items offered during the anniversary of death services (paper boats, paper dresses and shoes, a model of a house) (1940a: 29–30). Day's other writings concerned with popular religious practices, published in *The Chinese Recorder* and the *China Journal* in 1927, 1928, 1929, and 1940, are fascinating and lively accounts of selected rituals and a valued source of information on popular practices. These articles also contain brief references to paper offerings such as joss money (Gold and Silver Paper), cloud treasure money (corresponding to the contemporary First Treasure, *Yuan Bo*), and the modern White Money (these items are introduced in Chapter 1).

Another valuable study, conducted about the same time as Day's and marked by its scholarly attention to a wider repertoire (it includes actual specimens glued into the book), is that of Dard Hunter (1937). Hunter's book, *Chinese Ceremonial Paper*, takes up "... the use of paper in Chinese rites and religious ceremonies ..." and is devoted to paper-making in general, especially the Chinese handmade varieties. He, too, devoted a chapter to paper prints of deities, but included helpful passages on the popular use of ritual paper items (which he collectively termed spirit paper), a few descriptions of funeral offerings, brief but interesting depictions of paper shops and craftsmen, and selected examples of real paper to illustrate the text.[6] A complement to Hunter's work is Floyd McClure's study of Chinese handmade paper, conducted at about the same time. McClure lived in China until 1941, teaching at Lingnan University of Canton, but during the 1920s and 1930s he traveled about Guangdong Province visiting paper mills and collecting hundreds of samples of traditional handmade paper. The resulting book, which was his master's thesis of 1928, was published posthumously in 1986, and contains forty actual samples of handmade paper, eleven of which he described as suitable for making paper offerings, mostly spirit money.

Lewis Hodous (1915, 1929) makes a number of useful but fleeting references to paper offerings. He mentions idol paper for the Foochow (Fuzhou) ceremonies for welcoming the spring. He also noted various forms of paper money in conjunction with ritual, and a special New Year custom: "When the shops are shut up for the night a few sheets of idol money are fastened between the boards which, in many parts of China, are used to close the front of the shop. The following year when the shop is opened for business the paper is burned before the door as an offering to the guardian spirit of the door" (1929: 158). A note on printed pictures of warm clothing and other items needed by the dead complete his few references to paper offerings.

While all these early twentieth-century writings give a tantalizing look at paper offerings during the Republican era and just before the Second World War, glimpses of an even earlier world of paper are provided by J. J. M. De Groot and the Rev. Justus Doolittle. In the general preface to the six volumes comprising *The Religious System of China*, published from 1892 to 1910, De Groot asserted that, despite the many good books on China, research on Chinese religion was still incomplete and that he need not apologize for adding yet another study. His massively detailed work was devoted to the study of funeral rituals, of disposal of the dead (the grave), the soul, ancestral worship, demons, and religious priesthood, and contains long discourses on the classical referents to, and the history of, all practices. It is fully referenced with Chinese characters, so that modern counterparts of the materials and practices De Groot described can be identified, and each volume is well illustrated with drawings or photographs. Yet, the paper offerings themselves receive less attention. Given his topic as death and its attendant practices, some space is given to funeral offerings, and in Volume Six he includes a long discussion on the exorcising powers of almanacs and charms.

Justus Doolittle's celebrated studies of Chinese life, *Social Life of the Chinese*, were published in two volumes in 1865. Doolittle exhaustively explored practices and events in Fuzhou, Fujian, where he was a missionary for fourteen years. Few aspects of everyday life escaped his attention, and his writing on these topics is as fresh and engaging nearly 150 years later as it was in his own time. Doolittle is especially strong when describing domestic religious practices and public holidays and ceremonies; it is easy to follow the progress of a ritual by reading his description. Although no characters were included (only romanization of terms), his attention to detail makes possible a reasonable identification of the same rituals today, including a comparison of the materials used. Doolittle's study allows a greater appreciation of the history of both practice and accompanying paper offering, and of my respondents' frequent assertions of the antiquity of both their trade and the items they craft. Each of Doolittle's chapters is prefaced by a detailed summary of the contents, so references to ritual or to paper offerings are easily found.

The above studies make it possible to appreciate contemporary paper offerings in a historical context, at least for that of the late Qing, and a number of paper items described in such sources are still recognizable 150 years after such writings appeared. These classical writings on Chinese religious practices will be referred to throughout the book, but their appearances are most useful as reference points, as a reminder that paper offerings have long been an important component of everyday worship. Further, these sources provide a historical context, a background setting, for the items in use today. Including such references in this account should not, however, be interpreted as an assertion that Hong Kong's current practices of worship are as those of the past. Nor does their appearance in the text assert that the paper offerings now used in Hong Kong are themselves exact replicas of past counterparts;

this is not the case, despite the remarkable resistance to change shown by some items. Finally, such references do not imply that the meanings paper offerings now hold in their Hong Kong context are exactly the same as the meanings held in the past places so loved by these authors.

More contemporary studies of Chinese religious practice are both rich and varied (see for example, Ahern 1973; Liu 2004; Lopez 1996; Shahar and Weller 1996; Smith 1991; Teiser 1997; Weller 1987; Wolf 1974; Yang 1994). Much attention has been given to the nature of the relationship between deities and humans, and studies related to ancestral worship and numerous studies have enriched our understanding of the meaning of ancestors and ancestor worship (see for example, Ahern 1973; Freedman 1967; Newell 1976; Wolf 1974). More recent studies of Chinese religion and ritual have placed greater emphasis on the debate over the existence of a general Chinese religion (see, for example, Anderson 1988; Freedman 1974; Watson 1976; Wolf 1974; Yang 1967) to a variation on that theme of the nature of Chinese popular religion, or to the relationship between religion and culture (Bell 1989; Feuchtwang and Wang 1991). All these valuable studies would be complemented with explorations of paper offerings emphasizing the material aspect, the physical representation of worship and belief. There are notable exceptions in the form of discussions of specific items and their social and cultural contexts, and items such as spirit money (Gates 1987; McCreery 1990; Seaman 1982) and offerings for gods and ancestors (Scott 1997a, 1997b; Segawa 1986; Szeto 1993; Topley 1953) have been illuminated. It is surely appropriate that the complement of paper offerings, so varied, beautiful and significant, should have a more prominent place in the academic explorations of contemporary Chinese religion and practice, not as rivals for scholarly study of other, classic concerns, but as important complements to the growing understanding of popular practices.

Acknowledgements

A great many individuals have contributed to the study of paper offerings, and who deserve thanks for the contributions they have made to the manuscript. The project work would never have been completed but for the hard work of a number of dedicated research assistants who worked with me on the many paper projects: Ms Tam Mei-mei, Ms Florence Lui

Yuk Lin, Ms Elizabeth Lai Ching Man, Ms Brenda Cheung Lai Shan, Ms Mabel Kwan Chui Yi, and Ms Cindy Wong Shuet-ying. I share with them many happy moments in paper shops, factories, and the homes of worshippers, and am grateful for their many helpful insights and comments for improving the research. Dr Cheung Siu-woo, Ms Lau Shuk Fong, Dr Liu Tik-sang, and Ms Naomi Szeto Yin Yin, former students and now colleagues, helped immeasurably during the earlier forays into the field and provided valuable advice during the earliest studies of offerings. I am particularly indebted to Dr Liu for his insights into the worship of Tian Hou. I could never repay the assistance of Ms Viona Lee Wing Sum, research assistant, artist, and photographer extraordinare, who photographed the great majority of the collection and helped establish a database for visual storage of the collection. Ms Ursula Chan Wai Ching provided valuable assistance in translating the insights from the project into self-access teaching materials for classes in Hong Kong's traditional culture, and Ms Wallis Chan Yin Fan assisted with material processing and character checking. Much gratitude is also due to many former students and student helpers enrolled in my classes in anthropology and sociology, who assisted in collecting newspaper clippings, in making observations, visiting shops, and in other ways too numerous to count: Ms Emily Bales, Mr Larry Ho Lai Yin, Ms Zelma Cheung, Ms Vanessa Hung Sun Hau, Ms Janet Jik Siu Hang, Mr Lee Hoi Ming, Ms Florence Lee Lai Fan, Mr Li Wah Li, Ms Ng Yuen Man, Ms Tam Shuk Wan, Mr Timothy Tsang Ching Chuen, Mr Wong Chi Keung, Dr Wong Heung Wah, Ms Tammy Wu Sau Ling, and Ms Yeung Yuk Man.

While researching and writing on paper offerings, I have always been fortunate to be surrounded and supported by many friends and colleagues who could be counted on to share their expertise towards the uncounted questions that arose in the course of the study. All contributed innumerable insights and comments on earlier drafts of this manuscript and on the independent essays related to paper offerings. Professors James L. and Rubie S. Watson, from the beginning at the Universities Service Center, encouraged my passion for these objects and contributed many insights and ideas that have sharpened the analysis. With Professor Charlotte Ikels I shared many visits to temples and events of religious holidays, not to mention collecting expeditions. Colleagues at Hong Kong Baptist University and elsewhere were always generous with encouragement and sharing of their considerable expertise: Professor Lauren Pfister, with his mastery of Chinese texts and philosophy; Professor Michael DeGolyer, for his practical experience in apprenticeship and research design and his unfailing instinct for the most important questions; Professor Peter Baehr, for endless encouragement and willingness to read and criticize earlier stages of the manuscript; Professor Gene Blocker, who provided useful critiques of earlier essays; Dr Elizabeth Teather, Dr Jacqueline Adams, Dr Odalia Wong, and Professor Chan Kwok-bun for useful criticisms and encouragement on earlier chapter drafts; Professor Grant Evans and the anonymous reviewers of an earlier stage of the manuscript, for much helpful advice; Dr Joseph Bosco and Professor Ho Puay-peng for their support of research into the offerings for Tian Hou and for their helpful editorial comments on earlier essays; Dr Gordon Mathews for his comments on an earlier draft of the first chapters; and Professor Keith Stevens, with his vast knowledge of Chinese gods. I also thank Dr William Guthrie of the University of Macau, for his helpful insights and gifts of paper offerings. I will be forever in debt to Ms Anna Lo Siu Po and Ms Christie M. K. Tang for their endless patience and good humor with all my requests for computer assistance and advice on daily details. And in all, I could never repay Ms Jennifer Wun Chi-yee for decades of encouragement, friendship, and inspiration.

I owe a great debt of gratitude to the Fairbank Center for East Asian Research at Harvard University, where as a Visiting Scholar and an Associate in Research I was able to spend many productive months of study leave writing and thinking over the materials. I am very grateful to the director in 1993, Professor James L. Watson, for his many kindnesses and support of the research. Many thanks are owed to the staff of the Harvard Yenching Library in Cambridge for their advice and assistance. They could always be counted upon to help me secure even the most obscure and hard-to-find reference, and working in the vast collections was always rewarding and pleasurable. Gratitude is also due to the staff of the Peabody Museum of Archeology and Ethnology of Harvard University, who allowed me to explore their collection of paper offerings from the late 1800s and the 1920s and 1930s; special thanks must be given to Professor Rubie S. Watson, Howells Director from 1997 to 2003, and to Ms Kathleen Skelly. I am also grateful for permission to obtain photographs of certain items. I owe a particular debt of gratitude to a skilled editor, Ms Pamela Summa, for her good work and support. She provided not only careful copy-editing, but the talent for catching anything obscure or illogical; the manuscript is much clearer with her comments. A very special thanks to Dr Colin Day of Hong Kong University Press for his wise advice and patience during the preparation of the manuscript, and to Ms Clara Ho for her skilled editing. I am also deeply grateful to the Hong Kong Branch of the Royal Asiatic Society, and to the Sir Lindsay and Lady May Ride Memorial Fund, for their encouragement and generous support, without which this publication would not have been possible.

The research on which this book is based was made possible by generous support from a number of agencies. The first forays into the field and initial investigations of Hong Kong's paper items were sponsored by a grant from the Institute of Chinese Studies of the Chinese University of Hong Kong. The author is grateful for such assistance at an early stage of the research. During my tenure at Hong Kong Baptist University, additional investigations into such topics as the meanings of selected pitched New Year items, the empowerment of everyday offerings, and the place of traditional offerings in contemporary expressions of ethnicity, were supported by Faculty Research Grants in 1986, 1993, 1994, and 2003. The author is greatly indebted to the University for both its encouragement of this research topic and its sustained support. The large project from which much of the data in this book is taken was carried out from 1989 to 1992 and was supported by an Earmarked Grant for Research (HKBC 3/88; RSC/88–89/02) from the (then entitled) University and Polytechnics Grants Committee of Hong Kong. This funding not only provided support for the intensive interviews and observations on paper offerings and their meanings, but allowed for the making of a large collection of contemporary forms of ritual papers. The author is deeply indebted to the Committee for its generosity. An additional allowance for supplementary research into offerings for the goddess Tian Hou were provided by Dr Joseph Bosco and Professor Ho Puay-peng, organizers of the conference, "The Tianhou/Mazu Temple: Iconography, Architecture, Social Organization" held at the Chinese University of Hong Kong on January 3–4, 1997.

The research base for the study of paper offerings includes in-depth interviews conducted at over eighty urban paper shops in Kowloon, the Sha Tin District of the New Territories, and Hong Kong Island. Interviews were also conducted at ten companies wholesaling paper offerings, and at eight workshops specializing in funeral offerings. Interviews conducted with eight master craftsmen for Pinwheels, three masters of Golden Flowers, and three of Flower Cannons were also included. In addition, 282 in-depth surveys of consumers of paper offerings were completed, with a matching sample investigating young people's knowledge, and nearly 1,000 indicative (non-random) surveys concerning Pinwheels were conducted at temples. A separate set of fifty-five interviews with consumers was completed on the empowerment of selected specimens, and a second set of interviews with worshippers and shopkeepers investigated the uses of paper and genuine comestibles in worship. The bulk of the information contained within the text, unless otherwise specified, comes from these interviews and surveys. The author was also able to include a subset of questions relating to offerings and worshipping practice in a telephone survey conducted by the Hong Kong Transition Project in June of 2003; I am very grateful to the Project for this opportunity. Whenever data from this survey is referred to within the text, it will be clearly identified and accompanied by response percentages.

A collection of nearly 1,500 examples of paper offerings has been assembled. This collection includes not only examples of everyday and special occasion items used by the Cantonese community, but the distinctive items unique to the different Chinese ethnic groups in Hong Kong, notably the Chaozhou and Hong Kong's fishermen. It also includes certain items for the Shanghai community, and, although very rare, a few examples for worshippers from Fujian and Dongguan. The collection also includes twenty-one sets of Spirit Reds, nearly 150 Pinwheels, and 173 pairs of Golden Flowers. While the storage requirements of the larger examples of pitched paper offering, notably the Flower Cannons and certain of the funeral offerings, make their purchase impractical, the collection does contain numerous smaller examples, especially from subset of funeral offerings and offerings for the ancestors and the gods. Examples collected within the category of the items of everyday use for ancestors include: replicas of electrical appliances, food, personal items, and clothing. The majority of these items have been photographed and the images transformed into CD form, creating a visual source which, when added to the interview and observation records and other data from the research, constitute a large historical archive for the future. In May of 2005, the bulk of this collection was transferred to the Hong Kong Museum of History.

Finally, the greatest debt is due to all the paper shop owners, workshop managers, and paper masters who gave so generously of their time and expertise. It would be difficult to find anywhere a group of respondents as helpful and generous. I am particularly grateful to Mr Ho Kan, Pinwheel master and indeed to all members of the Ho family, for their continued support and concern, as well as for their magnificent Pinwheels. I am further indebted to the late Mr Chan, The Master of

Tak Wo, for his advice and explanations of apprenticeship; to Mr and Mrs Lau of Nam Shan Paper, for permission to film in their shop as well as interview; to Mrs Tang and Ah Bo of Hang Fung Tai and to Choi Wai Ying (Ah Ying) of Ying Kee, who continues to send me paper objects, expecially the lanterns of which she is a master crafter. Deepest appreciation also goes to Mr Ng Shek Fai of Kwong Fuk, Mr Carlse Li of Kwong Fuk Lan, Mr Chan and the Chan family of Chan Cho Kee, the Dai family of Kwong Fuk Hing, Pinwheel master Mr Poon Tsuen Kai, and funeral paper master Mr Lam of Lam Tak. May their businesses continue and prosper.

To best appreciate paper offerings, it is helpful to present them within differing settings, including: the world of the paper masters and the contexts of manufacture, the formal features of design and appearance, and the everyday patterns of worship which give them meaning. To better illustrate these settings, certain of the items will make multiple appearances within the book. Their appearance and reappearance in a variety of contexts should serve to illustrate the many ways in which items are seen and used by makers and worshippers. However, at the end one always returns to the objects. To choose only one example, the great Flower Cannons offered to Tian Hou (discussed in detail in Chapter 3) embody a wide range of contradictory messages — the support of local identity as well as pan-community unity, and cultural and social integration as well as separation. Yet, on seeing Flower Cannons for the first time, neither observers nor worshippers likely see any of these social possibilities. Transfixed by the sheer magnificence of the cannons themselves, viewers see only a "so beautiful" offering given to an equally beautiful deity (Scott 1997b).

While bright with materials for worship, the entrance to a typical paper shop displays only a fraction of the paper offerings within.

On any day of the week, one can see any number of worshippers giving offerings to Wong Tai Sin in his temple in Kowloon. After offering their gifts of foodstuffs and paper, they will ask for the god's blessing and seek his advice by throwing the *chim*, or divining sticks. The number on the first stick to hit the ground indicates the deity's answer to the inquiry.

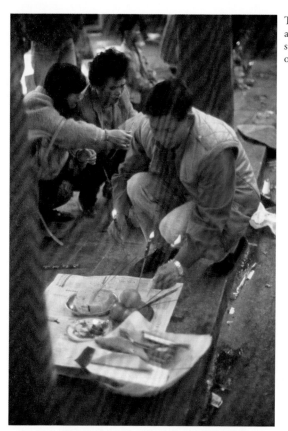

This worshipper at the Wong Tai Sin Temple, already prepared with folded Gold Paper, is using h[...] stack of oranges to hold red candles. Small offering[...] of candy and cakes are set in place.

Worshipping is not solely the concern of the elderly. On ritual holidays to commemorate the ancestors, such as Chong Yang, younger members of the family assist their parents in arranging the offerings within the paper chests.

Worshippers of Tian Hou come well prepared with the handcrafted packages of clothing made especially for her. The youngster on the right carries his own package, topped with a splendid paper hat.

No festival, but especially that for Tian Hou, would be complete without a Good Fortune Chicken. This example, accompanied by three chicks at its feet, is complemented with wings and tail trimmed with resplendently colored genuine feathers. A good luck couplet written in gold on red is attached to the base (photo: Viona Lee Wing Sum).

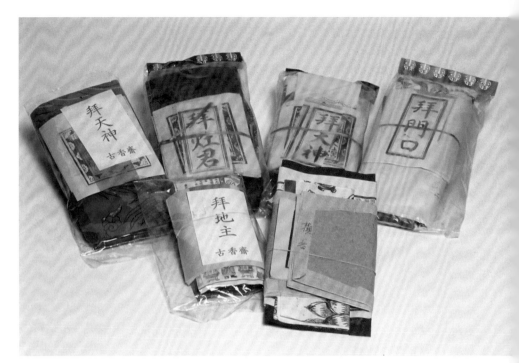

Here is a selection of pre-assembled worshipping packages for the deities: one each for Men Kou and Di Zhu, one for the Kitchen God, and three for "big gods" (photo: Viona Lee Wing Sum).

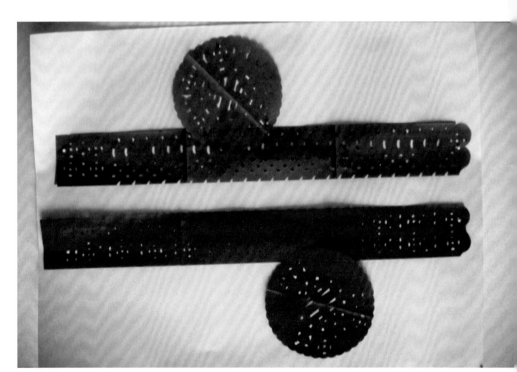

A set of rectangular and circular forms of the Honorable People Papers. Honorable People Papers are found in nearly all worshipping assemblages.

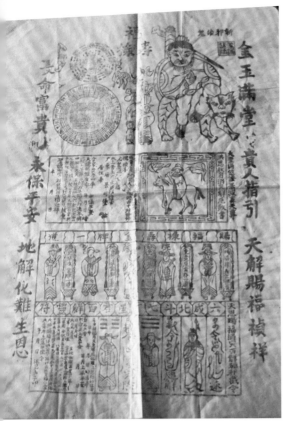

A large example of the Solving of 100 Problems, one of the most popular of everyday paper offerings (photo: Viona Lee Wing Sum).

Examples of the Five and Seven Colored Paper, burned to the dead in the next world, so that they may be used by the dead to fashion their own clothes (photo: Viona Lee Wing Sum).

A trio of everyday offerings: Longevity Gold, Gold Paper, and First Treasure Paper. The coarser First Treasure is marked with characteristic edge stripes of red and green (photo: Viona Lee Wing Sum).

The many sizes of Gold and Silver Paper are folded into shapes according to the native place or family practices of the worshipper. Most worshippers will fold such papers into ingot shapes of varying forms. However, Longevity Gold is not usually folded, and the very largest varieties, as shown here, are looped once and put together in the form of a ruff before being offered.

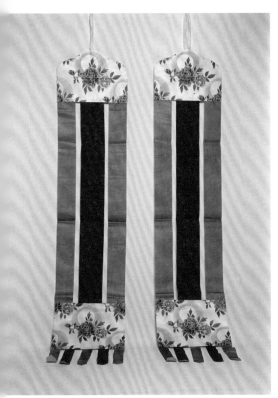

A very fine pair of Long Pennants: they are used to thank the deities for their care and protection in curing illness or relieving misfortune. The Long Pennant may be accompanied by offerings of First Treasure, Big Bright Treasure, Longevity Gold, and foodstuffs (photo: Viona Lee Wing Sum).

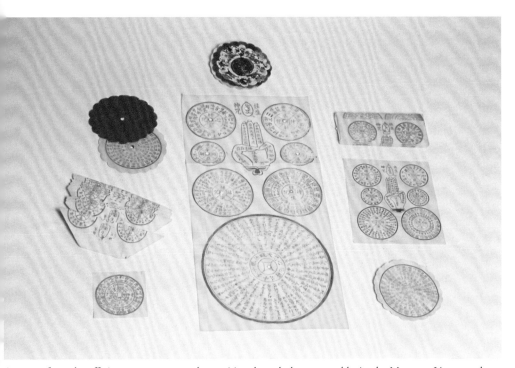

A group of popular offerings to ensure a speedy transition through the next world: circular Money to Live, complete with rose-colored and ornamented paper toppings, and the larger Seven Voice Incantation. Money to Live may be burned in the thousands by relatives of the deceased seeking to ease the soul in rebirth (photo: Viona Lee Wing Sum).

The small Fate Changer (literally, Lucky Money or Luck Paper) assists those worshippers who wish to obtain good luck and change their fate for the better (photo: Viona Lee Wing Sum).

Lucky Basins are a common variety of pitched paper offering, gaily decorated with Honorable People Papers and folded Longevity Gold (photo: Viona Lee Wing Sum).

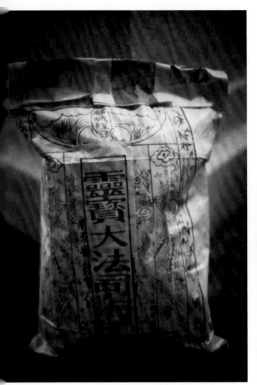

At festivals such as Chong Yang, offerings for the ancestors are presented packed into Fu Jian bags to ensure the neat and tidy sending of materials to the next world. This one bears the Label and is closed with Gold Paper. It is likely filled with a combination of folded Gold Paper, Money to Live, Hell Money, White Money, and even small packages of clothing.

The younger members of the family begin early in learning about ritual holidays; this one is the Chong Yang holiday to honor the dead. This young boy assists his family by holding on to one of the Fu Jian bags filled with offerings. The name of the recipient can be faintly seen written in the middle.

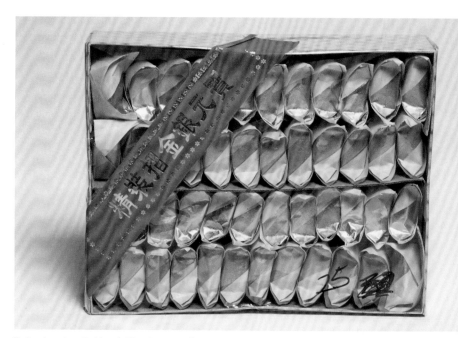

Before burning Gold and Silver Paper to the ancestors, many families still prefer to fold each sheet by hand into its proper ingot shape. However, some paper shops have recently begun to sell packages of pre-folded Gold and Silver Paper for customer convenience (photo: Viona Lee Wing Sum).

In the 1980s, paper offerings could still be burned directly in ovens set up within the temple grounds. This one was kept busy with the offerings for Tian Hou.

Offerings to the deceased are commonly burned in large metal ovens. These ovens may be rented by individual families and set up on city streets and village lanes, but during holidays they are also made available for the burning of larger quantities of paper offerings.

Offerings for the wandering spirits are increasing in their number and variety. Such offerings, given during the Festival of the Hungry Ghosts, include many everyday offerings: Longevity Gold, Honorable People Papers, White Money, and Gold and Silver Paper. These two packages are Chaozhou offerings, identified by their inclusion of Chaozhou Gold, Lonely Clothing, and the red and green Peaceful Money. The Fu Jian bag is seen in the middle.

Bird-keeping remains a popular pastime in Hong Kong. The ancestors are not denied this pleasure, for a paper cage, complete with lively bird, may be ordered for their enjoyment (photo: Viona Lee Wing Sum).

A full range of banking facilities are available in the next world, and the ancestors are provided with all that is necessary: bankbooks, credit cards suspiciously like those of American Express, and savings books — all bearing the image of the King of Hell. In addition, deceased who wish to travel are provided with passports and tickets from Hell Airlines (photo: Viona Lee Wing Sum).

Residents of the next world may be provided with a full complement of Hell Money and gold and silver, the latter in the form of ingots and coins (photo: Viona Lee Wing Sum).

Models of servants are traditional components of the basic set for the dead. Classic versions may be quite large, but by the 1990s, small models had become available in retail paper shops. These two pairs are clothed in old-style pant suits, and have modeled faces carefully painted with eyes, noses, and mouths. Their fingers are carefully cut out of fine white paper (photo: Viona Lee Wing Sum).

No detail is too insignificant when caring for the ancestors. Departed relatives with dental problems need not fear, for they can be provided with a full set of dentures. Even the toothpaste and toothbrush to care for these dentures are provided (photo: Viona Lee Wing Sum).

A house and garden is a component of the basic set for the dead. Classic versions are large and detailed, and are still burned at the funeral. However, by the 1990s, customers could purchase a variety of small models at retail paper shops. Such models were just as detailed and carefully crafted as was the funeral version, as can be seen in the inclusion of paper servants (photo: Viona Lee Wing Sum).

Houses for the dead are finished with an eye for detail, including sets of finely made furniture such as this set (photo: Viona Lee Wing Sum).

Vices as well as virtues are provided for in the next world. If the ancestor was a smoker, a supply of cigarettes and cigars can be burned, in sets completed by lighters (photo: Viona Lee Wing Sum).

Paper foodstuffs are becoming more common as offerings, even if customers do not agree about their value. A wide array of *dian xin* selections are now available, so that the dead can continue to enjoy the family pleasures of weekend *yumcha*. Each popular selection comes in its own paper steamer, just as do the real ones (photo: Viona Lee Wing Sum).

The number of paper foodstuffs available in retail paper shops has been increasing since the mid-1990s. Relatives can choose from a variety of items to burn for their departed kin, including cans of soda, beer and tea, canned meats, candies, and luxury foods such as abalone (photo: Viona Lee Wing Sum).

...ncestors are well provided with clothing wrapped in the old-fashioned packages. Customers can purchase for both ...nen and women (photo: Viona Lee Wing Sum).

Modern and stylish clothing is increasingly popular with customers. Paper shops stock a wide range of complete sets of clothing for formal and casual ware, including shoes and accessories (photo: Viona Lee Wing Sum).

Care is taken to provide all the comforts of home in the next world. This paper fan comes complete with movable blades, settings, and electric cord (photo: Viona Lee Wing Sum).

The King of Hell is a majestic figure, presiding over the lost souls during the Festival of the Hungry Ghosts.

Female deities may be offered a variety of dainty footwear, including tiny boots and shoes for bound feet, decorated with flowers of painted metallic paper (photo: Viona Lee Wing Sum).

This gown, made especially for a big god, is identifiable by the dragon motif in the center; this charming depiction is surrounded by colorful swirls and floral designs. As part of a specially ordered set entirely made by hand, it is accompanied by a set of golden boots, a finely decorated hat, and a paper flywhisk symbolizing authority (photo: Viona Lee Wing Sum).

Handcrafted gowns for the big gods are painstakingly crafted in vivid colors and with fine detailing. These are hand-painted with auspicious motives, such as the dragon on the chest of the lower red example. The upper robe is adorned with painted roundels bearing the character for long life (photo: Viona Lee Wing Sum).

A particularly lovely offering for the big gods, but especially for Guan Yin, is the Gold First Treasure (or, Golden Pineapple) made of painstakingly folded sheets of Longevity Gold. When the top cone is removed and the item lit, it burns down evenly and completely, a feature appreciated by worshippers. These objects are made in a variety of sizes and are featured prominently during the ritual events associated with the goddess (photo: Viona Lee Wing Sum).

Monkey is offered an assemblage of offerings which includes an elaborate crown, a pair of cloud-hopping boots and a pair of buckets. Also included is a paper sheet marked to mimic his furry pelt (photo: Viona Lee Wing Sum).

A handmade assemblage of clothing for Lu Ban, the patron deity of the skilled trades connected to the construction industry. The set includes a splendid red robe hand-painted with abstract designs, a red belt with golden inserts, a pair of red and blue boots, a hat, and a fly whisk (photo: Viona Lee Wing Sum).

Worshippers of Guan Yin may wish to express their devotion by making special orders for completely handmade and hand-decorated paper clothing. This set, of cream colored paper, consists of two elaborate hats, an apron, a pair of "embroidered" red shoes for bound feet, a second pair of taller boots in gold and red, and a gown wonderfully painted with flowers, especially the lotus, her symbol. In front are examples of more common machine-printed paper clothing, including the most commonly purchased gown, made of white paper and printed with an elaborate collar and auspicious elements such as lotus flowers and seed pods (photo: Viona Lee Wing Sum).

Golden Flowers are among the most beautiful of paper offerings. This large pair is suitable for temple worship and is adorned with two pairs of peacock feathers each (photo: Viona Lee Wing Sum).

This close-up of a large Golden Flower shows two small wax images of deities, each colorfully dressed and with features carefully painted. Such wax figures are no longer made.

A box of Spirit Reds, ready for purchase and placement with the household's Golden Flowers.

An example of a Gold Money Pinwheel.

Rows of Pinwheels in the sunlight are irresistible attractions at the Wong Tai Sin Temple.

Every Lunar New Year, some craftsmen will create a number of very large Pinwheels to sell. This one is adorned with flags, a Spirit Red, a pair of lanterns, numerous lucky phrases, and painted metallic cutouts of fish.

Another splendid Pinwheel, this one adorned with a pair of red plastic lanterns, golden bells and painted metallic cutouts of dragons.

At the Wong Tai Sin Temple, an offering of various fruits, cakes, and candy, accompanied by five red glasses of wine and five sets of chopsticks. After worship is completed, the worshipper will likely take the foods home to eat.

The Chaozhou Heart of Money, in three sizes, is purchased traditionally with accompanying folders termed Money Ingots, trimmed with Gold and Silver Paper and red inserts (photo: Viona Lee Wing Sum).

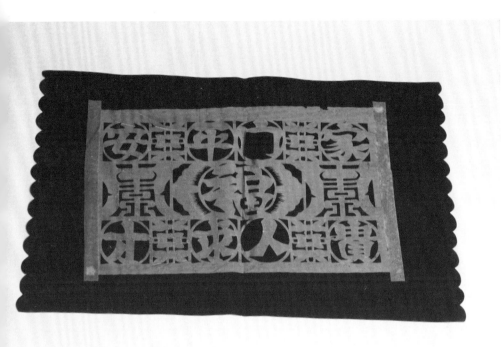

The Chaozhou Peaceful Money bears motives carefully hand-cut in this older example (photo: Viona Lee Wing Sum).

During the Lunar New Year, the Chaozhou offer varieties of Cake Money, each elaborately trimmed with hand painted motives (photo: Viona Lee Wing Sum).

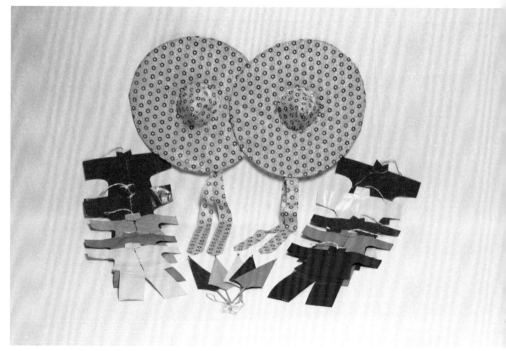

Hong Kong's fishermen burn a distinctive assemblage of paper offerings, including these charming examples of clothing and hats for the ancestors (photo: Viona Lee Wing Sum).

Depending on the sea, many of the offerings used by fishermen are directed to fish; these are two Fish Gates directed to more plentiful catches (photo: Viona Lee Wing Sum).

lower Cannons are the largest of the pitched paper offerings, and require at least one pair of strong worshippers to
arry them into the temple grounds. This is especially true if the Cannons must be maneuvered off a boat and onto a
ickety boardwalk to the shore (photo: Li Wah-li).

This splendid Flower Cannon is decorated with the
characteristic Spirit Red at the top, then a colorful
bat, pairs of lanterns, images of the deities, and a
variety of auspicious flowers and animals (photo:
Wong Heung-wah).

Many of the Flower Cannons hold clusters of red dyed eggs, attached by the members of the Flower Cannon Associations who have had children during the preceding year. Such eggs are then eagerly sought by couples who wish to have children during the next year.

Flower Cannons are exuberantly decorated. This one, in addition to the red eggs, holds a fancy lotus lantern trimmed with tassels. Below it, a colorful fish makes an appearance.

splendidly dressed images of heroes and deities are integral parts of a proper Flower Cannon.

All Flower Cannons include images of bats at the top, made of painted cloth, and representing the desire for good luck and good fortune. Staring straight ahead, they fix their eyes on the temple and on the deities to whom the Flower Cannon is dedicated. This bat shares space at the top with an old-fashioned painted cloth lantern in the shape of a butterfly.

Dragons are particularly auspicious animals and take pride of place, with the bats, on Flower Cannons. This one's chin appears to rest on the golden lantern.

While the majority of paper offerings are made by anonymous craftspeople, pitched objects provide clues as to their makers. The bases of the Flower Cannons make it easy to identify their crafters, as the names and telephone numbers of the shops are painted on in clear view.

1

The Practices of Paper Burning

It was the middle of the month, when people burn paper offerings to the gods for luck and protection. A young woman, obviously a shop assistant from the trendy boutique behind her, carried a battered old oil tin with its top removed across the sidewalk to the curb. She was dressed in the height of fashion — leather mini skirt, lace bra and matching blouse, rhinestone-studded hip belt and knee-high red boots — and with hair sculpted and tinted pink. She opened a large red plastic bag, and took out a variety of spirit money, mostly gold and silver, with flashes of red and yellow, and placed them in the tin. After taking a moment for a prayer amidst the streams of passers-by, she set the papers on fire. She stirred the lot from time to time as she added more papers from the bag. She made sure that everything burned down completely. When all the papers had been burned, she emptied the ashes into the street and took the tin back into the shop. That the person burning the ritual paper was not the elderly owner of an ancient establishment selling traditional goods but the obviously up-to-date employee of an equally up-to-date fashion house was nothing out of the ordinary.

Through Fire and Smoke

The first feature to understand is that paper offerings[1] are burnt to ashes so they may go beyond the confines of the living world — to the gods, the ghosts, and the ancestors.[2] Even the most magnificent and beautiful examples, which can represent days of labor, must leave this world to reach their destination in the world of the spirits. Accordingly, customers do not buy paper offerings to hoard or display, and even the large quantities that worshippers purchase to prepare for a festival are not kept for very long.[3] Burning changes the nature of the offerings, for in their original form they cannot go anywhere; burning accomplishes the vital transformation which sends the items to the ancestors, the gods, or the ghosts. As Sangren explained for the burning of incense, also an integral part of worship, "A transformative process is represented, and it is fire that possesses transformative power" (1993: 567; see also Sangren 1987: 162–5; Teiser 1993). This transformative process is even more pronounced for paper offerings, for example, funeral offerings. "Effigies made of coloured paper are burnt at the graveside in the hope that they will be translated into the spirit world for the assistance of the manes of the dead" (Williams 1976: 181). Even earlier, De Groot noted that for silver money for the ancestors, "These sheets ... are, according to the prevailing conviction, turned by the process of fire into real silver currency available in the world of darkness, and sent there through the smoke to the soul ..." (1892: 25). Paper offerings possess a shape and a form within the world of the living, and can be handled, measured and recorded using the same methods as are other artifacts and items of material culture. In that sense, they are real items (albeit identified as replicas) for the living. However, these same offerings are only tentative, replicas in a state of becoming, and it is burning which transforms them into real objects at their destination in other worlds.

The burning of paper offerings also echos the traditional Chinese respect for printed paper, which went hand in hand with the reverence for literacy. Any paper bearing the written or printed word was treated carefully (Baber 1882; Ball 1926; Cave 1998; Doolittle 1865b), even when it was being discarded.

> All classes of Chinese, from the aristocratic scholar with his silk robes and horn rimmed spectacles down to the most illiterate coolie who carries bulky burdens upon his head and engages in all manner of menial toil, have a pronounced reverence for

every scrap of paper, written, stamped, and printed … The lowly Chinese who has not been schooled to read or write the seemingly-intricate characters will gather all scraps of paper and deposit them in baskets or boxes that schoolmasters and scholars place before their houses, each receptacle bearing a red paper label upon which is inscribed these four characters 苟惜字紙 meaning, "Respect all written paper and treat it with care" (Hunter 1937: 75).

Such scraps were burned reverently at temples, and the ashes stored until they could be disposed of properly. Many Chinese communities had lettered paper associations, devoted to collecting these ashes from temples and disposing of them in water, usually in a nearby river (Doolittle 1865b: 168–9; see also De Groot 1910: 1019–21). Proper disposal of lettered paper was believed to bring prosperity and long life to the devout, although by 1937, when Hunter was writing, many such practices had already faded (1937: 79). While modern paper offerings (also called sacred papers or ritual offerings) do bear characters, written phrases, or long passages of the printed word, they are burned for reasons beyond the respect for literacy, but respect for printed paper remains.

People burn paper offerings to the gods to give thanks for blessings or to beg for assistance in times of need; to the ancestors and departed relatives to express love and devotion; and to the ghosts to ease the sufferings of these unknown and neglected dead. Charitable offerings to the ghosts are believed to ease the suffering of the souls of those who died violently or unknown and far from home, so that relatives could not care for them properly. Due to the circumstances of their death, these spirits lack food, clothing, and shelter, and their misery is extreme. Sending them paper clothing and money helps ease their lot. Items for the ancestors are intended to provide the comforts of living to the dead who are known and loved, and can be more personalized. People believe that the ancestors will wear the paper clothing and accessories, live in the paper house and garden, drive in the paper car, use the paper appliances, and spend the paper money, just as they would in this world. Such thinking was also prevalent during the Republican period. Dard Hunter observed, "the paper craftsmen also construct full-sized carts, horse, and even automobiles, the thought being that when these fragile representations go up in smoke they will eventually assume reality in Heaven and the deceased will have horses and vehicles at his disposal" (1937: 6). When I asked people what the gods do with the money and clothing sent to them — after all, why would the gods need money or clothes — there was no single answer, but a perception that benefits were redistributed between this world and the next. Many respondents suggested that when burning the items, the worshipper hoped the deity would bless him or her (or the family) with the blessing implied by the item. For example, if an item bore the character for long life (壽), then the deity would reward the worshipper with a long(er) life — the deity does not require this. Another perception was that the deities take note of the worshipper, accept the offerings, and then redistribute them to needy spirits in the other world.

The modern world of paper offerings in Hong Kong is as multifaceted in meaning as it is in beauty. To fully appreciate its subtleties and complexities, it is best approached by looking first at the varieties of paper offerings available, their appearance and physical features, and their generally accepted meanings and uses. Following this, some common characteristics of where people worship, and common worshipping practices as performed in domestic, temple and ephemeral contexts, will be explored. This chapter will consider the offering typology, the purpose and appearance of items in the everyday collection, followed by some general features of worshipping practices, and the physical locations and social and personal contexts in which offerings appear — in short, the most common practices regarding these papers. With this framework, closer attention can be given in subsequent chapters to more detailed examinations of the manufacture of paper offerings, and of the more specific personal and social contexts in which individual paper offerings play a part: the human world with its concerns and desires, and the worlds of the gods, the ghosts, and the ancestors.

The World of Paper Offerings

Dard Hunter's 1937 study referred to paper offerings as "spirit paper," "bamboo ceremonial paper," "ceremonial paper," or "joss paper" (1937: 8, 31, 58). In Hong Kong, there are also differing names for paper offerings, joss paper or clothing paper (衣紙) being but two of them. Other common referents in the literature are variations on the theme of horses for paper offerings. "Simply speaking, 'paper horses' are joss paper printed with images of gods, scriptures, charms or talismans, which are mostly burnt during Chinese religious practices and rituals"

(Szeto 1993: 12). Horse imagery is of some antiquity, appearing in such terms as "best horses" (Dore 1917: 425; Goodrich 1991: 23), "horse sheets" (Day 1940a), "divine horses," or "first-grade horses" (Szeto 1993: 12). All have appeared in the literature to describe both everyday and funeral offerings. It has been suggested that the reference to horses was adopted during the reign of Shihuangdi (秦始皇帝, reigned 221–210 BC) when paper horse models were sacrificed instead of real horses, to avoid diminishing the fighting capabilities of the Qin army (Day 1940a: 6).

Just as there are many accepted terms for the paper offerings currently in use, there is some variety of opinion on how many individual items are contained within the full complement of paper offerings. Some shopkeepers assert that the number is many hundreds and growing if the ever-changing special items for ancestors are included. This great variety presents a problem for understanding the world of paper, for it is not accompanied by any absolute or overarching typology recognized by both trade professionals and worshippers; rather, there are multiple, overlapping typologies based on features of equal significance. Trade professionals have developed a system of classification based on the techniques of manufacture. Paper items are distinguished according to whether they are flat or foldable soft pieces of printed or painted paper, which will be called non-pitched in this book, or built on a bound-together frame of bamboo or wire. The second form, which literally means made by binding (紮作), will be termed pitched throughout this book. Yet, even among these masters of the trade, there are differing opinions on how (or whether) to separate the items recognized as pitched (such as the funeral offerings, Pinwheels, Flower Cannons, and Golden Flowers taken up in this book) into even finer subcategories. Some masters (the lumpers) recognize few subcategories and some (the splitters) see more, opinions stemming from their individual experiences or from respect for the categories of pitched items used by their own masters.[4]

In fact, a third "in between" category could be constructed for items of papier-mache, but even these items begin with a frame and it is not absolute that craftsmen see them as different from any other pitched item. Objects of papier-mache are hard to find in Hong Kong now, except for the brightly colored Good Fortune Chickens available at the New Year and during the festivals celebrating the birthday of Tian Hou, the Empress of Heaven. Roosters are believed to ward off demons and specters, as they herald the sun which drives evil away (De Groot 1912: 36). The Hong Kong chickens, with a chick or two placed between their feet, are still modeled of papier-mache, then gaily painted in red, yellow, and green and finished with natural glossy or brightly dyed real tail feathers. They also wear small mirrors on their chests to deflect evil, carry brightly colored silk tassels dangling from their beaks, and most are accompanied by a lucky phrase or two brushed onto a red paper slip attached to the base on which they stand.

If the professional distinction based on technique of manufacture (pitched or non-pitched) seems widely accepted among trade professionals, it is unlikely that customers, while understanding the distinction, use it as a model to organize their paper offerings. They purchase and use offerings according to other dimensions of the worshipping process, resulting in additional distinctive typologies parallel to those based on technique of manufacture. Customers and trade professionals also categorize paper offerings according to the entity being worshipped or cared for, a form of classification reflecting classic distinctions among gods, ghosts and ancestors. This is the most common manner of classifying, as concern about one or another of these entities underscores most rituals. Accordingly, offerings are divided with regard to whom they are being burned, although, as will be seen, such distinctions are sometimes blurred. Worshippers and professionals may also divide the paper according to the holiday being celebrated, although it is sometimes difficult to separate the event from the object in such cases. That is, while some lunar calendar events such as the Dragon Boat Festival (端午節) have distinctive papers firmly fixed on the festival itself, papers for other events, such as the birthdays of the gods, are more clearly directed towards the deity.

Paper offerings can be further divided according to the specific ritual that needs performing. When purchasing at the shop, customers may say, "I need materials to worship the Lady of the Bed" (a deity who protects sick children), or "My child is ill, so I need a package of materials for Passing the Gate" (another ritual to overcome sickness). In these examples, it is the personal concern or the ritual purpose that determines the classification of the papers. Finally, as the personal element is so significant in worship, there are idiosyncratic styles of conceptualizing offerings unique to individual worshippers. Such diversity in conceptualizing and classifying the offerings is recognized in the world of paper, and an individual item of paper offering may appear in multiple contexts and be spoken of in different ways, thus underscoring the complexity of the repertoire and its resistance to a single typology. In this chapter and in Chapter 6, which takes up the crafting of offerings, paper offerings will be introduced using the framework based on the professionals' non-pitched and pitched distinction. However, when these items are reintroduced in other chapters, they will be discussed according to their place in the worshippers' minds and in the contexts of worship.

The Non-Pitched Offerings

Nearly all everyday offerings for domestic or temple rituals fall within the two-dimensional, soft paper, non-pitched category. The term "everyday" is one used to highlight the most common items. It does not imply that such items are offered on a strict daily basis, but only that they are the most commonly used. Such items appear in many different contexts and are available in all places where paper offerings are sold. These paper items are usually packaged in multiples of one kind, or as separate components in assemblages of different paper offerings.[5] Individual worshipping practices and use of these materials vary considerably. They may be used singly or in multiples, used just as they are or, in the case of paper currency, folded into a variety of shapes. In addition, certain items are made in different sizes; which size to buy depends on individual habit, for all sizes of an item carry the same meaning and benefits, and may be used in the same ways and for the same occasions. Use of these items for the gods, the ghosts, and the ancestors has remained rather stable in living memory, except that the boundaries of what is appropriate to offer to these three categories of otherworldly beings show some blurring. For example, speaking of paper currency, in the early 1980s, shopkeepers and customers would agree that White Money (溪錢, introduced below) was basically for the ghosts. Yet, twenty years on, White Money is commonly found in offerings for ancestors and for deities. On the other hand, Longevity Gold (壽金, also discussed below) remains an offering to deities. A discussion of these everyday items begins below, beginning with paper currency, a category which has received scholarly attention as a separate entity, but which will be treated in this book as a form of everyday offering. Selected items will reappear in subsequent chapters, to be discussed a second, or even a third time, so that the differing contexts of the item in the paper world (its manufacture, actual use, and design) may become clearer.

Paper currency

Within the everyday offerings are included the various forms of paper currency, often referred to as "spirit money" (Cohen 1977; Seaman 1982), but also called "joss money" (Day 1940a), "idol paper money" (Hodous 1929), "mock money" (Dore 1914; Hunter 1937), or "ceremonial paper" (Hunter 1937). Paper currency is important in the history of paper offerings generally, as many of the proposed dates for the appearance of paper offerings concern spirit money. Dard Hunter wrote that by the reign of Ho Ti (He Di, 和帝, AD 89–106) paper was already a substitute for genuine coins, and paper cut into coin shapes was being burned to the spirits by the beginning of the Three Kingdoms Period (三國) from AD 221 to AD 420 [AD 220–265 Ebrey 1996: 338]. By the Tang (唐), imitations of real paper money appeared during the reign of Kao Tsung (Gao Zong, 高宗) (Hunter 1937: 28, 29). Dore (1914: 118) also advanced a Tang date, while others (Hou 1975) argue that the shift to spirit money took place during the Song (宋), when urbanization expanded the use of money and encouraged the growth of paper bank-notes (Gates 1987: 272).

Whenever it appeared, paper currency has long been crucial to all forms of worship. "The practice of burning some of this mock-money on almost all occasions of worshiping the spirits of the departed or the gods seems to suffer no abatement … No family is too poor to procure mock-money when occasion demands; and no heathen family is so intelligent, or so free from the trammels of customs, as not to be in the habit of buying and burning it" (Doolittle 1865b: 278). On arriving in the next world, the soul of the dead needs money to pay the heavy ransom demanded by the King of Hell for its release, or to satisfy other creditors waiting there who need funds for *their* release (De Groot 1892: 80). Thus, large quantities of money are required. By the twelfth century, paper money had become a standard item in funeral ritual, to meet this demand for release. "Each person was born into this world by borrowing money from the bank of the underworld. Each person stayed alive only so long as the term of repayment had not ended. At death, each person was required to repay in full the loan contracted at birth" (Teiser 1993: 133–4). "The paper money burned at funerals and other rituals in China is symbolic of the merits of the living whose acts of love and giving are like banknotes in hell, drawing interest to free the souls of the deceased into eternal life" (Saso 1997: 455). Doolittle explained that among the funeral gifts, there is a "small paper money-chest of a particular kind" which was, "to pay the debts of the deceased, whether known or unknown to him … His surviving relatives do not wish him to be annoyed by demands presented in the other world for the debts of this and therefore furnish a box of cash for the express purpose of liquidating these liabilities" (1865a: 194). This idea still shapes the burning of paper currency even in contemporary Guangzhou, where the burning of Gold Paper assists in paying the soul's expenses during the forty-nine days it is believed necessary to traverse Hell (Ikels 1996: 256; 2004: 99). The use of paper currency in all its forms is still an important component of worship in Hong Kong. Five themes shaping the use of paper currency which are also relevant to Hong Kong practices have been advanced: the perceived superiority of imitations over real objects, the need to burn offerings, the division of sacrifices into those within and those outside the house, the one-year effectiveness of rites, and the belief that the spirits of the dead are always hungry and require offerings (McCreery 1990: 7; quoting Hou 1975).

Worshippers burn Gold and Silver Paper (金銀紙) for ancestors,[6] Longevity Gold Paper (壽金紙) for major deities, and White Money (literally, Brook Money, 溪錢, but the term White Money will be used in this book) for lesser deities, ghosts, and ancestors. Also for ancestors and ghosts are the Bank of Hell notes (冥錢) or Hell Money, which bear a variety of names, including, Unreal Money (假銀紙), the Silver Money (銀錢), and the Yin (shady) Administered Paper (陰司紙). Finally, there are cardboard coins covered in gold and silver foil and different forms of Gold Ingots (金錠) which are given to the ancestors. Gold and Silver Paper for the ancestors and White Money for the gods, ghosts, and ancestors, are included in many pre-packed assemblages, and are burned or scattered in great quantities at ceremonies and holidays honoring the deceased.[7] Longevity Gold Paper, usually simply called Longevity Gold and bearing the character for long life (壽), is also burned to honor the deities on their birthdays, on major holidays, or at other occasions as the worshipper wishes. It is given to the gods, to thank them for blessings already received, or to ask for long life. Longevity Gold comes in many sizes, including a very large version of eleven by twelve inches, and may be offered singly, in a pack, or folded into ingot shapes or other forms.[8]

Everyday offerings also include the rather coarse, brownish colored First Treasure (元寶) on which the other offerings are placed. Some decades ago, Clarence Day wrote of this item, which he termed "paper merit money" and described as made by "rubbing silvered sheets of metallic paper onto a coarse grade of brown paper" (1940a: 30). First

Treasure is still made of coarse paper with two painted stripes of green and purple (a color which some shopkeepers identified as red) along its outer edges. Shaped into basin form, First Treasure is often used to enfold and support the other offerings. Shopkeepers agree with Day's earlier observation in saying that First Treasure is not only a support for other items, but is itself an ancient form of currency used by both gods and ancestors, which now has no precise value. Many shopkeepers declared that the full meaning of First Treasure was too complex to understand, and no one could provide a truly satisfactory account of its history or ultimate meaning.[9]

A related item, the Big Bright Treasure (大光寶) is made of a combination of fine and coarse paper. Each piece is actually two sheets, the lower one of silver money mounted on a coarser backing sheet (in appearance this lower sheet matches Day's 1940 description of First Treasure). The upper sheet consists of a variety of Longevity Gold also mounted on coarse backing, but edged with fine white paper. The whole is also used to support the other offerings. Worshippers use Big Bright Treasure notes of three sizes: the Large First Treasure (大元寶), the Two First Treasure (二元寶) and the Small First Treasure (細元寶). More recently, some shops have stocked this item with the top sheet printed on brilliant white paper. Some worshippers prefer to use Big Bright Treasure at the bottom of the stack of offerings, packing the coarser First Treasure further up. Others use the First Treasure only for the lesser deities, while others give greater deities combinations of First Treasure and large Big Bright Treasure papers.

Other everyday items

The Honorable People Papers (貴人紙), which are usually called simply Honorable People (貴人), are burned to the deities in nearly all acts of worship, as the worshipper hopes for the assistance of these helpful people sent by the gods. Honorable people are real people who appear when help is needed. As the shopkeepers explained, "The honorable people are those who help you. For example, if you get into a dispute with someone, and a stranger steps forward and helps you, then that is an honorable person." The Honorable People Papers are made of thin red and green paper, either rectangular (長貴人) or circular (圓貴人) and bear the punched-out figures of eighty or 100 small individuals representing these honorable or helpful people. The figures are not delineated in any great detail, but are nevertheless identified as small individuals. A more recently appearing version of the Honorable People Paper bears on each sheet the image of Guan Yin, the Goddess of Mercy, flanked by the gods of longevity and wealth, two bats for prosperity, and two peaches (signifying immortality), and bordered by images of the Prosperous/Green Horse (祿／綠馬, a lucky animal bearing gold ingots on its back) and additional peaches. The individual honorable people are, in this version, quite clear, as each sheet contains 100 cutout faces, clearly printed with eyes, noses, and mouths in black.[10] The Honorable People Charm (貴人符) is a third version, a red paper and a yellow charm combined; it is composed of two or three smaller papers. These different versions will be discussed in more detail in Chapter 2, where the ritual use of the Honorable People Paper will be explained.

Another paper, the Lucky Basin Paper (運盤紙) in its non-pitched or two-dimensional form, is directed to the gods in the hopes of obtaining good health and good luck. This is a brightly colored paper (despite the name, it is not in the shape of a basin) bearing a pair of green bats for prosperity and the images of the Three Star Gods (三星, 福祿壽), the deities representing happiness, affluence, and longevity. Another good fortune paper is the Five Treasures Document (五寶牒), which thanks the gods for blessings and seeks good fortune. This item is actually a package of five to six separate items, including a Lucky Basin Paper (above), both a circular and a rectangular version of the Honorable People Paper, a Great Luck Document (鴻運牒), one piece of the Solving of 100 Problems (discussed below), and an Honorable People Charm. Sometimes, the Lucky Basin Paper is just used by itself, but the combination packages are very common.

The yellow Solving of 100 Problems (百解, also referred to as a "hundred remedies for crises and predicaments," see Szeto 1993: 19) assists the worshipper in escaping from disasters and difficulties, and ranges in size from twelve inches wide and twenty-one inches long to large sizes of twenty-one inches wide and thirty inches long. It is sometimes called the Forgiving Book (赦書), as the item is viewed in two parts: the upper one-third of the sheet is the Forgiving Book and the remaining two-thirds, the Solving of 100 Problems. The upper Forgiving Book bears depictions of a horoscope, a bat for prosperity, a deer for longevity, and an image of Zhang Tianshi (張天師), the First Heavenly Master of Daoism and great destroyer of demons (Stevens 1997: 78, 106). It also contains two circles, the uppermost to assist Zhang in ridding the worshipper of problems, and the lower (the eight trigrams, 八卦) to act as a charm for dispelling any troublesome ghosts. The Solving of 100 Problems comes in varying sizes, with some shops stocking a much smaller version called a Small Solving of 100 Problems (細百解), but the overall meaning and use is the same, no matter what the size. Worshippers use it in nearly all contexts of worshipping the gods, for they wish to be protected from harm.

The Towards Life Money (往生錢, or the Towards Life Spirit Incantation, 往生神咒) will be termed Money to Live in this book. It is a round yellow paper with scalloped edges, printed in red with Buddhist scriptures or incantations. Dard Hunter included an example of this item, which he referred to as "money for the hereafter" in his 1937 publication (1937: 30; also described on an insert between pages 40 to 41); its size and appearance are much the same today. Used in Buddhist ceremonies, Money to Live assists the soul in rebirth. As one paper master explained, "This Money to Live is a Buddhist incantation used so that the ancestors may be reincarnated earlier. [It is] For those ancestors who are distant, and for those who are the newly dead, for they still suffer in Hell and need this incantation." Most Money to Live have a hole burned in the middle of the yellow roundel; this means a Buddhist monk or nun has recited a prayer over the paper. In the past, the nuns (or even elderly lay worshippers) would read the prayers over the sheets one by one, burning the hole in the center of the paper with an incense stick, but nowadays most recite the prayer just once and burn a hole through an entire package of papers.[11] However the holes are burned, worshippers believe that papers with holes are more powerful; these versions are accordingly more expensive. Shops sell the Money to Live in packages in which the sheets are divided into stacks of varying amounts (some 100 sheets, some only thirty) by sheets of rose color, which also bear the printed prayer and may be burned. With some packaging of Money to Live, the top rose-colored sheet is set behind and shows through an additional painted metallic paper roundel with cutout flowers and the symbol for long life, adding beauty to the object. Also available in Hong Kong is a much smaller and less expensive version printed on square paper; lacking some of the outer circles of the full prayer and the holes, it is therefore not as popular with local worshippers.

Shops also sell a larger and different item, but one with the same meaning, called the Seven Voice Incantation (七言咒), although some shops identify the Money to Live by this second term. This version, which literally bears the name, Towards Life Spirit Incantation (往生神咒), is a yellow sheet printed with seven roundels and a Buddha's hand, all in red. Each of its printed roundels, and the printed name as well, has a hole burned in the middle, for a total of eight holes, making this paper very auspicious. In addition, on the larger seven roundel versions, the bottom roundel is very large and complete, being a special incantation to Guan Yin separately identified in some shops as the Incantation of Big Sorrow (大悲咒).[12] The Money to Live and the Seven Voice Incantation are burned during festivals to honor the dead (such as Qing Ming and Chong Yang), or during Buddhist ceremonies in the funeral home at the time of death, to ease the transition of the soul and ensure successful rebirth. The Money to Live is a very popular item during such commemorations, and relatives of the deceased may burn many tens of thousands of these papers.

Many popular non-pitched items are used under more specific circumstances. For instance, many different kinds of clothing and accessories are offered to the gods, the ghosts, and the ancestors. A popular item is alternately called the Five Color Paper or the Seven Color Paper (五色紙 or 七色紙, although a minority of professionals call it the Seven Color Money, 七色錢), and is composed of packages of flat sheets of colored paper representing actual cloth, for the ancestors and ghosts to use to make their own clothing in the next world.[13] Other offerings for the ancestors, cut in the form of clothing from paper of the same colors as these five color papers, bear machine-printed or hand-painted tailoring details; still others are cut from paper printed in various decorative motives and alternate colors. These items of paper clothing look like the real thing and are accompanied by a wide range of accessories, from boxes of miniature jewelry, to personal grooming aids, underwear, and footwear (more detail will be provided in Chapter 4). The crafting procedures, design and color, and symbolic content of paper clothing and accessories will be taken up in more detail in Chapters 6 and 7. Other distinctive non-pitched papers for special rituals accompanying such events as curing an illness or moving into a new home will be discussed in Chapter 2.

While quite diverse at first glance, all these examples of non-pitched offerings are made of flat paper, and are two-dimensional. Other papers are folded into elaborate forms by the craftsman or worshipper, giving the appearance of truly pitched, three-dimensional items, but lacking the frame. The most common example of "not really pitched" are the sheets of Gold and Silver Paper, especially the former, which are generally folded into a variety of elaborate shapes representing the traditional ingots (tubular, rectangular, in crown shape, even perfect cube) before burning. While Gold Paper is normally hand-folded by the worshipper, more recently shops have begun to sell pre-folded ingots in cardboard boxes for customer convenience. Not really pitched items also include the paper tigers which are part of the packages sold for such events as the Frighten Festival (驚蟄), an occasion for overcoming disasters. These tigers are fashioned of lightweight cardboard printed in varying tints of yellow,[14] with the tigers' physical details printed in black and cut out in the general outline of the tigers' bodies. There are two tabs at each end. When these tabs are pulled together and glued, the resulting cardboard shape makes a tiger. A separate piece printed as a ferocious head is then attached. The result is a charming and (not so) fierce little figure of a tiger. Still other three-dimensional but not pitched items are found among the offerings for the dead, as many of these items are made of paper or light cardboard carefully folded or pasted into shape; there is no real frame supporting the form. The sets of miniature furniture made up for the paper residences burned to the dead are examples. More recently, retail shops have begun to stock smaller, but fully crafted, versions of the homes burned to the dead once available only by order from funeral workshops. These new and smaller versions of homes (see Chapter 4) are made entirely of folded, glued or stapled thin cardboard. All these non-pitched offerings, both folded and not folded, are still made entirely of paper or similar combustible material, and are completely or nearly completely burned when set alight.

The Pitched Paper Offerings

The second category of offerings recognized by the trade is that of pitched paper items. Pitched items are three-dimensional replicas made up from a frame of bamboo strips. Earlier references speak of kaoliang stalks being used (Lowe [1940–41] 1983: 115), or sorghum straw covered with pasted colored paper (Wieger 1913: 567). Cave refers to pitched items as " 'paperworks', three-dimensional models often made to order by skilled craftspeople" (1998: 10). Most pitched products are built on bamboo frames, including many of the funeral offerings for the deceased, such as houses, cars, servants, and numerous smaller items (see Chapter 4). Other items include the pitched form of the Lucky Basin Paper given for birthdays, and sometimes the elaborate hats included in custom clothing assemblages for the gods. Also included are lanterns (not taken up in this book), the Pinwheels (風車), purchased at temples after worship, the Golden Flowers (金花, also known as Spirit Flowers, 神花) purchased to honor and adorn the gods, and the magnificent Flower Cannons (花炮) offered to the gods.

A very popular paper item unique to Hong Kong, quite subtle in meaning and complicated in the nature of its efficacy, is the Pinwheel (which will be revisited in Chapters 6 and 7). Pinwheels are made by affixing a number of pinwheels to a frame usually shaped in a round or gourd form, which is then adorned with a variety of auspicious trimmings. While glorious in their design and color, especially when viewed in their massed displays at the Lunar New Year, Pinwheels are far from merely decorative objects or irresistible toys for children. Revolving in the wind, the Pinwheels are believed to bring in and then multiply certain desirable spiritual benefits for the worshippers, including the changing of bad fortune to good. Golden Flowers, always used in pairs, are objects formed in a triangular or elongated inverted kite shape. Formed of bamboo and wire, they are covered first in gold foil, and then adorned, depending on their size, with a great many auspicious elements. These wonderful elements, attached in layers to the underlying framework, make Golden Flowers the most gloriously colored and intricately crafted examples of the paper master's art. They are accompanied by red "ribbons" of varying length and thickness called Spirit Reds (神紅). Finally, the great Flower Cannons are not really cannons, but large towers, ten to fifteen feet high, constructed of bamboo. Crafted to hold images of the god to whom it is dedicated (often Tian Hou), it is composed of levels, each level containing a bewildering array of trimmings, all of them beneficial elements with auspicious meanings, and capped with splendid replicas of bats for good luck.

The largest pitched items, such as the Flower Cannons and certain funeral offerings, may be quite heavy and awkward, requiring a minimum of two persons to lift and carry. For this reason, many genuine pitched items are not ordinarily available in space-restricted retail paper shops, but must be specially ordered, or purchased directly at the workshop where they are made. Other pitched items, such as the Golden Flowers and Lucky Basins, are available in shops year round, although the available stock for the former consists of only the simpler and smaller versions; larger and more elaborate varieties are obtained at the Lunar New Year. While popular offerings, pitched objects are not strictly everyday items, because they are usually purchased only once a year (at the Lunar New Year for Golden Flowers and Pinwheels, or for the deities on their birthdays) or for special or unpredictable events (birthdays, funeral objects at death). Pitched items will also be taken up in more detail in following chapters.

How to Burn Paper Offerings

As already explained, most paper offerings are burned, for only by being totally consumed by flame will the object reach its destination, and be usable by the recipient. However, the exact procedures for burning are decided by individual worshippers. Assemblages of different offerings, whether for the gods, ghosts, or ancestors, whether pre-packed or assembled at the time of purchase, are burned at the same time, as one item. All everyday items purchased in individual packages of many pieces can be burned piece by piece, but most often are not, because they are burned in such large quantities that burning that way would be very time-consuming. These large quantity items for ancestors include the Gold and Silver Paper, the Money to Live, and the White Money; which are generally gathered in quantities in burning bags and set alight all together. When using such bags, many worshippers *do* separate the individual sheets of each item and place them in the burning bags one by one, or at least, spread them out to separate partially separate before adding them to the bag. While it is rare to see anyone burning such items outside of the burning bags one piece by one piece, this is, again, decided by the worshipper.[15] At one time, the Honorable People Papers were cut as individual figures, with more physical detailing, and burned one by one, but about sixty years ago in informants' memories this form[16] was replaced by the now common circular and rectangular forms bearing more numerous and more stylized images. Each Honorable People Paper may be burned alone as one piece, but they are generally included in assemblages and burned along with other items. In addition, as for the terminology of paper offerings, there are different ways in which to talk about the act of burning them, and for the act of worship. Informants used such terms as "burning paper bound offerings" (燒紙紮祭品), "burning Gold and Silver Paper" (燒金銀衣紙), "burning paper sacrificial offerings" (燒紙祭品), "burning First Treasure" (燒元寶), or the also familiar terms of "worship the gods" (拜神) or "worship the ancestors" (拜祖先).

Despite all the ritual importance of burning, certain paper

offerings are not in fact burned as a condition of use. Depending on the occasion and the intended recipient, paper offerings may be scattered for troublesome ghosts (the White Money), pasted or hung into position for ancestors and gods (charms), reverently returned to the temple (Pinwheels), or presented as offerings of respect, gratitude, or adornment for the gods (Golden Flowers). The Qing Ming Festival offerings of Red Money and White Mountain (紅錢白山) or Mountain Money (紅錢山帛), which are small strips made of Red Money (紅錢) attached to a sheet of white paper cut into "peaks" along the top and bottom, are not burned but affixed to the top of the gravestone or the traditional horseshoe tombs.[17] After a year of exposure, these offerings, which become faded and torn, are replaced with new ones.

Charms are also not always burned. Paper charms, which are obtainable at most temples and at some paper shops, are applied, in a general way, to the misfortunes of life such as quarrels, bad health, bad luck and poverty, and the evil intentions of malicious spirits.[18] The most common form of charm is the *fu* (符) amulet of mystic writing and symbols on a piece of paper (Topley 1953: 63, 1967: 110–1; see also Ch'en 1942; De Groot 1910; Mark 1979; Ruitenbeek 1993). Charms are popular in Hong Kong, and may be obtained at the temples or from the shops associated with the temples, such as those at Wong Tai Sin. Made of yellow paper and printed in red, charms are usually folded into elaborate small shapes and carried around for good luck. They may be worn as amulets, fastened to walls, set above the doors of houses, pasted up on a door or a bed curtain, or even worn in a bag or in the hair (Doolittle 1865b: 308). Charms may also be burned at the end of rituals seeking heavenly help, or burned when seeking healing from illness, the ashes then drunk in water, tea, or soup (Anderson 1970: 173; Hayes 2001: 50; Topley 1953: 68–70).

The pitched paper offerings present more difficulties for the conscientious worshipper. Certain of them, such as the Golden Flowers and the Pinwheels, were defined by craftsmen as items that originally needed to be burned but that are burned no longer. Others, such as the Flower Cannons (taken up in detail in Chapter 7), have their constituent parts distributed by auction or by lucky draw during the festival to the deity to whom they are offered; these individual elements are deemed very auspicious. Further, individual Flower Cannons deemed particularly lucky are auctioned intact and placed in ancestral halls for good fortune. When this happens, neither the intact Flower Cannons nor their individual parts are burned. Other pitched offerings that continue to be burned are problematic. For one thing, they may be quite large, such as the houses or cars burned for the dead; it is difficult to ensure that all parts of items so large are actually consumed. Pitched funeral objects for the dead may be set alight at the huge incinerators in the funeral parlor itself, or in large three-sided metal ovens rented from the paper offerings workshop or from funeral parlors. Mourners have these ovens taken to the curbside, or some other location, where they feed the offerings to the flames. While such pitched offerings are mostly consumed, bits of blackened bamboo from the frame may remain after burning. In addition, pitched items in their modern forms contain plastic, metallic paper, tin foil, staples, wire, and other non-combustible materials. The use of such materials makes it more difficult for the worshipper to achieve the goal of having the items totally consumed by fire.[19]

To be sure that their offerings burn evenly and completely, so that the objects reach the other world in their entirety, many worshippers are careful to purchase only those everyday, non-pitched items made of higher quality paper. Paper offerings are made with different grades of paper, which affect both the way the material burns and the time needed for all to burn completely; the coarser varieties leave more residue. There is a special kind of high quality handmade white paper that the shopkeepers called Jade Fastening Paper (玉扣紙), which burns down evenly into a fine ash. Machine Made Paper (機器紙) is also used, but it is coarser and heavier and when burned leaves an undesirable black ash.[20] As one shopkeeper explained:

> Jade Fastening Paper is the best; this is also true of white paper money. The white paper money which is really white in color is not as good as the red [i.e., white paper having a reddish tinge]. The red is made of the Jade Fastening Paper paper while the white one is made of Machine Made Paper, which blackens after burning and is heavier. If you buy Machine Made Paper, one catty of it is the same as one and one half catties of the Jade Fastening Paper, so you get less paper. Comparing two stacks of the same weight, the Machine Made Paper stack is very thin.

While at one time it might have been true that wandering ghosts were offered coarse, unattractive offerings, this no longer holds true in Hong Kong, as worshippers may give many of the same offerings to them as are given to the honorable ancestors. Hence, ghosts may receive offerings of the finer quality paper, and even the common White Money, while not expensive, is itself made of very delicate, thin paper.

In the past, urban families burned their paper offerings (except at funerals) in a variety of containers such as cooking oil tins. Now it is more common for urban worshippers to use the red enamel portable metal ovens, for sale at most retail paper shops. These ovens are sold complete with lid, elevated interior platform to ensure air circulation and even burning, side cutouts in the form of auspicious stars and gourds for air circulation, and wheels for ease of movement.[21] At one time, people were allowed to burn paper offerings within the older public housing estates and the pre-Second World War private housing blocks; residents and visitors to these estates recall seeing the paint and plaster of stairwells and lift lobbies blackened from the smoke and scorching caused by careless burning. In the more recently built modern private and public housing estates, burning in the stairwells and other public spaces is now prohibited as a fire hazard.[22] Paper shop owners in a number of new estates, interviewed in the early 1990s, explained that paper burning was prohibited in such public areas. By 2003, a number were lamenting the possible negative effect this would have on worshipping practices.

> As you many know, there are lots of people in Hong Kong and housing for Hong Kong citizens is getting smaller and smaller, the corridors in public housing are getting narrower and narrower, the ventilation in the corridors and the stairwells is getting worse. The fire-proof doors always need to be closed. In such poor housing design, how can the culture of domestic worship continue? Worse still, our government does not support the local traditional worship either, it would even block the paths for grave sweeping.

Residents must now decide whether to burn fewer offerings, to perform such rituals within their own flats (using the red enamel ovens) and hope for the best, or to burn their offerings at a temple. Many have opted to take offerings to the temples, affecting the practice of domestic worship.

People living in rural areas, or in squatter or cottage areas in urban districts, also use the red enamel ovens, even though they have more open space (wasteland) for safe paper burning. The larger temples in the urban districts have restricted burning due to air pollution from the billowing smoke of countless offerings and incense sticks. The Wong Tai Sin Temple in Kowloon, originally surrounded by the blocks of the Wong Tai Sin Estate, now sets firm limits on paper burning, with temple staff continually clearing away spent incense sticks, candles, and paper offerings.[23] Worshippers now gather up all paper offerings after worship and deposit them in large plastic trash bags set around the plaza facing the temple; when these are full, workers come and take them away for burning elsewhere. While papers can no longer be burned in the temple, worshippers continue to offer incense, although workers also remove incense regularly, even when those sticks are not fully burned down.

Putting It All Together

The number of sheets of any particular paper offering that must be burned is a matter about which even the professionals have quite different opinions. For example, while there is some agreement that First Treasure paper should be used in ten pairs, the ten pairs representing ten treasures (十寶), some shopkeepers felt that five pairs were sufficient for domestic deities. A rule of thumb is that even numbers of items are best if the worship is for a happy event and inside the home, and odd numbers are used for rituals against evil. There are times when this odd/even rule is switched, however. For example, the Red Money used during the Lunar New Year is purchased in sets of three, five, or any odd number. Made of fine deep red paper, flecked with gold and adorned with rows of perforations, it is glued above the main door. Sets of three glued above the entrance to one's home suggesting "three number ones reach [home]" (三元及第), representing the hope that three children will achieve the ranks of numbers one to three in the Imperial examinations, while sets of five represent "good performance in five generations" (五世其昌) or "five blessings knocking on the door" (五福臨門) (Knapp 1986: 118).

While shopkeepers could explain odd and even, customers were less concerned about the numbers of even the most common items. As many items are set into packages at the factory or shop, most customers will just buy the package and not stop to count all of the contents (although some will flip through the contents to make an estimate). If the customer did not specify an amount (when buying items not already packed into bundles), some shops just gave them an even-numbered amount. The forms of currency such as Gold and Silver Paper, Longevity Gold, White Money, and the Money to Live are, however, normally sold in larger packages of multiples of ten, while paper clothing may be purchased singly or in sets of six or more. There is also some ethnic variation in the amounts used. Shopkeepers explained that the Big Gold

(大金) used by the Chaozhou community[24] to worship the gods was generally used in twelve pieces, but some customers used twenty-four or even thirty-six pieces (all multiples of twelve, however). The rule of thumb is that a worshipper deemed "more serious" in worship burns more than usual of any item.

While customers may purchase only one item of paper offering, they usually buy a combination of items. Paper shops have always assembled offerings into sets as the customer ordered them; there is a term in the trade, to fold (疊, or 疊出來, to fold up) which refers to assembling offerings into a set. Beginning twenty to twenty-five years ago, retail paper shops and wholesalers began to pre-pack these sets for particular deities or the ancestors.[25] These packages are identified by a slip printed or handwritten in red and gold, bearing the name of the deity for which it is used, or marked as "worship the ancestors."[26] Each package is wrapped in plastic and contains all the needed paper items, although some packages do not contain the incense and the wax candles.[27] People may use these packages as is, or combine them with additional offerings. While their convenience makes them extremely popular for customers worshipping the gods, experienced or elderly worshippers nevertheless examine the contents carefully for correctness. Reflecting customer concerns and because they believe the assemblages packed by Mainland workers can be inaccurate, retail paper shops assemble their own packages or purchase packages only from wholesalers of good reputation. The larger Hong Kong wholesalers assemble their own packages in their warehouses, which are then sold locally or exported. Such sets are available only for gods and ancestors, and not for ghosts, who have other packages assembled for them during their festivals, and not for rituals directed towards a specific situation (such as house moving) or problem (such as illness). Packages for these personal concerns must be hand-assembled on the spot by the shop or the customer.

Combining various everyday items amplifies their efficacy, as each item reinforces the good meaning of the others; that is why so many assemblages of offerings contain the same familiar items. For example, the assemblages for the gods are designed to simultaneously ask the deity for assistance and express gratitude for favors, hence, all contain Longevity Gold and Honorable People Papers because all worshippers want the gods to bless them with a longer life and more helpful people to assist them during that long life. These assemblages also contain clothing, and White Money, which the deities need to help other unfortunate souls. It is important to begin by placing items in an overall circular or bowl shape, which has the meaning of completeness or wholeness. For example, when using White Money (by itself), some worshippers may tap open the stack, then fan out the sheets so the result looks like a plate or half plate. When worshippers assemble their own sets, they often arrange the items in a particular order, for they feel that the set is more efficacious if each item is in its proper place in the stack. However, as there are different opinions about the "proper placement" of an item, there are many variations in assemblages. A typical package of offerings, packed by a worshipper for the Earth God (Tudi Gong, 土地公), contained the following everyday items, moving from the bottom to the top of the pile: two sheets of white First Treasure placed as a cross, then ten pieces of coarser First Treasure, White Money fanned out into a plate shape, two pieces of circular Honorable People Papers, one piece of the Lucky Basin Paper, one piece of the Solving of 100 Problems, two sheets of the Honorable People Charm, two pieces of the rectangular Honorable People Paper, Gold and Silver Paper, and a set of wine-colored clothing for gods. Overall, this seems quite an impressive package, but is not unusual, for when assembling their own sets, customers often include many items. It is also a good example of how worshippers mix many categories of paper in their own ways; this one for a domestic deity contains three forms of currency, including Gold and Silver Paper associated with ancestors, and White Money associated with ghosts.[28]

While many customers prefer to assemble and pack their own sets, the use of the pre-packed offerings packages has become very popular among both novice and experienced worshippers. Such packages allow novice worshippers to learn about proper offerings, thus simplifying the process, but even elderly customers buy them, especially those containing clothing and accessories for the ancestors, as a convenient way to be sure that nothing is missed. Most retail paper shops stock them,[29] but they have been sold at Wellcome, a local supermarket chain.

Where People Worship

Hong Kong people burn paper offerings at many locations both private and public, informal and formal, permanent and ephemeral. While people worship in greatest numbers during the major events of the lunar calendar, many of Hong Kong's temples attract worshippers no matter what day of the week.[30] During the Qing Ming and Chong Yang festivals to remember and honor the ancestral dead, families give offerings at the graves of their departed kin. While the majority of Hong Kong's dead are buried in public or privately maintained graveyards in Kowloon, Hong Kong Island, and the New Territories, many graves are scattered within what are now country parks or in the New Territories countryside, some quite magnificent and accessible, others modest and isolated. Ancestors are also given respect in ancestral temples for clan and kinship-based rituals, or at home at the family altar, while spirits are given offerings at innumerable small shrines and ephemeral sites (see below).

Domestic worship

A vital component of worship, paper offerings are used regularly, which means that the average customer purchases on a recurrent basis (perhaps every two weeks). The amount used depends on the customer, for worship is a very personal activity and individual customers, not shopkeepers, set the frequency of worshipping practices. Shopkeepers explained that some customers bought paper offerings every day, some once a week, and still others purchased large quantities once a month. Faithful worshippers buy proportionately more supplies just before major events of the lunar calendar, such as the Lunar New Year, Qing Ming and for the Festival of the Hungry Ghosts.[31]

Worship is still conducted domestically and at businesses on the first and fifteenth days of each lunar month (初一, 初十五). In 1865, Justus Doolittle observed the special practices of Chinese businessmen on the second and sixteenth of the month (初二, 初十六), when any place of business or trade burned "a quantity of black coarse incense (but no candles) and mock-money and mock-clothing." This practice was to protect businessmen from purchasing worthless goods, or beginning unprofitable transactions (1865b: 155–6). In 1924, L. Newton Hayes wrote, "The majority of stores and shops made a regular practice of worshipping the God of Wealth every fifteen days" (1924: 95). The young shopgirl whose burning of paper offerings was described at the beginning of this chapter was following this customary practice. Domestic worship followed a similar pattern. "In many homes, there is a daily worship of the ancestors, the God of Wealth and the Kitchen God. Before the establishment of the republic it is probable that there was scarcely a non-Christian home in all the country that did not perform this rite of worship on the first and fifteenth day of every lunar month" (Hayes 1924: 95). It is difficult to know how many Hong Kong families still follow this practice; data from the surveys of 2003 indicated that 18.4 percent of the sample still followed such worship. Berkowitz, Brandauer, and Reed described the practice in the late 1960s:

> In addition to red lamps, most shrines are fitted with holders for burning incense and candles, which may be burnt on any day but usually only on the first and fifteenth days. On these days, one first cleans the shrine and then burns incense, once in the morning before going to work and once in the evening between dinner and bath time. The worshipper stands before the shrine, holding before him three sticks of burning incense. He then either simply bows three times, or if he wishes to show special reverence, he goes through the ritual known as the Three Kneelings and Nine Kowtows, kneeling three times and kowtowing three times each time he kneels. He then places the incense in the holder. (1969: 96)

Many Hong Kong families are often too busy nowadays to keep strictly to such old practices, or they feel that domestic worship conducted at other times is sufficient.

Private worship at home (拜神), whether on a daily or weekly basis, is generally a simple affair. Many worshippers give offerings to a small complement of deities. Many families worship the Sky God, who protects the home from evil spirits. Some identify this deity as a distinctive entity they call Tian Guan (天官), the Ruler of Heaven and "bestower of happiness, freedom and prosperity" (Stevens 1997: 56), but others maintain that the Sky God is a euphemism for all the major gods. Deities closer to home include the Earth God (土地公, Tudi Gong), who protects the house. One respondent described him as "the bodyguard of my family." The Earth God shrine is usually placed outside, near the front door of the house, where he prevents the entrance of malicious ghosts. The spirits of ancestors and deceased relatives are allowed to enter, because they would do no harm. Other popular deities include Men Hau (門口), and Cai Shen (財神), who protect the door and bring prosperity, respectively, and Di Zhu (地主), the Lord of the Land. The Di Zhu shrine is set up inside the house, so that he may oversee home security. Finally, the Kitchen God (Zao Jun, 灶君) still rules the kitchens of some homes. More exalted deities include Guan

Gong (關公), who supports business and protects the family, and the ever-benevolent Guan Yin (觀音), the Goddess of Mercy and giver of children. Guan Yin is particularly popular with Buddhists, and is probably the most common deity on Hong Kong's domestic altars. Wong Tai Sin and Tian Hou may complete the complement of deities. Personal preference determines which deities are worshipped and the order in which they are worshipped, but devotees often follow a rank order based on the hierarchy of the gods, a hierarchical pantheon which some have suggested connects the household to both wider community and state (Liu 2003: 380). Hence, the Sky God comes first, then those deemed "big gods" such as Guan Yin and Guan Gong, then the Lord of the Land, then the Earth God, and finally, the ancestors if there is a tablet or shrine to them at home, for families may keep the tablets elsewhere. Some families reverse this order, beginning with the ancestors and proceeding to the gods, and worshipping the gods themselves in no particular order.

Domestic worship is usually a simple affair, with offerings of incense, flowers, and food, but there is considerable variation in actual practice. The material content of home worship includes two or three sticks of incense, both morning and evening. Some people vary the number of sticks offered; three for the ancestors and powerful deities, but only one for the Earth God. Others give one stick to each entity, twice a day; others, three sticks to each, twice a day. Some offer five sticks, not three, to the Lord of the Land, because he protects the four corners and the center (五方土地). Whatever the practice, incense is rarely dispensed with, and even those who declare that they no longer worship in the old way may continue to burn incense. The use of flowers in worship also varies, with some families never using them, others using fresh flowers every week, and others only on selected holidays. Colorful flowers such as gladioli and chrysanthemums, especially in red, pink, or yellow and accompanied by a few sprigs of greenery, are still very popular in Hong Kong, although elderly worshippers prefer white flowers for Guan Yin. Younger worshippers select other varieties of flowers for their color and beauty, including roses, but some people avoid them for the thorns, which the deities would not appreciate. When giving flowers to the ancestors, people choose the flowers and colors the deceased most loved.

Food offerings are also very common, and a great range of individual practices may be observed. Many families offer apples and oranges, three or more in a pyramid, while others add candies, cookies or cakes, tea, and wine. Fruit can be replaced regularly, so that it does not spoil, but some families leave the fruit on the altar for a week, then replace it. During major holidays, domestic food offerings become more complicated. For example, during Qing Ming, the grave-cleaning holiday, families prepare roast pork, chicken, cakes, three cups of tea, and three cups of wine. At the grave, these items are offered first to the dead, and then consumed by the family on the spot. Offerings for the Chong Yang Festival are similar, although for both occasions care is taken to prepare gifts of the foods that the ancestor most loved. Because of this, a wide range of cakes and sweets, special treats, and even fast foods are offered now. On both occasions, worshippers take care to arrange the food offerings in attractive shapes and in such ways as to harmonize their colors, a practice seen in the offerings of fruit. During the Festival of the Hungry Ghosts, people give fruit, roast pork, roast duck, tea, and wine to the ancestors. Some families also take food to the street for the wandering ghosts, including fruit, bean sprouts, peanuts, tofu, and rice. If giving meat offerings, some people believe ducks are more appropriate than chickens, as they are better protection against evil. This may be individual belief, although duck eggs are used in the rituals of moving to a new home (see Chapter 2). Some respondents said that the sharp beaks of chickens could damage the colored paper offered at these times for the ancestors, and so ducks were preferred. During the Mid-Autumn Festival, fruit, moon cakes, roast pork, chicken, three cups of tea, and three cups of wine are offered to ancestors. Finally, at the eve of the Lunar New Year, vegetables, roast pork and chicken, fish, glutinous rice, and fruit are offered, while vegetarian dishes are prepared, with rice and tea, on day one. On day two vegetables, roast pork, and chicken are added. Some families prepare only vegetarian foods for days one and two. Popular during the Lunar New Year are the bouquets of vegetables (garlic, celery, lettuce, spring onions, parsley, lotus roots, red carrots, and more) tied together with red paper and sold in the markets. Many of these vegetables have good meanings. Celery signifies hardworking, lotus roots mean surplus within the year, onions represent cleverness. Whatever the actual food offerings during the holidays (and Guan Yin is only offered vegetarian foods), the deities are also given red candles, their own cups of wine (or tea for Guan Yin) and their own chopsticks, which are also red for good luck.

At the temple

As any visitor to a temple in Hong Kong will attest, religious activities are still significant. At both neighborhood and major temples, worshippers of all ages and backgrounds — from the very old to those youngsters in school uniforms, from those in business suits to those in hawkers' aprons — offer their devotion to the deities (for a general depiction of a Hong Kong temple, see Anderson 1970: 168–71). For an idea of how worship is conducted, we may visit the temple of Wong Tai Sin, the Great Sage Wong, the resident deity of one of the most popular temples in Hong Kong (for a full history of Wong Tai Sin, see Lang and Ragvald 1993). Built in 1921, the Wong Tai Sin Temple attracts numerous worshippers every day who fervently believe that the god can aid all those who seek his advice and assistance. While worship is particularly notable on Wong Tai Sin's birthday or during the Lunar New Year, occasions when the number of worshippers reaches tens of thousands as believers flock to the temple to seek out their fortunes for the coming year, any day is a good day to worship at the Wong Tai Sin Temple.

After exiting the subway stop or coming down from the adjacent housing, one first encounters a line of elderly beggars hawking small charms. These individuals are well organized, forming a line in which each takes her turn approaching a potential customer, and then, whether successful or not, moves to the end of the line and begins again. Moving past these ladies, one comes to a row of ten or so hawker stalls selling religious souvenirs and worshipping materials on the left, and more indigent elderly selling charms and fortune slips. These hawker stalls, all that remains of the many tens of stalls originally operating at the temple, sell most necessities, including packages of most common offerings, incense, and even fruit, but their main business is souvenirs bearing the name or image of Wong Tai Sin himself. The temple also contains a more formal enclosed arcade further to the left, maintained by the Tung Wah Group of Hospitals, in which small shops sell a wide variety of items for worship. In front of these stalls is usually a line of small portable ovens for burning items to the deity; however, most people take their offerings inside to be burned. Passing under the main arch, the visitor turns left under a second arch, and ascends a flight of stairs to the first platform. This platform faces the stairs leading up to the main platform in front of the temple. At the rear of this first platform is a long stone altar-like table which worshippers use to arrange their offerings. The table also contains a variety of small incense burners filled with sand to hold the dozens of sticks lit by devotees at a nearby glass and metal lamp. Both upper and lower platforms have a lamp of this kind, which contains a burning votive candle to light the incense sticks. Many worshippers spread newspapers on the stone floors of the platform and arrange their offerings before beginning to worship, but some come better prepared and have small mats to kneel on, kinder to worshippers' knees than thin paper on cold stone. While most worshippers prefer the upper platform closest to the deity, quite a few are content to conduct their worship on the lower one. During the major religious holidays the two platforms will be packed to the limit with worshippers, and every inch of space will be used. During these times, when crowds prevent the full complement of worship involving the spreading out of many offerings, many people just offer incense and fruit.

Devotees bring with them all that they need for worship. Both the small shops within the enclosed arcade adjoining the temple on the lower level and the small hawker stalls outside the gate stock the most common offerings, but they do a better business in temple souvenirs and small religious oriented gifts such as lucky jade pieces. In addition to a variety of paper offerings, most worshippers offer food to Wong Tai Sin. Recent visits have confirmed the constant use of the most popular fruits, apples and oranges, offered to the deity and also used as convenient holders for incense sticks and candles. I have also seen offerings of grapes, tangerines (lucky fruit at the New Year), bananas, and whatever fruit is in season. Some people bring roasted baby pigs, traditionally wrapped in red cellophane on a red bier, and sometimes adorned with one or two traditional red paper flowers. Others bring boiled chickens, slices of fried pork, whole cakes made of white radish, cakes and squares of tofu, boxes of vegetarian delicacies, a great variety of candy, oil and wine. If wine is offered, it will be served in three red wine cups (although some give five cups), which will be emptied onto the stone pavement after the worship is completed. Except for a few pieces of fruit, all these food offerings are taken home and eaten, having been blessed by Wong Tai Sin.

The style of worship reflects personal choice. After setting out the offerings, many press their foreheads to the stone a number of times. All will light incense sticks, "nodding" with them while praying, then place the sticks in the incense holders. Some hold the incense sticks, in the classic three or more often in clusters of ten or more, over their heads and bow, while others hold the sticks over their heads while kneeling in front of the temple. Many worshippers are busy folding the Gold and Silver Paper and the Longevity Gold into various shapes; some will pass the folded spirit money over the billowing incense smoke to obtain an extra blessing. Additional paper items such as packages of paper clothing and special creations for the deity will be kept close in bags or displayed on the paper mat. During the holidays, and especially at the deity's birthday, the offerings are more elaborate; handcrafted clothing being a favorite choice. After initial prayers some worshippers will ask Wong Tai Sin questions, throwing wooden divination blocks or shaking the fortune sticks to seek the god's advice. After all questions have been answered and all prayers of thanksgiving or supplication said, the worshipper leaves, gathering together all the paper offerings and placing them in nearby plastic containers, to be collected and burned by the temple staff.

Shrines and ephemeral sites

Worshippers also give paper offerings as well as fruit, flowers and incense at locations other than the home and the temple. These other locations, in both rural and urban areas, on street corners, lanes, and hillsides, may spring up and quickly disappear, or may turn into shrines, which Stevens (1980: 21) described as "miniature unmanned temples or open air altars often called in Chinese 'small temples' (小廟)." Shrines are marked by an accumulation of paper offerings, incense pots, ceramic images, or gifts of fruit. They might be left open to the elements if surrounding a natural rock formation or a tree or roofed and partly enclosed if protecting images of a deity or deities. The latter form of shrine can become quite complicated, assuming the appearance of a genuine small temple as it expands and accumulates internal altars. For example, larger street shrines in the urban area consist of a large altar with numerous images and framed prints of gods. These sometimes fragile, and often illegal, structures are maintained by a few elderly devotees (Stevens 1980: 21).

Shrines may also be situated close to natural elements, at the base of a tree or a rock, or the rock or tree itself may be considered a spirit (Stevens 1980: 21; Webb 1994), or as the abode of a spirit or spirits — the distinction is not always clear (Graham 1961; Berkowitz, Brandauer and Reed 1969). These locations are chosen as, "Believers in local religion also think that all animals and natural landscapes have their individual spirits who can chose to help people with their supernatural powers ... In Hong Kong and Macau, people may worship old trees, rocks with special shapes and Earth Gods represented by rocks" (Liu 2003: 377). Burkhardt's description of a simple shrine on Lantau Island is typical of such sacred natural locations, this one a combination of rock and tree:

> A conical stone is wedged in the roots, capped with red paper with the usual inscription. Sometimes a gilt talisman is pasted on the face of the stone, between two scrolls. A very primitive P'ai Lou, or honorific arch, is constructed of two forked boughs with a cross bar, roughly lashed with twine. Pasted on the uprights are two sets of Chinese characters. Pasted on the reredos rock is "Bless and Honour the Spirit". The altar is a level scrap of bared earth, with the usual incense burner and cups of wine. (1953: 124)

Burkhardt provided further descriptions of well and rock worship (1953: 123–5), which he felt were of considerable antiquity, and the latter of particular importance, as an emblem of fertility which was given tribute from engaged couples to ensure the perpetuation of the clan. Berkowitz (1975: 6) gave other examples of such worship, explaining how the personal gods "tied to locality, place, occupation and lifestyle ... resided in specific trees or rocks in or near the village."

How trees and rocks become shrines is not always clear. It may be that a natural site has gradually become a focus of attention due to actual events or personal belief, such as the notable "spirit trees" of the New Territories. An excellent example, the most famous of Hong Kong's spirit trees, may be found in Lam Tsuen (林村), the "Village in the Wood," southwest of Tai Po Market in the New Territories. Patrick Hase (2000) has described these trees:

> Near the Temple are two large and prominent trees. These are Spirit Trees, the residences of the local Earth-gods. These two trees, with other numinous trees and clumps of bamboo in nearby villages are very heavily worshipped. Worship consists of throwing a paper and a bundle of worshipping paper items attached to a string weighted with an orange — if the flag is caught in the tree, then the spirit will take note of it, and the request (often written on the paper) that came with it.

Some locations become shrines because they are personally meaningful to an individual worshipper or group of worshippers. The two spirit trees described above became famous when, just after the Second World War, a very sick fisherman dreamed of a deity who promised to heal him. When he was healed, he discovered that the helpful deity was the Tai Po Temple Earth God and he began to go to the temple to worship; the trees have attracted attention ever since (Hase 2000). Other shrines were originally locations that became significant for individuals suffering from illnesses believed to have been caused by disturbed or malicious spirits. Having found these places where the disturbance (and their illness) began, they worshipped at that location and got well. Hence, while such locations began as meaningful to a single worshipper, they gradually attracted greater attention and a more permanent shrine grew up. As Hase explained for the Lam Tsuen spirit trees, "This history is greatly fascinating, as it shows us a religious practice growing up from nothing to major proportions within fifty years" (2000).[32]

It is also possible that some shrines originated as repositories for images of deities no longer worshipped. This practice of "sending back the gods" was described by Berkowitz during the late 1960s resettlement of Hong Kong rural villagers (Plover Cove) into urban areas. As part of the removal process, villagers performed ceremonies to send to heaven the locality-specific gods — earth gods, door gods, and village gods — who could not go to a new setting and who would be replaced by new gods (1975: 5–11). A geomancer, assisted by three or four Buddhist monks, performed the ceremony, which ended with a banquet of food including pork and bean curd (Berkowitz, Brandauer, and Reed 1969: 78). In the urban areas, some informants maintained that if one decided to cease traditional worship altogether (for example, on becoming a Christian) or to cease worshipping a particular deity, then one must adhere to a prescribed ritual: first explaining to the deity why they wished to cease practicing domestic worship, then taking off the wooden board (the image of the deity), then preparing a red packet for the god, then wrapping the wooden board (with the deity's image) and the red packet together with red paper, and finally putting the god in a location where other such materials had been gathered, perhaps under an old tree. One lady explained that she bought the papers for worship from the shop, worshipped, then wrapped the gods' images and gave them to the rubbish collector. Giving him a red packet to do this for her, he took the images to the temple and placed them there. Other respondents felt that a "casual chat," to inform the gods that their altars were to be removed and that they should return to the temple or to heaven, was sufficient. Food or incense could be offered while the deities were being requested to leave, but this was a matter of personal preference. They believed that no one need take the domestic altar anywhere (some just threw it away), although very elderly worshippers might feel more comfortable removing it to the nearest shrine or temple.

Still other sites have acquired social significance by their tragic associations with real events from the recent past. During the Festival of the Hungry Ghosts this form of worship is particularly prevalent. The festival is celebrated beginning on the fifteenth day of the seventh lunar month (Ward and Law 1993: 59), at various locations: near temples in Hung Hom (紅磡), at the King George V Memorial Park in Kowloon, near the railway station in Tai Wai (大圍), and at the Morton Terrace Playground in Causeway Bay, to name but a few notable sites. It is just as frequently observed at specific locations identified with ghostly activities, such as sightings of ghosts. Many of these locations are remembered as the sites of fires, bombings, or atrocities from the Japanese occupation of Hong Kong during the Second World War. These sites are regularly visited during the festival by elderly worshippers who hope to ease the sufferings of the spirits of the dead who linger still at the sites of their death because they died violently, far away from relatives, or with no living relatives, and have been neglected, deprived of food, clothing and money in the other world. During this festival, Hong Kong is dotted with ephemeral sites where small offerings of fruits and candles and the remains of burned materials, such as spirit money and paper clothing, recall the attentions of the devout towards these lost souls. The same concern for souls extends throughout the year, not just at the Festival of the Hungry Ghosts, and small offerings may be seen from time to time at places marked by other fatal events, such as fires and traffic accidents. I recently observed such an offering on a sidewalk bordering a highway exit ramp; it consisted of three sticks of incense, two small candles, and a Flower to Thank God (還神花) stuck in a paper cup and placed on a newspaper with cooked rice. No matter how shrines and ephemeral sites acquired their significance, all are places of worship and devotion, as much as is any temple, and all are marked by items left for the deities or spirits, including paper.

This chapter is an introduction to the world of paper, focusing first on the general features of selected paper items from the complement of everyday offerings. The common features and patterns of worship were then examined, again with regard to the variations, before turning to the locations, both domestic and public, in which worship is carried out. The items of everyday paper offerings, appearing in a variety of contexts, are wonderful examples of paper art. Conceptions about their nature and use vary, and professionals and worshippers employ a variety of overlapping schemes of classification. No one scheme predominates and the major typologies, that of the profession based on pitched and non-pitched and that of worshippers based on recipient (whether god, ghost or ancestor), ritual, or purpose are complementary and not mutually exclusive. In addition, worshippers' behavior does not follow a consistent set of rules regarding which items to burn to which recipient. As seen in the example of paper currency, the original rule of Gold and Silver Paper to ancestors, Longevity Gold to the deities, and White Money to the ghosts is well understood, but there are variations. Such variations in attitude and practice are a theme in paper offerings, illustrating the great importance of personal motivations and individuality. To continue this exploration, Chapter 2 will describe some of the practices of individual worship designed to alleviate the worries and concerns of everyday life.

2
Individual Worship and Personal Concerns

Hong Kong's many temples are lively with devotees during the birthdays of the deities, the Lunar New Year, and other religious holidays.[1] At other times, worshippers visit the temple or worship at home for more personal reasons. As Marjorie Topley once observed, "A good deal of 'popular' religious activity — performances of the kind I would call 'Little Tradition' — is in fact individual. People act singly, or with the aid of a companion or sometimes a ritual expert, to change circumstances in their lives" (1966: 99). Topley classified rituals as either "regular" rites, those with broad objectives such as thanking the gods or requesting aid, which occur at annual festivals or at other propitious dates, and "occasional" rites, those dealing with more specific problems (1967: 99). The regular rites involve many of the items from the everyday offerings introduced in Chapter 1. But, as Topley discerned, occasional rites, while employing many pieces from the everyday repertoire, often involve more unusual paper materials.

Illness and Its Remedies

Among the most common of occasional rites are those dealing with illness. In a 1924 study of prayer slips collected in Chengdu, Suzhou, Tianjin, Shanghai, and Fuzhou, L. Newton Hayes noted that illness was the subject of the most common prayers for assistance to the deities, followed by concerns over marriage, protection during travel, and desire for wealth (Hayes 1924: 97). In Hong Kong, all illnesses are troubling, but illness is particularly distressing when children are affected; shopkeepers' comments indicate that youngsters' health is a great concern of their customers. While shopkeepers encourage treating illness through prompt visits to regular Chinese or Western doctors, they are prepared to offer advice on rituals based on the *Tung Shing* (通 勝), the traditional Chinese almanac (Couling 1917, Smith 1992). De Groot described the *Tung Shing* as a classical book which indicated days "fit or unfit for important actions, thus teaching man how to behave in accordance with the annual revolution of time" As such, it was deemed "an exorcising instrument of the highest order" (1910: 1022), excellent for protection against angry spirits (ghosts).

Many paper masters believed that if people remained ill over a long period, it could be because they inadvertently violated the rules of proper conduct and offended the spirits. Violations included actions such as tearing leaves off trees — which would put humans in contact with wandering spirits, described by Hodous as those "attached to wood" (1929: 160, see also De Groot 1912: 16–17) — or knocking over an incense burner and not apologizing; behaviors common to active and careless children. Prominent in all discussions of illness was being disturbed by (or disturbing) ghosts, the "dirty things" (污糟邋遢嘢) as some refer to them. Ghosts are particularly troublesome because they are often invisible and thus can easily be disturbed if they linger in areas busy with unknowing humans. Further, ghosts may have evil intentions and can cause illness and even death (Dennys 1876; Berkowitz, Brandauer and Reed 1969: 93). Yet, others feel that, because of their fate (命), which guides people to good or bad luck, some people run into ghosts when they are in bad luck and fall ill as a result; no conscious ghostly malice is involved. In other examples, as suggested by the offerings to offset the illness, perhaps the malice of what Hong Kong people term the "small people" (小人), a general category of annoying (and living) people, is involved. In all situations, to get well, rituals need to be performed and the practitioners need to make amends for their own behavior or for that of the sick person. In all such rituals, paper offerings act as mediators, providing the necessary link reconciling the entreaties of the supplicant and the distress of the offended spirit.

Getting rid of ghosts

Shopkeepers explained that sick customers usually saw a physician first, but if the physician's treatments were unsuccessful, they would turn to ritual. First, the sufferer tried to remember on what day the illness began and then consulted the *Tung Shing* to see what had occurred on that day. This process is termed "Checking the Foot of the Day," or "Worshipping the Foot of the Day" (查日腳, 拜日腳), to see when and where the sufferer has been disturbed by, or has himself disturbed, a spirit.

> When a worshipper is sick, he may refer to the almanac to see if he has the symptom as described in the almanac on that day. If he has, a set of paper offerings will be offered to drive away evil spirits or demons. For example, if a worshipper falls and hurts his leg or arm, he will worship at the location where he hurt his leg or arm. Once there was a customer whose mouth was crooked and the doctors could not cure it. After worship, he did recover. I cannot explain why but his mouth was really crooked, and once he worshipped, he recovered within a few days.

Even shopkeepers themselves follow the procedures when their own family members become ill.

> This rite is very useful when people run into ghosts, especially for the young people. I do believe that there is something to it because I had a related experience about it and it really worked. When my younger son was in kindergarten, he suddenly began to cry at midnight every night. I took him to the doctor, but it was no use. My mother then suggested that I check the foot of the day. I went to a shop and told the shopkeeper, who checked the Tung Shing and found that my son had offended a pregnant female ghost. I then worshipped at night in the junction of three roads, using white wine mixed with water, rice, a pear, and a set of paper offerings, including a Solving of 100 Problems. This paper was passed front and back of my son for three times before I began the worship, and then I did the rites in the street. I prayed and asked the spirit not to be angry. It was mysterious, but my son recovered soon after.

The almanac also provides guidance about the direction of worshipping. "The *Tung Shing* may say, 'In the northeast, you have encountered evil male and female spirits.'" Following this instruction, the sufferer must worship and burn offerings in a northeasterly direction.

With the assistance of the almanac, the customer tries to reconstruct where he or she was or what he or she was doing at the time.

> When you begin to be sick, you guess when you might have violated or encountered something while you were out [of your home, for one usually becomes ill when going out]. Then, check the almanac. For example, you went out yesterday, came back in the evening and got sick this morning. So, you check yesterday. But, if you haven't gone out but were still not well, then your home may have something wrong with it. You can check to see if your home has a problem.

The almanac also describes physical symptoms quite carefully. For example, "You have encountered ghosts of the newly dead and headless ghosts; the symptoms include pain in the bones and muscles, a high temperature and general irritability." Symptoms do not always match because not everyone can remember precisely when illness began.

> You must remember the date, otherwise, what the almanac says may not be correct. For example, the almanac may say that you have a fever, but you do not [so the date as remembered was incorrect] . . . Generally speaking, people would not come to buy paper offerings immediately when they feel sick, but would see the doctor first. As a result, [time passes] people cannot recall the things that happened some time before.

If the memory is clear, the customer can then take the appropriate paper offerings back to the location and burn them to placate the ghost or entity that was disturbed.

The contents of offering assemblages for curing illness are often specified by the almanac:

> The *Tung Shing* states what you should buy and use to worship. If, for example, it specifies 500 pieces of White Money, then we give the customer a pack of white paper money. If it doesn't mention what to use, then we pack a set 'casually' [using a standard amount of items considered efficacious]. If the sick person is a male, we pack a paper with a male on it; if a female, then a paper with a female. We include a paper boat and one set of First Treasure and candles. There is also a sheet for curing vomiting and pain, seven sticks of incense, a package of five colored clothing for the spirits,

paper money, and a paper horse to drive the 'dirty things' away. In all, there are about ten items to pack.

Another shopkeeper read out for a day selected at random: "Use 500 sheets of White Money, a paper horse or horses, paper clothing, First Treasure, and candles." Actual offerings will vary according to the directions given by the almanac for that day, and to the worshipping practices of the sufferer.

Each of the items included in the above assemblage has a specific purpose. The male and female figures are scapegoats (代人, 替身) who stand in for the sufferer and endure the illness or disaster on his or her behalf. Paper boats and horses assist in removing the ghosts by providing the means of transport. The Five Color Paper is included so that the ghosts can make clothing for themselves, while the spirit money can be used in the other world; both items help to satisfy the physical needs of these neglected spirits. Slightly more complicated packages for dispelling illness contain a package of eighteen sheets of First Treasure paper, one set of Five Color Paper, three sticks of incense, two small red candles, a paper boat in red and green with a center green seat, one package of Hell Money, a variable [ten to fifteen sheets each] pack of Gold and Silver Paper, a package of White Money, one sheet of the large yellow Solving of 100 Problems, and a *Bai Fan* set. Most of these items are placed in the package to provide either transportation or funds for the spirits, while the Solving of 100 Problems is to aid the sufferer to overcome the problem. However, the last item requires a bit more attention.

The name of this set, the *Bai Fan* (拜犯), literally means to Worship [Against] a Violation or Crime. In other words, the sufferer worships to offset a wrong or an error committed, even an inadvertent error (as in the case of disturbing a ghost). The set includes one sheet of yellow Closed [Gate] Paper (關紙) bearing a tiger head printed in green (for tigers are protectors against evil), a sheet printed with twenty-four charms, a second gate paper for passing the gate (overcoming the problem), an Eight Trigrams Charm (also for protection), and a Heavenly Teacher (Tian Shi 天師) Charm. If the sufferer is an adult, the gate paper is used without the tiger head. The Heavenly Teacher Charm refers to a helpful person who is skilled at driving away ghosts,[2] something like an exorcist. Both the Heavenly Teacher Charm and the Eight Trigrams Charm overcome evil and help to keep the ghosts under control. Some shopkeepers do not add the Heavenly Teacher Charm to the set, preferring to include just the scapegoat to take the place of the sufferer. The sheet of twenty-four charms, a yellow sheet printed with red charms, is for use when the sufferer cannot recall where or when the offense occurred; burned in its entirety, it covers all possibilities. Other items can be added, such as a sheet of the Solving of 100 Problems. The elderly master explaining the set for Worshipping [Against] a Violation also remarked that many people no longer understand these older papers and hence, when they wish to perform this worship, they use a second, more common set of four papers.

These four papers are the Yin Separation (陰隔), the Yang Separation (陽隔), the Restful Heart Document (息心牒) and the Compassionate Heart Document (慈心牒). The latter two papers ease the minds of sufferers bothered by spirits, and are burned with the intention of appeasing these spirits so they will cease their disturbances. The Yin and Yang Separation Papers are burned in a ceremony with Gold and Silver Paper, and the two document papers. The ritual also includes three spoons of rice (offerings to the spirits) and a pear or pears, because the sound of the word for pear (梨) is similar to that for "go away" (離).[3] In all, the first complement of papers, then the papers to Worship [Against] a Violation, and finally the set of four Separation/Document papers work together to ease the worries and calm the hearts of the patient, and provide all the apologies that the spirits desire so that they may be satisfied and cease their troublemaking.

A few shopkeepers added that customers very seriously ill for a long time can also add a very rare paper called the Written Accusation (狀詞). In two sizes, this yellow sheet printed in red characters explains to the offended spirits the reason for the offense the sufferer has committed. It is burned with the hope that the offended spirits will be satisfied with the explanation provided by the sheet and will then permit the sufferer to get well. Used this way, the paper resembles a sincere apology given face to face. Those continuously troubled by bad luck could also burn the Happy Event and Disgraceful Affair Paper (喜事紙, 醜事紙). If an individual feels uncomfortable after attending either a happy event (such as a wedding) or an unpleasant event (a funeral), this paper may be used. The paper is printed in red on white, in three rows of three small squares each; the middle row depicts pleasant events, and the bottom row depicts unpleasant events. The sufferer should cut out the center square and throw it away, then burn the remainder, put the ashes in water, and then drink some or all of the mixture. The central square represents the inner problem and the source of the uncomfortable feeling, so cutting it out removes the problem. Doing this is like taking heart medicine to be rid of troubles, and so removing the center square can be explained as "medicine for regulating/making just, the heart" (正心藥).

Shopkeepers used various terms to describe removing ghostly reasons for illness. Practitioners used the word expel (趕走), but there were variations on this theme: "getting rid of," or "expelling," or "driving away." Still others preferred to use the phrase "invite," or "invite to leave" (請走), a more polite way of persuading the ghosts to go elsewhere. As there is always a chance that the ghosts will not leave, the stronger terms, used in conjunction with rituals performed by Daoist priests, are considered more effective.

Passing the gate

Another common procedure for dealing with illness, particularly for children, is the Passing the Gate (overcoming the problem) ritual. Recorded by Doolittle in 1865, the ritual, which he termed "passing through the door," was practiced regularly by families anxious to secure the welfare of their children. Some families had it performed many times a year if the child was particularly illness prone, some every year, and some on alternating years, until the child had reached the ceremony of "going out of childhood" at the age of sixteen (1865a: 127). Doolittle's description was of an elaborate one-day ceremony involving Daoist priests, a specially constructed altar, elaborate rituals, and an array of food, mock money, and mock clothing for the spirits, culminating in the burning in the open court or street in front of the house of the bamboo and paper covered door used in the ritual (1865a: 128–32).

Nowadays, the version of this ritual as practiced in Hong Kong is somewhat simpler, using the Closed [Gate] Paper (關紙), a yellow sheet printed in green with the head of a tiger, minus the lower jaw (but with an upper row of bulging teeth).

> First the child (or an item of clothing if it is too sick to be present) is taken through the barrier either by the simple method of passing a small tiger-faced 'gate' over its head and then tearing the gate in two while it is held aloft, or by having a Taoist priest carry it in and out of a tall paper and bamboo gate structure which many temples keep for such purposes . . . Food is then offered to a deity, usually Kam Fa, the protector of children, and a charm paper depicting the gate the child has passed through is burnt together with some paper 'coats'. (Topley 1966: 112)

Paper masters added that worshippers needed the Closed [Gate]

Money (關錢), the fee for passing the road which is given to the officials in Hell, and the (literally) Closed Separation Paper (關疏紙), which is a form of report informing the deities that the child has passed the gate. To these items are added Gold and Silver Paper to pay for the ritual. Masters explained that this ritual of passing the gate, performed for children under twelve years of age, can be very complicated, because there are many and specific gates for various situations. Although the *Tung Shing* lists twenty-six gates, each representing a different problem, there are actually more than 100 gates, each with a specific name and meaning, and only a ritual expert (such as a Daoist priest) can determine just which gate needs to be passed. For this reason, the ritual is most often performed in the temple, although some masters said that it could be performed in the patient's home during evenings. Ill or disturbed patients should not go out at night, when they are more susceptible to harm.

Closely related to passing the gate is the ritual of *Han Jing* (喊驚, Shouting out Against Fear), or Calling Back the Soul, which must be performed by women of Dongguan (東莞) ancestry. When a child has been dull or stupid for some time, or has never recovered from a previous illness, then the child is suffering from "injury by fright" (Topley 1970: 429), or soul loss, in which the animating spirits have left the child's body (Topley 1976: 255, see also De Groot 1892: 243–4). If it is further suspected that demons or ghosts have maliciously made off with the soul, then "Haam-king rites to expel these malevolent spirits may be performed by Taoist priests, by female ritual experts, or by the mother or another female member of the family" (Topley 1976: 255). Our shopkeeper specified that only women of Dongguan ancestry (he could not explain why, other than the rite seems to have originated there) could help in such situations. Shouting the child's name, and tapping all over the house with the child's sleeping mat or chopsticks, she calls back the soul of the ailing child. Topley described this ritual:

> Another rite from the Tung Kwoon district requires the scattering of rice, the speaker coaxing the soul to come with her to the house. It is entreated to recognize its mother's name, and its own name, and again a list of things which might have frightened it — cats, rats, spiders, cockroaches, pigs, and dogs — is given, with an entreaty to become calm. The recitation ends with an announcement that the rice is all gone now and a plea to return to the bed. A garment is again waved, the bed patted, and spittle is put on the child's brow — explained as 'settling in' the soul. (1970: 432–3)

Berkowitz, Brandauer, and Reed (1969) recorded yet another Hong Kong example of Calling Back the Soul:

> The woman ran to the playground. There she faced the east, and waving the child's coat over three sticks of burning incense, she sang in a moaning voice, 'Sister, be good; sister, come back! Grandmother will take sister back! Don't be afraid! Sister, would you come back and get better day by day?' She carried on like that for about ten minutes. Afterwards she walked back to her flat. (1969: 94)

While the practitioner taps and calls, a set of paper offerings is burned, beginning with the *Bai Fan* assemblage described above, then a Soul Pursuing Charm (追魂符) which asks the Cow Ghosts and Snake Gods (牛鬼蛇神) to find the soul and bring it back to the house. As well, a paper boat, a paper horse, a scapegoat (substituting for the child), White Money, and Gold and Silver Paper are burned. Also included are the Compassionate Heart Document and the Restful Heart Document to beg the ghosts to be kind-hearted and to return the soul and cease disturbing the child. The paper horse is provided for the lost soul to return on, while the paper boat and the scapegoat are given to the ghosts as a substitute for the real child; the paper scapegoat child rides in the boat to stay with the ghosts. All these papers are, again, burned to provide apologies, transportation, companionship, and funds for the disturbed spirits. Nowadays, elderly paper shop owners explained, most people simply cannot find women of genuine Dongguan ancestry to perform the ritual (although apparently, some elderly women of other ethnic backgrounds also know how to "shout," or call back the child's soul to cure illness; see again, Topley 1970). If customers burn the assemblage for Worshipping [Against] a Violation in the street where the ghosts can get it, this action alone will usually take care of the problem without resorting to "shouting."

Adoption and fostering

A sick or fractious child may be fostered by a deity (see, for example, Topley 1974). The parents purchase a red sheet called a Three Star Card (三星卡). This sheet is eight by fourteen inches, of vivid red printed in gold with the three Star Gods, a bat, the representation of prosperity (福), representations of ancient gold money, and a lower border composed of a line of characters for double happiness (囍). On the sheet should be written, by anyone who writes characters neatly, a variation of the following phrase: "[Name of god] and [Name of child] today his/her parents represent him/her in asking for adoption from [Name of the god], hoping that the god will bless him/her to grow up well. Thanks to the god." Some shopkeepers say that the eight characters for the date and time of the child's birth (八字, the horoscope), as well as the names of the parents, should also be included. The worshipper burns a package of offerings containing clothing appropriate for the deity (for example, white clothing for Guan Yin), although some shopkeepers say this is not necessary. The child may worship the fostering deity on the deity's birthday, as well as on the child's own birthday, but the child's parents should keep the sheet until the child has grown up and is married, at which time the parents must burn the sheet and thank the deity. A description of how Hong Kong's fishermen conclude heavenly adoption is given in Anderson (1970: 176–8). One of my own research assistants, who was adopted by Wong Tai Sin after a series of childhood illnesses, told this story:

> My uncle was also adopted by Wong Tai Sin as a child. He grew up, got married, and he and his wife moved to the United States. After twelve years of marriage, he and his wife were always quarreling bitterly, and one night my grandmother, who is still living here, dreamed that she had not burned the adoption paper and thanked Wong Tai Sin. She was convinced that her neglect of this was the reason for the couple's problems, and so she went to the Wong Tai Sin Temple the next day with my mother and properly thanked the deity. After she did this, the quarrels stopped, and my aunt and uncle have had no more problems.

The Three Star Card also appears at marriage, at which time the parents of both the prospective bride and the groom write down their dates and times of birth (時辰八字) on two sheets, and the matchmaker uses these two sheets to assess the appropriateness of the proposed match. In addition, the parents of both the prospective bride and groom can use the Three Star Card to record the kinds and quantities of the wedding gifts. The parents exchange these sheets, which are kept as a checklist to confirm that the gifts given match those requested. Some families use the Five Star Card (五星東) a larger undecorated sheet, for this purpose, but this version is rarely seen. Doolittle's account of Chinese betrothal and marriage practices recorded an object with a similar meaning:

At the time of sending these presents to the family of the bride, there are also sent two large red cards. On the outside of one there is a likeness of the dragon, and on the other, a likeness of the phoenix. In the former are written the ancestral name of the bridegroom's parents, the name of the gobetween, and frequently a number of felicitous words and sentences. In the other there are written the ancestral name of the bride's parents, the name of the gobetween, and felicitous sentences. (1865a: 71)

In Search of Aid and a Better Fate

Hong Kong residents are often described as sophisticated, practical, modern and quick to employ the latest technological or scientific discovery to improve their personal and economic well-being. So described, they do not turn to what they popularly refer to as superstitious practices. Yet there is a sizeable number who supplement their everyday practical endeavors and scientific knowledge with a variety of rituals. Educated individuals who would never perform (or declare that they would never perform) any of the rituals here described, nor subscribe to the beliefs underlying them, have elderly relatives who have done so or who continue to do so, believing that the traditional ways of seeking solutions to problems or ensuring good outcomes are still appropriate. Constructing a mutually antagonistic relationship between superstition and modernity only obscures the actual practice (and assumes that modernity and tradition are antagonistic). Improving one's lot in life is one area in which tradition and modernity cooperate.

Honorable People and the Kindness of Strangers

The Honorable People Paper (or simply Honorable People), an elegant red and green item, is a necessary component of nearly all assemblages of paper offerings for the deities, or even, in the opinions of some shopkeepers, for the ancestors. Honorable People Papers are purchased in varying forms, but the most common are circular (圓貴人紙), with the basic meaning that the honorable people will go wherever the purchaser goes, and a long rectangular form (長貴人紙), signifying that honorable people will be available throughout the year. Circular or rectangular, with eighty or 100 people represented, as a charm or not, in two pieces or three, the Honorable People Papers are deemed very important by all customers, as these papers allow the worshipper to obtain good luck, blessings, and affluence. The phrase "honorable people" does not refer to any specific individuals known to the supplicant but to those who will help whenever difficulty arises. All people experience difficulties in life, and hence, all people seek assistance, which sometimes appears in unexpected places or comes from strangers. As one master explained:

> There are honorable people to help you wherever you are. For example, if you quarrel with someone, another person may come and help you. This is what an honorable person is. People want to have as many as they can, and each person's honorable people are distinct and special to him/her alone.

The search for more honorable people is never-ending, and worshippers continuously beseech the deities to send honorable people to help them.

Perhaps sixty years ago, Honorable People Papers were cut out individually, in the form of short figures with large feet, dressed in what resembled a tunic. The oval eyes, mouth, and nose were neatly cut, and the outstretched arms held two coins over the head. This form has been replaced by Honorable People Papers in circular and rectangular forms which appear to be one piece, but are actually formed of two identical sheets, one red and one green, placed back to back as one; a smaller number of shopkeepers refer to the second green sheet as The Prosperous/Green Horse (祿 / 綠馬). These papers are machine-punched along their surfaces in a pattern of ovals and rectangles which suggest lines of people, either eighty or 100 in number. Many retailers considered the eighty person form unacceptable; they asserted that it is "cheating" and they refused to sell anything but the 100 person form. Other shopkeepers said that while the 100 person form was common in the past, the eighty person form is more popular because it is smaller and less expensive. In their shops, only the very elderly asked for the 100 Honorable People version. Still others had no opinion on the matter and allowed the customer to chose, or they packed the smaller version in more complicated assemblages. In fact, the circular form is itself cut in different sizes, so the actual correct number of figures contained therein is difficult to discern. Circular and rectangular Honorable People Papers bear no printed characters, but circular papers bear the cutout character for longevity in their centers, emphasizing the benefits of long life, as well as affluence and divine assistance, which the item will secure along with the helpful people.

The picture is complicated by other offerings bearing the same or nearly the same name but looking very different. The Honorable People Charm (貴人符) is a flat red paper, printed in gold. It is folded in half, with each half bearing half of the phrase, "When Going Out, Encounter Honorable People" (出路遇貴人), at the top. Within the interior fold is a second item, a tiny slip of red paper like a charm and also printed in gold, again termed an Honorable People Paper. Some shopkeepers said that this combination could be used to worship the ancestors, in which case it was added to circular Honorable People Papers and burned. After it was burned, the entire family would be safe. Others explained the tiny slip as the miniature version of yet another set of Honorable People Papers, one containing three items: a Solving of 100 Problems, a Charm of Cheung and Lau (張柳符), and a sheet printed with two people and a galloping green horse, entitled an Honorable people and Prosperous/Green Horse (貴人, 祿 / 綠馬), the horse described by Stevens as a messenger (1977: 93–94).

The individuals represented in the Charm of Cheung and Lau are difficult to identity, a difficulty compounded by informants' insistence on the character for willow (柳) which has the same sound as that for the surname. The closest shopkeepers could come was that these were the original surnames of the two gods of He He Er Xian (和合二仙), the Immortal Twins of Harmony and Union, who oversee happiness in marriage (Stevens 1997: 125–6). Close inspection reveals that this tiny slip does indeed carry the symbolic elements of the three larger papers. Some shopkeepers asserted that the Honorable People Charm and its accompanying tiny slip may be ignored and the larger three-piece set used instead. It appears that the Honorable People Charm is a more modern, shorter form of the older, three-piece design, and many customers prefer its simplicity. Both forms and the horse, as well as the people, convey supplicants' messages to the gods and bring affluence and good luck to the worshipper; the red and green circular and rectangular forms of Honorable People Papers do the same.

Ethnic interpretations of the Honorable People Papers add to the complexities of understanding this so-called common object. One paper shop owner explained the Chaozhou people's use of these papers. For them, in addition to the standard forms, the Chaozhou Honorable People Paper comes in the form of a pair, one piece a red cutout in a recognizable human shape (albeit with two coins for the head) called the Honorable People Paper, and one piece a green paper horse, also individually cut out, called the Prosperous/Green Horse. These papers are nearly identical to what other shopkeepers had identified as the earliest forms of Honorable People Papers (see above). These two "paper dolls" are used during the ritual of Beating the Small People (discussed below) in which the practitioner seeks relief from troublesome people. During the ritual, the honorable person is hung up and the horse burned, so that the small people causing the trouble will be dispelled by riding the horse away. After worshipping, some believers burn the red honorable person, some dissolve it in water; it depends on their personal habits. The same customers also use the circular form of Honorable People Paper to ask for blessings and to give thanks.

The Small People

The reverse of seeking honorable people is avoiding or defeating the small people (小人). The term "small" refers not to the actual physical sizes of these people, but to their pettiness and mean-spirited natures. Small people are the troublesome, small-minded individuals whose actions cause trouble and who are harmful to the worshipper's self-interest (Chiao 1983: 138). From interviews at shops, it appears that sometimes there is confusion between ghosts and small people, even though the former has left this world and the latter remains; certain of the offerings used are spoken of as for ghosts as well as for the more commonly identified target, actual humans. Victims of such annoying people need not passively suffer; they can perform a ritual called Beating the Small People (打小人) any time they wish, on days of the month deemed most auspicious for such an action.[4] Beating the Small People also occurs at the occasion known as the Frighten Festival/Feast of Excited Insects (驚蟄 / 節) during February or March of the solar calendar (Burkhardt 1953: 9). The ritual may be performed at home or in public, for a fee, by elderly female practitioners.[5] This ritual has proven so popular that these elderly ladies can be found at regular locations around Hong Kong, at times other than the festival. The customer simply goes to the places where these women congregate, where on auspicious days the ritual can be performed.[6]

The actual ritual is rather simple. As Chiao recorded it, "When the ritual begins, two candles and three sticks are lit, food is displayed, then the small person paper figure wrapped in the 'small person paper' is fiercefully beaten with a shoe or pierced into pieces with a sword while a chant is being sung. Then paper 'credentials' are rolled and waved over the recipient's body before they are burnt together with mock paper money and other paper goods" (Chiao 1983: 140). The ritual comes to an end with divination with wooden divination blocks (*bei*, 杯) to see if the ritual was successful. If these crescent-shaped wooden blocks, each with one convex side and one flat side, lands with both flat sides down, the ritual needs to be repeated; if both the rounded sides end up, the ritual was successful (for another opinion on how to interpret their position, see Anderson 1970: 172). While it is recorded that a mixture of the two indicates uncertainty (Smith 1991: 1), some practitioners of the rite believe that this outcome, termed the three cup (三杯), is actually auspicious. A somewhat more complicated, eight-step procedure for the ritual of beating the small people has also been recorded (Chiao and Leung 1982). It includes lighting candles; assembling the papers for the small people; pounding the papers to pulp while chanting phrases to invite honorable people, dispelling the evil of the small people, and asking for the gods' assistance; burning a white tiger paper to further dispel evil; using honorable people papers to secure good fortune; scattering beans and rice to disperse the unlucky things and feed the small people; burning a package of colored paper [probably the Five Colored Paper, which the spirits can use for clothing]; and checking on the ritual's success through divination with wooden blocks.

The paper offering assemblage for the ritual may be purchased at any paper shop under the festival names of "Beating the Small People" or the Frighten Festival. The customer will receive a bundle containing a number of items. The exact contents vary from shop to shop, but there will be one each of male and female small people, printed in green on thin paper and dressed in modified Qing dynasty style; one yellow Solving of 100 Problems, usually in the small version; a small paper tiger to protect against evil; and a yellow paper called a Gold Flower and Silver Hand [palm] (金花銀掌) or a Small People Fan (小人扇) printed with soldiers and weapons (spears and tridents) for dispelling evil. Some shops include a Net of Sky and Earth (天羅地網). This is made of one square sheet each of vivid red and green paper, laid together and folded in half diagonally, then folded again into a shape resembling a paper airplane. It is cut through at intervals, so when fully opened, it is transformed into a square net. Used with the Honorable People Charm the net catches the bad elements, so that sufferers can be released from the harm they cause.

Also commonly included is the Paper of Five Ghosts, or Small People Paper (五鬼紙, 小人紙), printed in green, and representing the five small people and other evil things; some shopkeepers call this the Five Ghosts Charm (五鬼符). It bears the images of a pig for laziness, a tiger for cruelty, a snake for evil-mindedness, and an eagle-like bird, thought to represent troublemaking. It also bears a broom to sweep away the small people, and a chain to bind them and keep them from harming the victim (Chiao and Leung 1982: 118–9). Also important are the Black Small People (黑小人), with accompanying black paper chain. The practice is to cut out the black small person (it should be cut by hand at the time of packing this set, and is black in color because its heart is evil) and stick its head through one of the links of the black chain. Thus secured, the evil creature can be beaten by the Gold Flower and Silver Hand mentioned above while the tiger looks on. Other assemblages may also contain varying elements such as sheets of Hell Money, sheets of White Money, a few sheets of Gold and Silver Paper, sheets of First Treasure, various charms, an Prosperous/Green Horse Paper, and colored or white clothing (sometimes called the Small Clothing, 衣仔). All these are dispersed to the bad elements, to encourage them to cease causing trouble. Three sticks of incense and two small red candles are common accompaniments.

As with the honorable people, small people do not generally refer to any specific individuals known to the worshipper, but to a generic category of troublesome or unpleasant people. However, on occasion they can be specific individuals known to, or suspected by, the worshipper.

> Some performances of the 'Beating the Small Person' ritual even have a specific 'small person' as the target. His or her name, address and other information available such as the time and date of his birth, names of other members of his family are all written on a piece of paper which will be wrapped together with the small person paper figure to receive fierce beating. This practice is indeed close to black magic, though it was only intended to stop the target small person from making further trouble rather than to hurt him. (Chiao 1983: 143)

Observations bear this out; customers can have the ritual performed for such reasons as to get rid of a rival for a husband's affection, or to remove unruly friends who are adversely affecting the success of one's children at school.[7]

The Pinwheel

While beating the small people may be a popular activity in Hong Kong, many participants will shyly profess disbelief even as they purchase the package of offerings and seek out the elderly practitioners. A more serious aura surrounds other paper offerings dealing with uncertainties. A very popular paper item unique to Hong Kong, more subtle in its meaning and more complicated in the nature of its efficacy, is the Pinwheel (whose manufacture will be taken up in Chapter 6). Discussions with worshippers and interviews with craftsmen revealed that Pinwheels were not insignificant paper trifles but objects imbued with meaning and religious significance, whose reconstructed history revealed a steady accretion of meaning and significance over time. Pinwheels are made by affixing a number of pinwheels to a frame usually shaped as a circle or gourd, which is then adorned with a variety of auspicious trimmings. While glorious in their design and color, especially when viewed in their massed displays at the Lunar New Year, Pinwheels are far from merely decorative objects or irresistible toys for children. Revolving in the wind, they are believed to capture and then multiply desirable spiritual benefits.

Each Pinwheel contains from one to ten small red rectangular papers bearing a lucky phrase or meaning head (意頭). These lucky phrases take the form of four-character couplets, hand-brushed or printed, either singly or in pairs (pairs are referred to as a double blessing). The lucky phrases were once (roughly from the 1940s through the 1970s) brushed with golden calligraphy onto rectangles of fine red paper; this painted form is now found only on handmade varieties. Factory-based manufacturers now use machines to print out the phrases, in gold, onto cardboard or plastic rectangles which, while less attractive, are more durable. Pinwheels will contain at least one couplet-bearing rectangle, and the largest may hold as many as ten. The rectangles are glued or taped to the frame, most often near the top, but also at the center or along the sides. There is no fixed rule on number or placement; I have seen larger than normal rectangles containing four lucky phrases, and cardboard plaques in which the phrase shares space with a printed design such as an image of the deity, such as Wong Tai Sin.

Pinwheel masters estimated that while there were over 100 lucky phrases, only about a third of them were actually used.[8] Certain phrases have become archaic or represent desires that have become less popular (such as the desire for many sons), and so are not reproduced unless by special order. Choosing the proper lucky phrase is of great importance, for it is believed that its content is obtained as the Pinwheels revolve. Worshippers who are not so specific in their concerns, but who are worried about affairs in general, can purchase Pinwheels with multiple lucky phrases or one bearing the popular, all-encompassing phrase of "the desires of the heart come true" (心想事成), thus covering all possible wishes. Poor worshippers need not worry about finding an affordable Pinwheel, for the full range of lucky phrases is reproduced in all price ranges. Worshippers purchase their Pinwheels carefully, selecting the design and the lucky phrase harmonious with the wish they hope the deity will grant. The continuous revolving of the Pinwheels in the wind repeatedly brings the wish to the attention of the god at whose temple it was purchased.

Pinwheels are objects of true religious significance and not decorative items or toys. On this point, paper masters were quite emphatic.

> While it is true that people do not see the Pinwheel as part of the god, it is always regarded as something good. It can bring people safety and chase the devil away. This is because people buy the Pinwheel after worshipping the god, so they think it is a gift that is blessed by god. I have never heard of anyone who thought it was a toy; it is absolutely not a toy in my opinion.

The history of the Pinwheels, reconstructed from the collective memories of elderly masters, suggests that all began as toys but then, through a process still incompletely remembered, some forms achieved religious significance sometime after the Second World War. This process of empowerment was likely brought about through their being adorned with lucky phrases and other auspicious elements, their function as an integral part of worship and religious ritual (especially at the New Year), their close association with temples and/or deities, and their passing through the smoke of the temple incense. These features made them particularly evocative of the blessings of the god to whom they were dedicated, most notably Wong Tai Sin and Che Gong. The Pinwheels' association with temples is especially meaningful in the case of Wong Tai Sin, whose rise as a refugee god has been well documented by Lang and Ragvald (1993; see also Lang 1997). The increasing popularity of the deity in the 1940s and 1950s among Kowloon's refugee community, who believed in Wong Tai Sin's ability to provide assistance and meaning to their lives, likely strengthened the perception that the Pinwheels associated with him were able to satisfy meaningful desires. Yet, the Pinwheels' ability to assist worshippers in securing particular blessings is only part of their significance.

Hong Kong worshippers may employ a wide variety of traditional procedures for identifying difficulties in their lives or perceiving the outlines of their fate (for a description of classical techniques for discerning one's fortune, see for example, Dore 1917, Smith 1991). A very popular method, practiced at all Hong Kong temples, is a procedure termed *kauh chim (qiu qian* 求籤), in which the worshipper asks the deity questions. At the Wong Tai Sin Temple, a most famous temple for such divination, "The god expresses his answer to the worshipper's questions or petitions by selecting a number, corresponding to the number of one of the poems, through a procedure called qiu qian (Cantonese: kauh chim)" (Lang and Ragvald 1993: 106). Giving offerings, the worshipper shakes a container of 100 numbered bamboo sticks until one falls out; the number written on that stick is noted and the worshipper, after asking all questions, collects the pink *qian* slips bearing the numbers on the sticks.[9] These slips, which are printed with well-known stories taken from history or literature, are then read and interpreted as the answer of the Great Sage. On any day, not just on holidays, many worshippers can be observed performing this rite, but tens of thousands will try to perform it on the eve of the Lunar New Year. Worshippers also may seek answers to their questions with the pairs of wooden pieces, already mentioned in connection with the ritual of Beating the Small People. In both instances, it is believed that Wong Tai Sin (or any deity so approached) will answer truly all requests for advice.

Armed with such answers from the deity, and knowledge of their condition, worshippers purchase Pinwheels not only to obtain good luck, but to change their fate from bad or indifferent, to good. Pinwheels are bought new every year, purchasers selecting ones with different lucky phrases according to their needs. Worshippers assert that one must purchase Pinwheels annually at New Year, to secure blessing for the family and general protection. The interaction of the features of empowerment already explained (association with temples and with worship of a deity, the possession of lucky phrases, being decorated with numerous other elements bearing auspicious meanings, and being imbued with smoke of the temple incense) creates Pinwheels deemed truly efficacious that can bring about beneficial changes to individual or family situations, and ensure a good fate for the purchasers. As the popular phrase explains, "Pinwheels are bought to change fate," and for this reason, and for the general good luck they also bring, they have become objects of great significance to all worshippers.

Other methods of ensuring a good outcome

There are other ways of ensuring good fortune that involve non-pitched paper offerings, such as the item termed the Lucky Money or Lucky Paper (運錢, 運紙). As its purpose is to alter one's luck and thus, fate, it will be referred to here as a Fate Changer. Most Fate Changers are composed of five rectangular sheets of colored tissue paper, but some varieties contain six or ten. The internal colors include cream, blue, green, yellow, and orange; the outermost sheet is generally violet, but can shade into rose. Shopkeepers stress that these colors, which appear in different combinations, have no particular meaning, but are only for beauty. These colored sheets are folded in half and then cut along one side into connecting coin-shaped strips, which would produce a long ribbon effect if the sheets were pulled out, something worshippers would never do for fear of tearing them and thus cutting off their fates. Worshippers may hold the fate changer up on a stick, and rotate it to make the change, but Fate Changers are better used in the temple, where the priest can cut and rotate the paper while chanting a prayer. After rotation, the Fate Changer is burned to the big gods with one Five Treasures Document (itself composed of a Lucky Basin Paper, a deep red Great Luck Document, the red Honorable People Charm, one circular and one rectangular Honorable People Paper) and a Solving of 100 Problems (including a Forgiving Book).[10]

Some shopkeepers felt that burning the Fate Changer and the Five Treasures Document was sufficient for the ritual, while others said that these two papers must be accompanied by gifts of clothing for the deities, Longevity Gold, and First Treasure. In one sense, the Five Treasures Document is a general offering to all major deities, and has many purposes, but the items it contains individually bear the meaning of changing one's luck for the better. Burning it reinforces the meaning of the Fate Changer and increases the chances of a turn for the better.

A rarer item is the Long Pennant (or Banner, 長旛), which is used in the worship of the most powerful gods. Long Pennants can be obtained at temples or at retail shops, where they are made by special order in either cloth or paper. An example of a Long Pennant in the collection is approximately four feet in length and made up of three strips of fine colored paper, each strip three inches wide. These three strips, the central strip red and the two side strips green, are attached at both ends to floral paper cut to resemble pelmets. The bottom pelmet is finished off with five of these paper strips in alternating green and red. The Long Pennant is completed with the name of the deity written (in full honorific form) on the upper part of the right hand strip, and the name of the sender on the lower section of the left-hand strip. The middle red strip contains the written message of the sender, such as a wish for a blessing such as long life, or praise for the deity. Because the Long Pennant requires a talent for elegant calligraphy, many retail paper shops no longer stock nor craft such items, lacking the skilled hands for writing the essential characters. If ordered to thank a deity for curing an illness, the Long Pennant would be made of paper and would be burned as soon as the sufferer recovered. The Long Pennants made of cloth, which are purchased in the temples, are given to the deity in gratitude for care and protection, often at the Lunar New Year. They are painted with the appropriate phrases and hung (by the temple keeper) high inside in front of the image of the deity. While some families decide to burn their pennant after one year, others just leave it hanging in the temple as a sign of their gratitude. In either situation, the offering of the Long Pennant is accompanied by offerings of First Treasure, Big Bright Treasure, Longevity Gold and paper clothing for the god. Food is also offered, mostly chicken and fruit, but only vegetables and flowers if the deity is Guan Yin.

Protection from Uncertainty

Paper offerings are also used for more joyous occasions such as starting a new business, moving to a new house, or celebrating a birthday. The Golden Flower may be purchased for the first two events. A new pair of Golden Flowers is purchased for adorning the corners of the signboards for a new business, even if the existing boards are transferred to the new location. New ones are needed as well to adorn the images of the gods when the domestic altar is reset after moving to a new home. For both events, informants explained that the purpose of the Golden Flowers in these rituals was to adorn the images of the gods. On hearing this, I thought that the true underlying meaning of the Golden Flower might be to ease the actual transition, assuring protection during such potentially stressful events and facilitating the transition from one state to another. As such, the Golden Flower would be an object figuring prominently in the performance of rituals classically understood as the "rites of passage" (Van Genep 1960, Turner 1970). In such a capacity, it would act as a mediator and protector as the household passed through different states of being. When shop owners and master craftsmen were asked their opinion of this interpretation, they agreed on the situations in which a new pair of Golden Flowers was required, and further, that these occasions involved stress and uncertainty. While they agreed that the interpretation was interesting, they were not so certain that the Golden Flowers were such active agents in securing a successful transition, feeling that the rituals of worship performed at the time would be sufficient to secure the care of the gods.

Establishing a new business or moving to a new home involves risk, for one can never be certain of what events have occurred in the new location. What if the previous occupants were plagued by illness or bad luck, or even worse, if someone died within that space? To protect the family or business from the lingering evil influence of such unhappy events, people burn paper at the four corners (in a ceremony referred to as, Worshipping the Four Corners, 拜四角) and at the center (more precisely, the five directions of north, south, east, west, and center) of a newly occupied home. The procedure for worship was explained like this:

> This set of paper offerings contains five packages for each of the five directions — East, South, West, North, and Center. Before moving into a new house, one can worship these five directions with paper offerings and the following items: bean sprouts, bean curd, fat pork, white turnip, a pear, a duck egg, and leaves of the pomelo. All these are also divided into five parts for the five directions, except the duck egg and the leaves; the former is for the center only. After lighting the incense, one can worship the five directions one by one. After worshipping, you must take the duck egg out of the house and break it, so that the evil influence will go away. Then, sweep the house with the leaves to remove any lingering evil. The food offerings should be placed on newspapers, and not plates, for the evil spirits will not take the food offerings from plates.

Each of the five packets, one for each of the four directions and the center, is burned with an assortment of paper items: First Treasure, Gold and Silver Paper, clothing for gods in the sky (the most powerful gods), and paper clothing for the gods of the earth. Another respondent assembled a package containing White Money, Gold and Silver Paper, an Earth Cow Charm (土牛符), five pieces of small clothing, two packages of small-sized Hell Money, five sheets of the Solving of 100

Problems, five Honorable People Charms, Longevity Gold, and five circular Honorable People Papers. Another shopkeeper said that when she actually moved into her new shop space, after she had worshipped the four corners, she burned a package of Clothing for All the Gods (通神衣), and clothing for Di Zhu (地主, Lord of the Land), Men Kou (門口, the god of the door), and for Guan Di (關帝, the popular protective general). Others added a gold and silver dragon to the package to burn at the center, for this is beneficial to the house. As paper offerings are variable, so too, are the food items that are offered; duck eggs, bean curd, bean sprouts, pears, apples, carrots, and fatty pork have all been used. The pear, which has been mentioned before in connection with the rites to dispel evil, here again bears the association of "to leave or depart," which is what the occupants hope any evil thing will do. Some shops added carrots to the packages, cutting each carrot into five pieces (one for each pack). Some said that, if the worshipper had only one large piece of pork, then it could be placed intact in the package for the center of the house. Some said that duck eggs were not necessary, although Anderson reported the use of duck eggs during a fisherman's ritual because duck eggs drove away evil spirits (1970: 177). New owners can also burn a Yin Contract (陰契) to let the underworld know who has purchased the property. Other shopkeepers referred to this as an Earth Contract (地契), explaining that it should be burned to protect new owners from the possible evil effects of dead being buried under the property. These contracts are yellow when purchased for urban properties, but white for property in the New Territories; informants were not clear why.

Turning to a decidedly cheery occasion, shops also make up pitched round Lucky Basins (運盤) to celebrate long life. Lucky Basins have two purposes. The basic meaning is to change bad luck to a lucky fate through worshipping the gods; in this, they are similar to the Fate Changers already described. The second is to ask for blessings on one's birthday. The Lucky Basin comes in a pitched version and a flat paper version. The first is a charming item made by shaping a bamboo strip into a circle, to which bamboo "legs" may be attached. This circle is then covered with red paper, while sides are formed with alternating strips of red and green rectangular Honorable People Papers (usually four per basin) which have been pasted along the edge of the circle, hiding the legs. Hence, while its name contains the character for basin, Lucky Basins do not resemble basins, but tambourines with legs. The red top formed by the paper is finished off by pasting on a painted metallic paper cutout of the character for long life, and encircling this cutout along its edges with either ingots folded from Longevity Gold or circles of golden foil paper shaped into cones, referred to as Golden Tripods (金鼎). Most examples carry four of these golden ingots or cones.

According to some shopkeepers, pitched Lucky Basins should be burned only at the sixtieth birthday, at which time the person is said to "Hold the Peach of Longevity" (手執壽桃), and is likely to have grandchildren. Other birthdays must make do with flat Lucky Basin Papers. But other shops said if used for a birthday, the addition of Longevity Gold (an item usually offered to the gods) is appropriate as a trim, for the paper expresses the wish that the gods will grant an even longer life to the recipient. This is an instance in which an offering normally given to the gods is suitable for ordinary humans. Additional Longevity Gold is burned to the gods in the hopes of securing an even longer life. For some respondents, the correct amount of Longevity Gold to use was the same as one's years of life; if one was fifty, then fifty papers should be folded and burned. Other shopkeepers declared that, as one always wishes for a longer life, one should burn double the number of one's actual years; still others said that one folded ingot of Longevity Gold should be added for each year of one's life after one had attained "several tens" of years.

The Lucky Basin Paper, some shopkeepers assert, is only for worshipping the gods, and can be burned with a package of Fate Changers. The Lucky Basin Paper is also a necessary component of the Five Treasures Document (discussed above and in Chapter 1). Elderly shopkeepers explained that in the old days, the worshipper would take the Fate Changer and the Lucky Basin Paper to the temple, where the temple keeper would open the former to full size and hang it up during prayers. Or, the temple keeper would place the two paper items together and shake them over the worshipper's head as he or she walked past; this was part of the ritual for changing one's fate. They added that not many people now ask for this ritual to be performed. While burning (to the gods) is the correct procedure for both versions of the Lucky Basin, worshippers recognize the difficulty posed by the pitched form, which sometimes does not burn down completely. For this reason, shopkeepers felt that more worshippers, provided they understood how to use the accompanying papers, would now using the flat paper form for all occasions, even birthdays. While most shops craft neat but simple pitched Lucky Basins, some shops are known for their artistry. One retail shop sold us a particularly fine version covered in a construction of elaborately folded Longevity Gold; the finished creation resembled a mountain of golden papers and was very attractive, if not conforming to the more common examples in the sheer number of papers it contained.

3
Gratitude to the Gods, Charity for the Ghosts

The numerous discussions of the heavenly pantheon of Chinese religion (see, for example, Hayes 1924; Heinze 1981; Harrell 1986; Irwin 1990; Stevens 1997, 2001), describe a world populated by a myriad of supernatural beings. In old Hong Kong, gods were given honor as protectors (see, for example, Bone 1889a: 367) and many holidays have long expressed worshippers' gratitude for the gods' care and attention. Today, Hong Kong's temples (Savidge 1977; Stevens 1983; Lang and Ragvald 1993; Lang 1997) serve a significant population of faithful worshippers and seasonal visitors and house deities of diverse origins, both great and small. "In a few temples, it is quite obvious that the deities are all of one religion, either Buddhist or Daoist, but the altars in most temples bear a mixture of Buddhist, Daoist and folk religion images side by side" (Stevens 1983: 3). What worshippers believe appears to be in harmony with this mixture. While much has been written about the three strands (Buddhist, Daoism and popular belief, 三教合一) that dominate Chinese religious belief (see for example, Berkowitz, Brandauer and Reed 1969; Dore 1917, Hayes 2000, Smith 1986, Teiser

1996), strands which have been deemed "a powerful and inescapable part of Chinese religion," the whole is far more complex (Teiser 1996: 4), and not all scholars follow this line of reasoning (for a dissenting view, see Anderson 1970). Most paper shop customers encountered professed some level of general Chinese traditional belief, but the rest identified themselves as Buddhists, Catholics, or "Christians" (Protestants), faiths for which the burning of paper offerings to any entity is not a requirement. Nevertheless, shopkeepers say that these customers are reluctant to give up the practice of burning offerings, notably for ancestors, suggesting the co-existence of different beliefs and the strength of customary practice. This chapter will consider, first, the offerings for the gods, the meanings of such offerings, and the occasions on which offerings are made. It will then consider the second of Wolf's (1974) otherworldly entities, the ghosts, describing the ways in which worshippers deal with these sometime troubling spirits.

Honoring the Gods

Arthur Wolf's 1974 essay about Chinese popular religion described the gods (in the eyes of the peasants) as part of a supernatural bureaucracy, reflecting its earthly imperial counterpart (1974: 133–45, see also Stevens 1997). In Hong Kong, both shopkeepers and worshippers make a distinction between the big gods and the lesser gods, although just which god fits into which category varies according to individual belief. Within the pantheon of big gods or "gods in heaven" are the patron goddess of fishermen and sailors Tian Hou (天后), Wong Tai Sin (Huang Da Xian or the Great Sage Wong, 黃大仙), Guan Yin, the Goddess of Mercy (觀音), Che Gong (the Great Marshal Che, protector from disease, 車公) and Guan Di (the great general of the Three Kingdoms, 關帝), with Tian Guan (天官, Ruler of Heaven) ruling over all. The temple-centered birthday celebrations of these deities are among the most popular and elaborate festivals of the year. The lesser or local gods include Di Zhu (Lord of the Land, 地主), and Men Kou (god of the door, 門口) who are also part of a bureaucratic hierarchy of great antiquity (Baity 1977, Stevens 1997: 171–7).[1] They are worshipped at home, where their worship is often simpler (consisting of fruit, flowers and incense) but no less sincere. Some respondents refer to the gods of the earth and the door as yin (陰) gods, because, as protectors of the home, they come in contact with the ghosts always lurking about on earth.

The paper offerings for the gods include spirit money, clothing and accessories, and it is generally agreed that gods should receive Longevity Gold. In addition, while paper clothing is a popular gift to all three spiritual entities, clothing for the deities is usually imprinted with dragons, is cut in the style of classical robes and is often of good size. Most worshippers are not very clear about why the gods need such things, but some will say that the gods redistribute these items to the needy spirits in the next world; thus worshippers' offerings are a form of charity. Other worshippers believe that the gods will return to them the benefit exemplified by the offering (such as long life for Longevity Gold). However, as worshippers are giving offerings out of gratitude to, or love for, the deity, need is not the issue, but sentiment is. Nearly all of the popular gods are honored with pre-packaged assemblages of paper offerings. A typical pre-packed set of offerings for a big god normally includes a small package of Longevity Gold, a collapsible paper hat, a brightly colored gown printed with dragons, a packet of First Treasure protective paper, and a Five Treasures Document. Most sets also contain Honorable People Papers. While certain of the papers (the clothing and money) are for the god to use in helping others, other papers are to direct the god to human concerns. The Five Treasures Document (which contains both circular and rectangular Honorable People Papers, a Lucky Basin Paper, a Great Luck Document, and a red Honorable People Charm) is used to thank the deities for blessings received, especially at the end of the year. To this standard package, the customer adds incense and candles, and whatever additional papers seem necessary to them, such as extra packages of Longevity Gold. If not satisfied with these packages, customers can also make special orders for more elaborate handcrafted clothing sets consisting of hats, gowns, and shoes; anticipating this, such sets are crafted by the shops in advance of holidays.

Other worshippers prefer to assemble their own packages for the deities, packages which can become quite complicated. A respondent packed for us one such package for the Sky God, with the components layered as follows (from bottom to top): two sheets of white First Treasure placed in a cross shape, ten sheets of coarse First Treasure placed in an overlapping circle to resemble a bowl, two circular Honorable People Papers, one sheet of the Lucky Basin Paper, one sheet of the Solving of 100 Problems, assorted sheets of Longevity Gold (both flat and in ingot shape), two sets of the Five Treasures Document, two sheets of rectangular Honorable People Papers mixed with more Longevity Gold, and on top, a package of clothing. A hand-packed assemblage for a smaller deity such as Men Kou may contain small gowns, a package of Gold and Silver Paper (also used for ancestors), a few sheets of Hell Money, White Money, and the Solving of 100 Problems. A golden dragon is included in some assemblages, representing his concern for the house. The contents of all of these packages reflect the worshipper's desire for blessings and protection, as well as gratitude for the god's concern.

While White Money is usually burned for ghosts and is the least valuable spirit currency, many shopkeepers said that it can be burned to the lesser gods such as Men Kou and Di Zhu, for these gods use the money as small change or pocket money. Other respondents explained that Men Kou and Di Zhu are the lesser deities due to their close relationship with the earth, and so can receive White Money. More specifically, Di Zhu is responsible for ridding the house of ghosts, while Men Kou keeps them from coming in through the door. Fulfilling these responsibilities requires the burning of White Money, which they can use to "pay off" these creatures, ensuring that the residents of the house or apartment will be safe.

There are many ways to make up a proper offering, and both pre-packaged and hand-assembled sets specified for the same god may contain slightly varied materials. As explained, while Longevity Gold is generally agreed upon as a proper offering for the gods, worshippers are free to vary their offerings as they wish. Many will add other forms of currency such as Gold and Silver Paper, which others will assert is usually for offering to ancestors, and, as explained, White Money, which many give to ghosts, or to those deities they deem lesser. Paper clothing is a popular item, and clothing for the gods, no matter how crafted, should be adorned with dragons, but varieties of handcrafted, hand-painted clothing may be decorated with other motives. Both worshippers and tradespeople are concerned about giving appropriate and accurate offerings, but variations are acceptable as different interpretations of what this means.

Clothing the gods

"On their birthdays, it is customary to present the divinity . . . with a new suit of clothes" (Burkhardt 1953: 166). Paper shops offer a wide variety of individual clothing packages for the gods, equally termed Clothing for the Big Gods (大神衣), or Clothing for All the Gods (通神衣), which usually contain ten pieces of paper clothing, so that each god has one; these are either factory packed or assembled by the shop. Different, but equally popular, clothing packages for specific deities consist of long gowns of colored paper, printed with tailoring details (such as loops, buttons, pockets, and collars), or with a variety of ornamental designs in addition to the dragon motif. These are accompanied by a sheet of stiff paper imprinted with hats and shoes in full color. On special occasions, worshippers may special-order more elaborate handcrafted sets of clothing which can include pitched components. These sets are more expensive than either the manufactured items or the shop's existing semi-handmade assemblages.

The size of the clothing for the gods reflects their majesty; while many examples are normal (perhaps one to three feet in length) or within the size range of normal humans, a totally handcrafted gown is often quite large, a third beyond human life size. There are a few general agreements about appropriate colors. One shopkeeper explained:

> The colors of gods' clothing usually follow the traditional ways and so, follows the clothing of the gods' images. For example, the image of Wong Tai Sin often wears blue clothing, so I use blue for the paper. Strictly speaking, there should be different colors for different gods, females in red and pink and males in green or other colors, and most clothing for the big gods will be imprinted with dragons.

Many respondents also agreed that red was the single good color for all gods' clothing, using the phrase "big red and green" (大紅大綠) meaning very beautiful, to describe offerings of that color. There was in the author's collection a semi-handcrafted clothing package for Wong Tai Sin in which the manufactured gown was indeed red and green, overprinted with black dragons. It was accompanied by a pair of handmade red topped "felt soled" boots, and an emperor's style hat trimmed with painted, silver metallic papers cut into the shapes of flowers and the character for long life.

Within these general agreements, considerable variation exists from shop to shop, depending on the supplier or the inspiration of the craftsman or craftswoman, suggesting no absolute rules to follow when selecting colors for the deities' clothing. Manufactured clothing for the big gods (even for Wong Tai Sin, characterized as wearing blue clothing), is often made in bright purple and green, or rose and green. Many crafters do not strictly follow the old ways, and design clothing according to their own ideas of propriety. "People now do not care about it [the exact colors for the clothing for the gods] and there is no clear distinction of different colors to different gods. I often design them as I wish, although the traditional ways are best to follow." One exception is the goddess Guan Yin, who consistently wears white clothing stressing her purity and dignity. It is rare to see her clothing made in anything but white paper, printed or painted with the auspicious symbols of the lotus flower and lotus root associated with her. Also, the Kitchen God is given black or other very dark clothing printed with dragons and a black hat; the reason being that he is always in the kitchen, near the stove, and so is covered with soot and the residues of cooking grease.

A special handcrafted assemblage for Tian Hou included a long gown of high quality paper in a particularly vibrant red,[2] with white sleeve extensions of even finer paper. This gown was elaborately trimmed with numerous auspicious motifs including *ru yi* scepters (with the meaning of, "everything as you wish", 如意), and silver metallic cutouts in the shapes of flowers and the character for long life, all hand-painted in pinks and greens, with the addition of silver dragons and phoenix. The hem of the gown was painted in a stylized design known as the "mountain peaks and clouds" motif embroidered on real gowns and shoes during the late 1800s, and symbolizing long life and happiness (Roberts and Steele 1997: 70). This gown was complemented by a fly whisk of fringed white paper, the Buddhist symbol of authority (Eberhard 1986: 112–3), and a dainty pair of small red boots with green soles, trimmed with the long life character, small flowers, and the Buddhist mystic knot, symbolizing longevity (Williams 1976 [1941]: 291–2). The hats accompanying the clothing for Tian Hou and for other goddesses do not exactly copy any real-life counterparts, as some examples are composed of elements taken from the phoenix crowns worn by empresses (modified side phalanges formed from painted metallic phoenixes, fringe, and decorated lower band) and from the flat tops of Han emperors' ceremonial hats (Garrett 1994: 4, 20). Other hat styles are distinctly masculine in design, with flat tops resting on cone-shaped bodies. Still other examples of heavenly millinery are decorated with trios of mirror discs, red tassels, multicolored fringe, flowers of red crepe paper, and the colored pompoms also characteristic of traditional wedding crowns.

Individual devotees may add paper items such as dainty bound foot slippers in red and green, small packages containing replicas of jewelry, or combs and mirrors. Although most shopkeepers said that the latter items are more properly burned to ancestors, worshippers mix them with more standard offerings for the goddesses. In addition, while clothing and money may be offered to any deity, many gods receive items that have gradually become associated with them, even if no one remembers why. Monkey (Sun Houzi, 孫猴子, or Sun Wukong 孫悟空), was immortalized in the classic *Journey to the West*, in which he was one of the companions of the monk Xuan Zhuang (玄奘) in his journey to India. Monkey stole the Peaches of Immortality, thereby acquiring miraculous powers, and so the Jade Emperor gave him the title, "Great Sage Equal to Heaven" (齊天大聖, Qitian Dasheng) (Burkhardt 1953: 162, Ward and Law 1993: 69). Ward and Law date his special day to the sixteenth day of the eighth moon where he is particularly venerated at his temple in Sau Mau Ping Estate (秀茂坪邨) in north Kowloon (Ward and Law 1993: 69), but he is also worshipped on the twenty-third day of the second moon (Williams 1976 [1941]: 278; Burkhardt 1953: 162).

Monkey is deemed powerful in protecting worshippers from demons. Whichever day he is honored, he is offered "a gilt and paper crown, red jacket, and yellow cloak . . . The kit includes a tiny pair of white shoes, for cloud-hopping, and two red cardboard buckets slung at the ends of a carrying pole" (Burkhardt 1953: 166). Current packages for Monkey include a circlet crown in gilt paper, a pair of red buckets, and a doubled piece of yellow paper printed in green on both sides, rolled up and secured with a red strip or a metallic cutout of the character for long life. This paper, outlining in green what at first appears to be a tiger head, really depicts the monkey's own skin and the printed green streaks represent his fur. The golden crowns (金剛圈), may be simply constructed from a piece of gilt paper or be trimmed with paper chrysanthemums and red fringe. Some shopkeepers refer to this crown as the replica of the steel headband (頭筋圈), which was used for controlling this unpredictable deity. As Stevens explained, "Virtually all images show him wearing a tight fitting diadem or circlet with the two ends curled up and touching, in the centre of his forehead. This was placed there by Guan Yin to keep him under her control" (1997: 98). Even more complicated assemblages for Monkey consist of a pair of golden buckets, a pair of thick soled boots, a cape printed with his furry skin and overlaid with a red paper "apron" trimmed with metallic flower cutouts (these referred to as Clothing for the Monkey God, or 大聖衣), and an elaborate crown of gold with red paper fringe and stems of multicolored crepe paper flowers and metallic leaves. The two buckets are termed the Flower Basket (花籃) and the Water Bucket (水桶). The water brings prosperity to the worshipper, and both together represent "obtaining all things." The simplest combinations for Monkey are made of two sheets of yellow paper printed with a green fur pattern and a collapsible round paper hat of the kind given to all the gods, in green and white and bearing a cutout golden decoration.

Guan Yin, the Goddess of Mercy, is honored on different days of the lunar year; day nineteen of the second moon is her birthday, day nineteen of the sixth moon is her Enlightenment, while day nineteen of the ninth moon is the remembrance of the day of her death (Ward and Law 1993: 75). Guan Yin is immensely popular, a giver of children, a source of help, and a savior of endless compassion. While of particular comfort to women, she also protects farmers and travelers (Stevens 1997: 90). As a major deity with many devotees (women form societies to worship her, for descriptions see Irwin 1990; Topley 1954, 1963), Guan Yin is offered very fine items. While she could be given a large red paper gown as described for a big goddess, Guan Yin always "appears only in a dress of spotless white" (Hayes 1924: 100). The white clothing, when commercially produced, is generally embellished with a variety of motifs printed in red and green. These can include a classic nine sectioned collar, "embroidered" with printed flowers; images of phoenixes, pomegranates, and citrons (popularly known as the Buddha's hand, 佛手); and the flowers, roots, and seed pods of the lotus. Such elements reflect her influence on women's fertility (pomegranates refer to having many children) and her association with purity (the lotus). These printed gowns are accompanied by a sheet of thin cardboard printed with a pair of shoes and a phoenix hat. Hand-painted clothing for Guan Yin is more elaborate. In the author's collection were two gowns in cream paper, the body completely hand-painted in abstract flowers and swirls, strongly reminiscent of Tang and Song period archaic robe styles (Tseng 1977: 146). These gowns had attached red paper collars, sleeve bands, and side panels, and were accompanied by deep red boots with green soles trimmed with silver stars and an elaborate metallic paper roundel with the long life character. Guan Yin is also the recipient of a unique creation, purchased at temples or shops, made of Gold Paper or

Longevity Gold folded into three-dimensional "petals" and assembled into a form reminiscent of a pinecone or an artichoke. At some shops, the item is called a Gold Pineapple (金菠蘿) although others declare it is intended to represent a lotus flower, and so call it a Lotus Flower Basin (蓮花盤). Worshippers offer this item during the practice of making prosperity or blessings, or on other special occasions such as the various dates of birth of the goddess. When the top petal is removed and the item set alight, it is supposed to burn down evenly and perfectly, an effect greatly appreciated by worshippers. This object is given various names other than the Gold Pineapple mentioned above. Sold at the Wong Tai Sin Temple, where it is also given to Wong Tai Sin, the paper sellers call it a Gold First Treasure (金元寶).

Hong Kong worshippers also honor more specialized deities, such as the patron gods who protect particular trades or ethnic groups (see, for example, Cheng 1967; Goodrich 1964; Li 1990). Papermaking itself is associated with Cai Lun (蔡倫), and his temples are found in his home town in Leiyang and in Longting in Shanxi Province where he was buried in AD 121 (Cave 1998: 19). Cave described small shrines with paper images in his honor in paper mills and paper shops. The Kings of the Three Mountains are patron deities of the Hakka immigrants to Southeast Asia (Stevens 1997: 111). Some deities are popularly associated with social groups who are partly economic and partly ethnic. In Hong Kong, these include Tan Gong (譚公), who controls weather and protects those who live and work on boats (Ward and Law 1993: 41), and Hong Sheng (洪聖), who protects fishermen and all who make their living on the water (Ward and Law 1993: 29, 41). The most famous of these deities is the great goddess Tian Hou, who is revered by Hong Kong's fishermen and often described as a fishermen's deity (Ward and Law 1993), but whose appeal might best be understood in terms of her general benevolence and concern for all those in difficulty (Scott 1997b; Watson 1985).

The patron deities who protected trades and professions during the imperial period are still revered today. While certain of them were local, others were worshipped throughout China, as in the case of the poet Li Bo (李伯), acclaimed as the patron deity of rice wine merchants (Stevens 1997: 153) and Lei Zu (雷祖), patron of silk weaving (Stevens 1997; Williams 1935).[3] On occasion, different deities were revered as patrons by practitioners of the same trade (Stevens 1997: 126). Burgess' classic study of Beijing guilds (1928) included a section on the guilds' patron deities, which he referred to as "guild founders or masters" (1928:

177). The most popular guild deities were Cai Shen (財神), the God of Wealth, and Lu Ban (魯班), the patron of builders. They, and the other deities, were offered special foods, candles, incense, and paper offerings including "imitation money of silver and gold paper" and reusable "prayers printed on yellow paper" (Burgess 1928: 177, 181).

Lu Ban is patron of the skilled trades connected to the construction industry,[4] and is quite popular in Hong Kong. Specific industries under his care include:

> . . . bridge and house builders, stone and wood workers, brick and tile makers, plasterers, varnishers, painters, plumbers, decorators, earth construction labourers, mat and awning makers, table and chair makers, artists, god-carvers, irrigation and dam workers, wheelwrights and surprisingly, umbrella makers. As the patron of boat builders, he is prayed to and offered sacrifices in particular whenever a new junk or sampan is launched. (Stevens 1997: 126)

Lu Ban's birthday is celebrated on the thirteenth day of the sixth moon of the lunar year (July or August), when he is offered his own elegant clothing. An assemblage purchased for him included an elaborate red hat, decorated with painted metallic cutouts of dragons and the character for long life; a truly splendid pair of high boots in vivid red and blue, with thick soles; the white fly whisk of the sages (Williams [1941] 1976: 193); a deep red belt adorned with three golden squares and two hearts; and a long red gown, hand-painted in abstract designs of blue, green, white and lavender, with green sleeve inserts. As well, he receives Longevity Gold and First Treasure, both rectangular and circular Honorable People Papers, and sheets of the Honorable People Charm.

The Golden Flower

The splendid Golden Flower (金花) is a pitched item whose primary purpose is to adorn the deities. Golden Flowers are always bought in pairs and are accompanied by a red "ribbon" of varying thickness and length called the Spirit Red (神紅), itself centered with a rosette of the same material and a silver metal disc.[5] The Spirit Red is placed behind the Golden Flower (laid out flat and by itself, this Spirit Red resembles the first place ribbon at county fairs). Both Flowers and Spirit Reds are of varying sizes, depending on the size of the image on which they are to be set. They are placed on the heads of the wooden or plaster figures of the deities (at home or at the temple) or on the ancestors' tablets on the domestic altar. More precisely, each individual Golden Flower is affixed to the temples or to the hat or crown of these figures, one flower on each side of the head. The central rosette of the Spirit Red is set in the center of the head and then each of the two side ribbons is draped along the sides of the body, each behind a flower. If the figure of the deity is small, the Spirit Red is not used and only the two flowers are so affixed. These are often the very smallest Golden Flowers, which are no more than a simple triangle of embossed golden foil embellished with a tiny sliver of red feather or with three red dots. Larger figures of deities found in the temple sport quite large flowers of elaborate construction, but the largest and most lavish varieties are set at the corners of the board above the altar.

At home, people use the small to medium-sized examples of Golden Flowers, but larger and more elaborate varieties are purchased by businesses and set at the sides of the old-style wooden name boards that face the main door. Many paper shops, including the paper shops themselves, have Golden Flowers set in this manner, or placed over the altar at the back of the shop. Smaller varieties are affixed to the incense burners (many shopkeepers say this is a practice characteristic of Hong Kong's Chaozhou community). Golden Flowers and Spirit Reds are purchased in greatest quantities during the Lunar New Year, when thoughts of renewal are on the minds of worshippers, and the deities should be given new ones as part of the worship. Isabella Bird noted the practice and explained, "they are much used for the New Year offerings in the temples, and for the annual redecoration of the household tablets" (1899: 161). In all their forms, Golden Flowers represent good luck and good fortune; hence, their popularity at the Lunar New Year and on other happy occasions.

Some respondents explained the order for the setting ascending from ancestors, then to the smaller gods such as the Kitchen God and the Earth God, and then to larger gods such as Guan Di, Guan Yin, and Tian Hou. Responses varied as to the actual number of pairs set (after the ancestors, some people set pairs for as many as six other gods) but indicated the importance of the worship of the gods most dedicated to the protection of the family. Further, many shopkeepers noted that, if a family was to place images of gods in their homes, then they were careful to purchase new Golden Flowers each year for each god. "Some women are very superstitious. If they set five gods in the house, that means they need five pairs of Golden Flowers. If I gave them one more pair by mistake, they would scold me."

Respondents gave many reasons for the setting of the Golden Flowers during the New Year. First, the Golden Flowers helped to make the gods more beautiful. "As people get new clothes during the New Year, so should the gods get new things to wear." Providing a new pair of Golden Flowers and a new Spirit Red makes deities even more beautiful and expresses believers' love and devotion. Some shopkeepers assert that this is the primary function of the Golden Flower and there is no need to construct more elaborate interpretations or to mystify the process. Second, the Golden Flower reflects the sincerity of the household; if one is sincere, and serious about worshipping, then the altar must be fully set. Using Golden Flowers to complete the setting means that the worshipper is inviting a god into the house with a sincere heart and treating them with "welcome, prestige, and respect." Using a Golden Flower and a Spirit Red is a way to welcome the gods into your house, and give them gifts.

One shopkeeper explained that:

> People think that after pinning on the flowers and hanging up the red, the god will have unlimited power, so that the god has the power to protect you . . . The Golden Flower is part of the god's altar, it is a necessity of a god's altar. It is not that an altar with no Golden Flowers will have no god; [the meaning] is not so strong. The Golden Flowers and the Spirit Red are like a hat for god. If you are sincere in worship you have to make it [the altar] complete. This practice is inherited from tradition and the Golden Flower is a necessary item for the worship of god.

The use of a Golden Flower is a significant aspect of traditional worship, without doubt at the New Year, but also whenever divine favor is being sought. While there are a variety of reasons for using Golden Flowers, worshippers overwhelmingly stress that proper worship requires them. "As I have set a tablet for the Buddha and for the ancestors, so I must buy the Golden Flower to worship them." Some purchasers said they followed the lead of other family members. "When I was a child, my mother asked me to buy the Golden Flowers, so after I got married, I continued to buy them for the safety of my family." Or, "I buy Golden Flowers now because the old people in my family did it and I am doing what they did." Others bought Golden Flowers because they had a good meaning, or because the gods would bring good luck to their families. "I am hopeful that the gods will bless me, give me good luck, achievement and prosperity." Others simply appealed to tradition, saying it was customary for Chinese to do this.

Sympathy for Unhappy Ghosts

Hong Kong's residents, however sophisticated and worldly, are nevertheless quite wary when it comes to ghosts (*gui* 鬼); even local newspapers carry stories about the ill effects of encounters with ghosts.[6] There are many motion pictures focused on ghostly doings, urban legends about places where ghosts may be found, and even university campuses are replete with their own much-repeated versions of ghosts and strange events.[7] Arthur Wolf's classic depiction of ghosts puts them at one end of a continuum with the true ancestors at the other. While the living are obligated to their ancestors, they have little or no obligation to ghosts (Wolf 1974: 159); the living care for their own ancestors, and these ancestors will ensure their success, but ghosts cannot ensure any good thing. Wolf further explained that ghosts are a symbolic reflection of the outcasts of the human social order (1974: 170–2), an interesting possibility occasionally recognized by respondents. One explained, "Generally speaking, the difference between ghosts and ancestors in our daily speaking is that ghosts are generally poor creatures without descendants to do the worshipping. This is quite similar to our social hierarchy, in that poor ghosts are like beggars in our world." Another added, "The poor ghosts who threaten people are different from our ancestors. They are similar to beggars in our world, because they do not have descendants to give offerings to them and so they do not eat as often as our ancestors do." It has also been proposed that sex and gender may be pertinent to the understanding of Hong Kong ghosts (Bosco 2001), as it is for certain categories of ghosts in Taiwan (Harrell 1986), but it is difficult to decide the opinion held of ghosts by urban respondents. The process of separating the ghosts from other categories of dead requires more information, beginning with how one becomes a ghost.

The first important component of the thinking about ghosts is the nature of the death itself. The Neo-Confucian scholar Zhu Xi (Chu Tzi) explained that the ch'i (*qi* 氣, material force) of someone who had died a premature, untimely or unnatural death, or of someone who refused to submit to an unjust death "can linger about and transmogrify into a ghost or spirit", or even an evil monster (Gardner 1995: 611, 602), suggesting that the form of death and not the nature of the relationship to the living is the main factor behind ghostly existence. However, "As the unexhausted and stubborn ch'i of those who meet with premature deaths finally disperses, their existence as ghosts and evil spirits reaches a natural and inevitable end" (Gardner 1995: 603), thus ghosts and spirits should dissipate over time. The themes of ill fortune and tragic and unjust deaths underlie many descriptions of ghosts found in the literature, and are understood by both shopkeepers and worshippers in Hong Kong.[8]

The lack of caregivers is another significant characteristic. As Lewis Hodous explained ghosts' condition:

> It should be remembered that in the realm of shades there are spirits to whom no offerings are made. Formerly these spirits were living men and it is not known how they died. Among them are those who died of wounds in battle. There are those who died on water, in fire, or were killed by thieves . . . There were those who died by disease sent by Heaven. Some were killed by ravenous beasts and poisonous insects. Some died of hunger and cold . . . Some who died left no children. These orphaned souls without anyone to supply their wants are worthy of great pity . . . They wander to and fro under the light of the stars and the moon calling piteously in the wind and the rain. (1929: 159–60)

Hodous' examples reflect Zhu Xi's classical thinking. Ward and Law added:

> Some died without children; others were unlucky enough to have all their descendents die out; still others have been unable to reach the world of the dead because they had no proper funeral. All these are the underprivileged dead. They get none of the food, paper clothing, and *spirit money* that are showered upon *ancestors*, and none of their great respect. And they resent it. That is why they are dangerous. (1993: 59)

Shopkeepers to whom we spoke explained the situation in much the same terms:

> If someone passed away and had no relatives, or he had relatives who did not worship him, then he had no money to use and no clothes to wear, so he [now a ghost] had to ask for things from other people.

If you placed an altar in your house with an ancestor tablet, it means your family members who had passed away would be cared for by you. These ancestors would receive things from you at festivals and other times. Therefore, they need not bother other people.

Another component of beliefs about ghosts centers on their nature; more precisely, whether or not they are harmful. An element of unease about ghosts runs alongside the recognition of their miserable deaths. Ancestors are revered while ghosts are still often referred to as the "dirty things" (污糟邋遢嘢), especially by the elderly. Some paper masters considered all ghosts to be dirty, while others said that people who did good deeds while alive could not become true ghosts (meaning, malevolent). Customers who were certain that ghosts were evil were not convinced by these or any other fine distinctions such as who was a stranger or who was an ancestor, who led a good life or who led an evil one, who died a natural death or who died unnaturally, who was an outcast or who was socially accepted during his lifetime, or whether the ghosts simply represented psychologically-based projections of the living worried about sex or the unexplained events of life. They simply believed that all ghosts must be avoided because they were dirty things that caused trouble and sickness.

Other worshippers, less convinced of ghosts' evil natures, explained that ghosts were considered dirty only because they looked ugly, but this frightening appearance depended, once again, on the type of death.

> The reason that there are so many sayings depicting ghosts as ugly, terrible and dirty is because that is the way they are shown in horror films. Normally, ghosts look like they are alive, just like people in our world, but in soul form. However, there are exceptions, such as those who died in accidents, through injustice or as suicides, for they will look ugly and terrible. This is because they died unwillingly or with anger, so they look ugly.

Those who refer to ghosts as dirty things also fear them for the illness and ill fortune that they are believed to bring (see again Chapter 2). Yet, not all informants who accept that ghostly encounters result in illness also believe that ghosts behave this way out of general ill intent. "I think people always feel sick after running into ghosts because they are shocked by these ghosts. But, I think ghosts will not harm people deliberately, since ghosts only want to take revenge on those who harmed them." Those who are not fated to meet ghosts, and those who have done no harm to these spirits have nothing to fear from them. "I am not afraid of them. I believe that they would only harm people who used to harm them when they were alive. I have not harmed them, so they would not harm me, and I do not need to fear them," so explained one woman.

Urban respondents' thinking about ghosts is informed by yet another observation. Wolf explained that, "The crucial point is that the category 'ghosts' is always a relative one. Your ancestors are my ghosts, and my ancestors are your ghosts, just as your relatives are strangers to me, and my relatives strangers to you" (1974: 173). This insight into the relative nature of the definitions of ghosts and ancestors is one understood in Hong Kong.

> Ancestors are the people we cherish and remember. They are our passed relatives and we know who they are. Basically, ancestors are a form of ghosts, since "ghosts" is only a term for people who are not here. The difference between ghosts and ancestors is only that ancestors are the ones that we know, but ghosts are the deceased that we don't know. Therefore, my ancestors are ghosts in your perspective, while your ancestors are ghosts in my perspective.

Or, "Ancestors are also ghosts, as I say all people who die will become ghosts. But, the difference between ghosts and ancestors is only that ancestors are our relatives, our family members, whereas ghosts are the general people that we don't know." This suggests a somewhat more benign, matter-of-fact attitude towards ghosts with no mention of malice.

Following the theme of care and compassion (as this is shown to ancestors) another attitude molding behavior towards the wandering spirits is that of pity and compassion for these miserable souls, a sense of pity likely influenced by Buddhist teachings and practice.

> I was afraid of ghosts in the past, because I did not know much about them then, so I believed that they were terrible and I was afraid of them. But, when I went to more lessons of Buddhism I realized that ghosts are only poor and pitiful creatures. If I do more good things, then I believe good fortune and happiness can result. I now believe that the ghosts deserve pity and I am not afraid of them.

This perspective harmonizes with the previous assertions that the wandering spirits are neglected and uncared for. Hence, if there is a concern about ghosts, much of it can be offset by the burning of offerings. Put simply, ghosts who are given offerings do not have to be feared, for they are satisfied and do not harm anyone; giving them offerings is a pious act of charity. To ease the suffering of these neglected souls and thereby neutralize their pain, worshippers burn offerings to give them what they require for a more comfortable existence in the other world. Such worship can be performed individually, as explained by one woman:

> We give offerings to the ghosts once a year, on a date chosen from the almanac, to ask for their forgiveness if we have troubled them and to ensure our safety. We do this in the daytime [many give offerings at night, when the ghosts are most active] at the village Earth God shrine. We offer uncooked pork [no reason given] a steamed chicken, a steamed fish, candies, fruit, bean curd, tea, and wine. We also give paper offerings such as gold and silver, and paper clothing.

Another respondent explained how she used three pieces of incense and candles set into an orange, and three cups of wine. Then she burned two pieces of First Treasure set into bowl shapes, each containing Gold and Silver Paper, White Money, Money to Live, Hell Money, and paper clothing. At the Lunar New Year, the ghosts can receive offerings for their comfort, a sensible act given worshippers' desire for a good start. Older accounts mention paper printed with pictures of warm clothing burned to the wandering sprits on the last evening of the old year (Hodous 1929: 158). Pious Hong Kong worshippers continue to offer to the wandering spirits throughout the year as a form of good works. In the words of one respondent, "When we donate money to the Tung Wah Hospital, we are doing charity to the living, but when we burn things to the ghosts, we are doing charity for the dead."

While unhappy spirits can be sustained by individual acts of worship, the greatest concentration of offerings for the wandering dead is burned during the Festival of the Hungry Ghosts. During the few days of this festival, which occurs on the fifteenth day of the seventh moon (late August or early September), the gates of the Underworld are opened and spirits can leave Hell. They roam about, being entertained by the operas performed for the gods and for them (for more information on these operas, see Ward 1979), and collecting the various offerings burned on their behalf. At the conclusion of the festival, the King of Hell (or his representative) will see to their return, suggesting that these spirits are once again safely resident in Hell. However, both respondents' comments and scholarly observations suggest that ghosts continually lurk about the world of the living, waiting to cause mischief. Depictions of the Da Jiao (打醮), a major religious festival in southern China, has among its many aims "to cleanse the district holding the festival from the presence of restless 'hungry ghosts' and other ill-disposed or dangerous spiritual forces" (Hase, n.d.). The wandering ghosts are called to the festival grounds by rituals, then collect the offerings burned for them. At the end of this festival, the image of the King of Hell is carried to a place outside the ritual ground and burned. This image is always made with a large stomach so that he can "eat" all the ghosts that have been summoned, and the burning sends both him and the captured ghosts safely back to Hell. That the Da Jiao is performed regularly suggests that there are always new, unsatisfied ghosts wandering about, a belief again reminiscent of Zhu Xi, for there are always unfortunates who die untimely deaths or whose sins have outweighed their good deeds (Teiser 1993) and who then are forced to linger about the world of the living. These must be regularly gathered up and safely sent on their way.

Ghosts can make their needs known in a quite direct fashion, as one shopkeeper related.

> Sometimes, we even see the ghosts. For example, there was a boy who moved here and told his mother that he saw an old man sitting on the chair every night. His mother told me about this, and then she worshipped and gave paper. After that, everything was all right. She said that her son no longer saw the old man after she had made the offerings.

Another shopkeeper told this story:

> After coming home from the last July festival one boy and one girl couldn't stop jumping up and down although four people had held them tightly. Some family members held the fingers of the girl and asked the ghost what he wanted as they believed that both the boy and the girl had met some dirty things. The ghost told them that he liked that girl and asked them to give him the girl. The girl's family asked the ghost what he needed, and then burned paper such as gold and silver to the ghost. After a time, the girl got well. It is hard to believe but you have to believe it.

The shopkeeper did not remember what happened to the boy.

Offerings for the Ghosts

A common paper offering for these unlucky wandering spirits is the Brook Money (溪錢). Better known as White Money (but also termed Long Money 長錢, Treasure Heart 寶心, or Scattering Money 散錢), it is approximately three inches by six inches and perforated with crescent shaped slits. People of Shanghai origin burn another form of White Money, a very large (twelve inches by fourteen inches) sheet in white or yellow, each sheet cut with twenty-five square holes. In use by the seventh century, White Money was also termed mock money (Cave 1998: 2). Hunter's 1937 study includes an example of White Money, of which he remarked, "The first mock money was probably made in imitation of round metal coins pierced with square holes for stringing . . . [white paper, representing silver coins] are not as valuable to the departed spirit as the yellow, or gold, paper representations" (1937: 34–35). Dore's studies of Chinese ritual practices contain drawings of mock money (Figure 56, Volume 1, 1914) resembling sheets of coins much like the White Money of today (see also Day 1940a and Serebrennikov 1933). De Groot also included a description of mock money cut with parallel rows of small scalloped incisions, which he termed treasury money (庫錢), and which represented metal coins, but these were burned to the ancestors (1892: 78). Hunter (1937) agreed, saying that the mock or treasury money was burned to ancestors. This practice is also followed in Hong Kong, even if White Money is frequently associated with the wandering spirits.[9]

White Money is considered of low value, representing small denominations, perhaps ten cents to one dollar in Hong Kong currency. "For these wandering spirits it is enough to offer paper imitations of a small coin called a cash, a cheap brass coin with a square hole in the centre" (Serebrennikov 1933: 192). Hong Kong shopkeepers explained that the spirits and the ancestors use White Money in much the same way that the living use coins. "If the White Money is burned to ancestors, it acts as small currency of low value (散錢), and the ancestor could use it to buy clothing or food. Compared with our world, [each piece of] White Money is like a one-dollar coin, while the gold and silver is as the $500 or $1000 notes." The square holes and surrounding crescent perforations do closely resemble small coins, so the association is easy to understand.

White Money may be burned or scattered, thrown into the air to keep wandering ghosts from interrupting a funeral or doing harm to the newly dead. "This paper money is destined for the malevolent spirits who, according to the popular conception, prowl about everywhere and infest streets and thoroughfares . . . swarming chiefly on the roads where coffins have to pass, for the express purpose of robbing . . . every deceased person of the money wherewith the living have so unselfishly enriched him during the funeral rites" (De Groot 1892: 154; see also Cave 1998: 68; Hase 1981; Serebrennikov 1933: 192). When used in this way, the White Money was termed "paper to buy a passage" (買路 錢), as the dead needed to pay off the ghosts clustering around them to ensure their own safe passage into the next world. Gamble also recorded paper money used in this manner, which he termed, "money to buy the use of the road" (Gamble 1954: 390). Ancestors may also use White Money to pay for transportation in the next world. While White Money was once scattered, to divert the attention of the wandering spirits and keep the road clean for the corpse, Hong Kong shopkeepers explained that this was no longer approved, as it contravened the modern rules of traffic safety.

Some respondents declared that brothels and illegal gambling establishments used White Money to lure customers inside.

> Nowadays, only the vice establishments and the mahjong parlors would spread White Money. They think that there are many dirty things lying about outside such places so that one will give White Money to these ghosts, hoping that the ghost could entice or otherwise persuade some rich customers to go inside. This is bribing the ghosts, for if the customer did not originally wish to go inside, the ghosts will just push him in.

Another version of the "helpful ghosts" story was that the ghosts waiting near the door were only given a small amount of White Money, after which they became impatient for more, and possessed customers, who would then go in.

> While the scattering method has no meaning, the gambling shops and the prostitutes would scatter White Money over a larger area in front of their shop or building, believing that the more is scattered, the more ghosts will come. It is like dirty money. The ghosts would help them to keep the eyes of their clients closed, so that their clients would walk into their establishments unconscious. The more the ghosts receive White Money, the more help these businesses get.

Other respondents declared that ghosts were passively obstructing the doorways and keeping away the customers. "They [proprietors] believe that the ghosts are blocking the door. They think 'Why is there no business tonight?' So, they spread the White Money outside in order to keep the door clear. They think that when they throw it on the street those ghosts will rush to the street to get it, leaving the doors and allowing the customers to come in." For other respondents, this supposed relationship between White Money, ghosts, and vice establishments was absolute nonsense.

White Money can be burned or scattered at any time, not just at funerals or at the Festival of the Hungry Ghosts, although more is used during this holiday. It is included in assemblages offered to ghosts, gods, and ancestors and a component of the bags of offerings burned to ancestors during the Qing Ming and Chong Yang festivals to honor deceased family members. In the ancestors' packages made up at a shop, White Money is set in the middle, between the First Treasure and the Gold and Silver Paper. When placed in this way, it is termed the Treasure Heart. Although Hong Kong worshippers use Longevity Gold for the gods and Gold and Silver Paper for the ancestors, sometimes they also burn the latter two for the hungry ghosts in addition to the White Money.

In addition to White Money, ghosts are offered clothing packages. One such package is termed both the Thirty-six Hell [literally, secluded] Clothing set (三十六幽衣) or, alternatively, the Clothing for the Spirits (孤衣). This is a small assemblage which includes the Contract (契), a slip of paper enabling the ghosts to claim the paper clothing. Shops also provide the Seven Color Paper or Five Color Paper (七色紙 / 五色紙), very attractive sets of rectangular papers, which are equivalent to each other despite the different numbers. Both are made up in either a coarse paper representing cotton, or in a finer, smoother paper representing silk. These papers may be rolled up before burning, in which case they become bolts of cloth from which the spirits can make their own clothing, or left unrolled, so that they turn into clothing in the next world. The Seven Color Paper is actually comprised of six colors (eighteen sheets each of green, yellow, deep purple, coffee, cream, and rose), colored on both sides.[10] While some respondents thought that these two colored papers should only be offered during the Festival of the Hungry Ghosts, most used it at any time they wish, including Qing Ming, when it may be burned to the wandering souls (遊魂).

The same item appears more elaborately as the Thirty-Six Hell Clothes Hell Green (三十六幽衣幽綠), consisting of a piece of clothing for Guan Yin (the Goddess of Mercy who distributes the clothing to these wandering spirits), thirty-six pieces of simple clothing made of Five Colored Paper, and thirty-six green and white sheets termed the Spirit Soul License (神魂執照). The Spirit Soul License enables the wandering spirits to go anywhere they like to collect offerings, instead of being confined to the place where they died. Nowadays, these three items are assembled into one set; one or two sets are referred to by the term Small Hell (小幽), while three sets (representing 108 pieces) is called the Large Hell (大幽). Some worshippers are content to burn one set of this item (representing the original thirty-six pieces), while those desiring more protection from wandering ghosts burn two or three (representing seventy-two or 108 pieces).

While most worshippers do not burn complicated or special-ordered items for the hungry ghosts, there is nothing to prevent the very pious from doing so. During the Festival of the Hungry Ghosts, it is quite common to see numbers of elderly ladies burning offerings at the street side (literally, "worship [the] street," 拜街) to ease the sufferings of the dead. Shopkeepers say that some elderly customers burn White Money every night of the festival, to give the ghosts money to spend. Others give the ghosts clothing packages that most people deem appropriate only for the ancestors — namely, paper robes and undergarments with tailoring details printed on them. There are no pre-packed sets if offerings labeled for ghosts as there are for the gods, but during the festival shops will pack their own assemblages for sale, offering them to the customers in plastic bags. While most worshippers do not spend much money on the wandering spirits, the assemblages made up at shops (clearly identified by shopkeepers as Clothing Burned [for ghosts] at the Street, 燒街衣) can be quite elaborate, reflecting a more generous attitude. One such set collected contained no less than fifteen items: two packages of Seven Colored Paper (one fine and one coarse) for clothing, a package of Gold and Silver Paper, two forms of Hell currency, one package of Money to Live, one package of rectangular gold bars, one package of gold bars in the form of traditional Chinese sycee, one package of White Money, incense, two painted and ten plain red wax candles, First Treasure paper, two varieties of Longevity Gold and a single printed paper gown of fancy design. The contents were surely more than sufficient to satisfy the needs of any deprived spirit. In its inclusion of Gold and

Silver Paper and a printed paper gown, this package further illustrates how opinions on the proper usage of different types of offerings may lessen the distinctions between offerings to ghosts and offerings to ancestors, suggesting both the primacy of personal opinion over strict rules governing what is burned to whom and the growing feeling of sympathy for the neglected souls.

4

Remembering the Ancestors

A 1939 photograph of the elaborate funeral procession in Beijing for the leader of the Zhili clique Wu Pei Fu (吳佩孚, 1874–1939) shows three nearly full-sized paper soldiers, mounted on horseback and fully uniformed, and no doubt meant for the lord's protection in the next world (Zhu 1997: 450; see also Bonavia 1995: 85–97; Schoppa 2000: 199). H.Y. Lowe's [Luo Xinyao] 1941 writings in the *Peking Chronicle* describe a set of three paper houses, one a storehouse holding paper ingots and a model of an automobile, all destined to be burned for the funeral of the old grandfather of the fictional family whose lives Lowe had been describing (1983: 115, 118). Even earlier, in 1913, L. Wieger recorded the following description of funeral paper offerings:

> Before the funeral day, paper-stickers are called in . . . papers of different colours are bought in the bazaar, to make the figures . . . there are a great variety of figures — let me enumerate some of them. First, four old men and four young men; then Buddha calling out of the infernal regions; a crane and an antelope; two cash boxes, two big lions, and the general guardians of the door;

all these figures are commonly used; they are seldom omitted
. . . All these dolls wear rich costumes, according to the latest
fashion. The heads are made of clay and the eyes depicted with
ink. (1913: 567–9)

These examples illustrate how mourners provide for deceased
family members. Traditional belief demands that deceased members of
families and clans be remembered, and the ties between the dead and
the living maintained (Yang 1994: 30). One way to do this is to give
gifts to the dead at regular intervals, which involve:

The transfer of food, money, and goods from the living to the
dead. Mock money and paper models of items to be used in
the afterlife (e.g., houses, furniture, servants, vehicles, etc) were
transmitted by burning. In addition to food, the basic set of
material offerings to the deceased included mock money and
incense; all other offerings were thus optional. (Watson 1988a:
13)

Offerings to departed kinsmen are a most significant part of both
the funeral ritual and the rituals of commemoration, for the dead are
dependents after death, needing the family to supply what they require
(Weiger 1927: 56). So important is this that the Neo-Confucian
philosopher Zhu Xi included comments on the making of grave goods in
the funeral section of his manual instructing the private performance of
ritual. "Carve wood to make carts and horses, male and female servants,
and all the things needed to care for the deceased" (Ebrey 1991: 109).
When referring to departed kin, respondents vary in their views about
the next world in which these ancestors reside. Most are vague about
where the next world is located and about where in the next world the
offerings are going. They say simply that the items will go to the next
world. Others are more specific, believing that the next world is parallel
to the world of the living and very much like it. Hong Kong's fishermen
believe that "the heavenly soul goes on to live in a world almost exactly
like ours but not visible to us" (Anderson 1970: 151). Some respondents
explained that what is known as Hell is only one part of the next world,
the part where those who did evil are punished. However, even classical
depictions of Hell, which contain vivid depictions of the Courts
of Punishment, do not make clear the destination of these funeral
offerings.[1] While not all respondents believed that the next world was a
terrible place (because only Hell is the grim place of punishment), their
concerns about burning items to kinsmen still echoed something of the

old sentiment that Hell is grim and the souls residing there are suffering (Thompson 1989: 33). Whatever the belief, the paper offerings are a significant and necessary component of the funeral rituals (Scott 1997a: 224).

In addition to the more durable objects made of metal, wood, or ceramic (Ebrey 1991: 109, n. 133), it appears that the use of paper replicas began to appear during the Song Dynasty (960–1279). The ceramic artifacts mentioned, echoes of the "Vehicles of clay and souls of straw" (De Groot 1894: 807; see also Smith 1986), had themselves been replacements for actual human sacrifices, but the use of paper took this ceremonial substitution a step further. "From the time of the Sung, folded paper burial items generally replaced ceramic funeral artifacts used traditionally, so shops appeared in towns and villages for folded paper and 'paper horses' " (Qin 1958: 11; see also Szeto 1993, 1996). By the Song, the imagery of the horse became the general referent to paper offerings in shops providing the items that by this time were considered necessary for the deceased. A similar sequence has been advanced for currency: from commodities to real money to imitations of money (Gates 1987: 272; Hou 1975).

Whether the preceding summary accurately reflects the precise timing of the shift to paper offerings is of less concern than the general sequence: funerals began with the offering of real objects, people or horses, to the use of replicas in durable materials,[2] to paper models, a sequence reflecting how "the Chinese at an early period of their history replaced the articles of value and domestic appliances which they had been accustomed to bury with the dead, by less valuable and even worthless things" (De Groot 1894: 806). By the late Imperial period, the use of paper funeral offerings was well established. In a ceremony connected to the ritual of "calling back the soul," offerings in the form of paper representations of carts, attendants, horses, chests, clothing, and other items were provided (Naquin 1988: 40). Other paper objects were offered during mourning observations after the initial ceremonies (Naquin 1988: 40, 45). While today's paper offerings are not fully comparable to those described for the late Qing, they appear within the same contexts.

Offerings are given during the funeral and the subsequent ceremonies held on regular seven-day ceremonies after the death. Gamble described the rituals and offerings, including paper, for the twenty-first and the thirty-fifth days after death, two special memorial days for the dead, as well as for the first day of the tenth moon (1954:

391). Such dates follow the old custom of assisting the departed spirit with ceremonies every seven days until forty-nine days have passed; these ceremonies may be accompanied by elaborate paper offerings (Waters 1991: 122; see also Hase 1984: 155–61; Ikels 1996, 2004: 99, 256n.). Other important occasions for offering to the departed include Qing Ming (清明), which occurs during the third lunar month and is the most significant festival for remembering the deceased. At Chong Yang (重陽), a festival for avoiding plague, people also visit their ancestors' graves. Families gather at the gravesite to clean the area and repair the graves of the departed, and to make personal offerings of food, paper offerings, flowers, and incense. If the dead are interred in modern columbaria, they are still offered bags or chests of spirit money and other useful paper items. In addition to these yearly commemorations, relatives may burn paper offerings on other meaningful occasions, such as on the birthdays of the deceased, although this is not as frequent a practice.

Ordering Paper Funeral Offerings

Mourners go to retail paper shops or funeral workshops to make their orders. Nowadays, many modern funeral halls also provide standard funeral goods. If the family orders from a retail shop or workshop, they may consult a list of funeral offerings before making a selection. While many customers are knowledgeable about these items, having attended or arranged other funerals, others are not aware of all the possibilities, and the list is a useful beginning. While placing an order in a workshop, customers may observe the objects in the process of manufacture, or consult the shop's photo album with pictures of previous orders. Simply seeing these objects, either as real items in the workshop or in photographs, is comforting to the grieving families; they can appreciate at first hand the variety and quality of objects and feel confident that their relative will receive the best that they can provide.

While the bereaved family usually orders the funeral offerings, they are not the only ones involved. Masters explained that some elderly customers paid for their own funerals, as they had no relatives in Hong Kong, a common enough situation considering the history and circumstances of emigration from Mainland China. To secure their comfort in the next world, these elderly residents trusted the master to craft and have burned all they required when the time came. Paper masters also implied that some of the customers who ordered in advance did in fact have living relatives in Hong Kong, but did not wish to be a burden to their families, were concerned that relatives would not provide the correct offerings, or were estranged from their relatives altogether. To assure their comfort in the next world, they preferred to order in advance their own set of funeral goods. One master explained:

> There was a man who had two wives, one of the wives was afraid that after she died no one would take care of her, so that she gave money to my father about ten years ago. My father wrote down the name of the paper pitching [what she wanted]. My father promised to do this for her. Her family [after she died] brought the receipt to me and said that my father promised this, and I gave them the goods.

Another classic alternative, although much less common nowadays, is for the elderly person to join a society to save for funeral expenses. Each member deposits a set sum each month, and at death, the society pays for the coffin and for offerings; membership in such societies provides a form of insurance most comforting for the old.[3]

Shopkeepers said that some very tradition-minded elderly among the Chaozhou community, practice "sending treasury" (寄庫) in which they burned the paper offerings for themselves in advance. "Those who perform the 'worshipping for prospects' are those who have no relatives, so that they know no one will do it for them after their death and that they must do it in advance." Another added, "Before death, one goes to the Earth God on the street and burns several cabinets bearing one's name. The Earth God will keep the cabinets and the items with him for that person until death." The items burned were mainly large quantities ("several thousands") of folded Gold or Silver Paper. Shanghai customers, who also have such a practice of sending treasury, place their folded Gold and Silver Paper into a special pitched paper item called an Assembling Treasure Basin (聚寶盤) to hold the folded gold and silver. Other masters described this item as a cabinet with a lock, similar to a safe, for the storage of this money. These items were burned tied with red strings (or sealed with red paper) for a protective good meaning, as the burner of goods was after all, still alive, and hoped not to die soon, but to have a long life. The name of the sender was also attached so that the materials could be reclaimed in the next world. As to who was to hold this money for them in the underworld, other than the Earth God, one master told us the following story from the Tang Dynasty:

When Tang Tai Zong (唐太宗) went to Hell, the judges in Hell told him that he should use money to comfort those soldiers who died on the battlefield. As he had brought no money with him, he borrowed money from two people who were already there. Then Tang Tai Zong returned to the human world, he returned the borrowed gold to these two souls. I believe that "mailing for prospects" began then.

This story also refers to the reasons discussed earlier for burning paper currency to ancestors; one must pay one's debts. Another basis for this practice is explained as the need to repay the obligation incurred at birth to the bank of the underworld. To pay off this debt, most people sent the greatest amounts at death, but "One could send installment payments during one's lifetime in order to lessen the amount due on the final payment" (Teiser 1993: 134). However or whenever this practice began, advance burning is only a preparation, to ensure that goods are stored in the next world, protected by underworld officials and ready for use when needed. One shopkeeper was not certain that it was really needed. "Actually, there is no point in the elderly being afraid [of not receiving what they need in the next life]. If they are really afraid, they can simply reserve a space in a retirement home connected to a temple, and after they die, if their children really do not care for them, they will still be secure. There is no need to be fearful." Yet, the fear of not being cared for after death is very real among the elderly, as is evidenced in this earlier anecdote recorded by Burkhardt, of a widow living outside Beijing. "She replied . . . if she abdicated [stepped down from responsibilities and then died] she had no guarantee that her interests would be respected . . . she . . . invested in a magnificent coffin in advance" (1958: 8).

When the purchasing of proper funeral offerings is entrusted to family members, some individuals may mention their wishes beforehand or inform their favorite shop. It is difficult to know precisely how many elderly Hong Kong residents discuss their funerals in advance with their families, however, and in what manner the discussion is initiated; recent studies of Mainland practice (Ikels 2004) suggest that families must and do make advance plans for funerals. Some masters assert that those who knew they were near death told their offspring what special objects they wanted, just as they told them if they wished to be buried or cremated. Others said that these dying individuals would not specify what they wanted, but would instead give their relatives the name of the trusted shop from which they themselves had purchased paper offerings during their lifetime. Another group of masters believed that the elderly would inform relatives even if they were not sick or failing, because they all knew they would die some day and wished to be prepared. Still others believed the practice of discussing funeral preparations before death to be quite rare in Hong Kong, given the fear of death and the accompanying reluctance to discuss it for fear of bad luck or danger (for an extended discussion of this fear, see Watson 1988a). Many people still avoid speaking directly of death, preferring to use euphemistic terms such as "go" (去了), "go to fairyland" (仙遊), "passed away" (過身), "not here" (唔喺度), or the longer phrase, "Go to San Francisco to sell salted duck eggs" (去舊金山賣鹹鴨蛋). While reluctance to discuss death while living remains the most common attitude, this may be changing,[4] and it is difficult to know the frequency of individual solutions. As long as someone is responsible for arranging the purchase of the funeral offerings, and individuals can be sure that they would be cared for after death, any reasonable arrangement is acceptable.

After death, the departed may decide that they need additional items, and the requests for such items must be conveyed to the living. Fortunately, there are means by which the dead may communicate their wishes. Dreams are one channel that paper shop customers often mentioned because "Ancestor worship taught that when people died, their spirits did not die but could associate or make contact with the souls of the living" (Fang and Zhang 2000: 45). In the dream, the deceased informs the relative what is lacking or makes a complaint about conditions in the next world (L. Thompson 1988; Waters 1991: 126–7). The relative, thus informed, purchases and burns the designated item or items. "One of my customers bought a lot of gold bars, saying that he had dreamed about his father. His father told him that he had opened a goldsmith shop in the underworld and needed stock. I cannot judge whether this is true or not, but have heard much information of this kind since I began this business." Another shopkeeper reported:

> When I worked in Tsuen Wan [荃灣, a district to the northwest of the Kowloon peninsula], I made a car with a driver, whose head was movable. On the day after it was burned at the funeral, a woman who had not attended told me that the driver's head was in the wrong position. I asked her how she knew, and she said that she dreamed of her mother, who told her it was wrong. It was very strange. I asked the priests whether this was true or not and they said it was. I then made another driver for the family.[5]

Sometimes, dreams can report on offerings given to the deceased by second parties.

> One customer came to me to buy clothing for her deceased nephew, who lived in the Mainland. Her younger sister (the child's mother) dreamed about her son walking into her room and wearing a suit different from those that she had burned. She told her sister in Hong Kong, and her sister said that the suit had been burned by her in Hong Kong. So what do you think? Is that true? It is hard to say, but since I began operating this business, I have heard many stories like this.

It appears that such dreams can cover even greater distances. Another shopkeeper told us:

> One of our earlier female customers went to live in the United States. After some time, she came back and I said to her, "I seldom see you buying here. Are you new?" She said, "Shopkeeper, let me tell you a story. I am an overseas Chinese and have just come back from the United States, where I have been for many years. My ancestors are buried here. I had three dreams, in which my relatives said, 'What a good life you have now. But no one cares for our home. We have no house to live in, no money, nothing at all.' At first, I didn't believe it, but the next day my husband had the same dream." So, she had no choice but to fly back to Hong Kong, where she came in here and bought paper offerings to worship those ancestors. You can believe this or not.

Other ways to determine the conditions of loved ones in the next world is to use divination, for which there are a number of popular techniques (for detailed accounts, see Doolittle 1865b; Dore 1917; Smith 1991). In 1908, the Reverend J. Macgowan reported his observations during a session between the mother of a deceased daughter and a medium whom he termed a "witch." The girl replies, in answer to her mother's questions, "I am living in the house that mother had made for me and that was burned at my grave, so that in that respect I have nothing to complain of" (1908: 215). In the New Territories of Hong Kong, another means of communicating with the dead is through a skilled elderly woman who can act as intermediary between the village world and that of the supernatural. These women, termed shamans by Potter, perform valued services such as predicting the future, recapturing kidnapped souls of children, and caring for the souls of girls who die unmarried (Potter 1974: 207). Customers of the urban paper shops may seek the services of still other professionals, whom they refer to as the Man Mai Po (*wenmipo*) or literally, the "Ask Rice Woman" (問米婆), to contact the dead on their behalf (David 2000; Liu 2003).

> One customer told me she went to find the Man Mai Po; when she did, the words the Man Mai spoke were just like those of her mother-in-law and the Man Mai knew everything about her family. She was told to burn more paper gold ingots to her mother-in-law, who owned a gold shop in the next world. Another woman whose mother-in-law passed away was told by the Man Mai, who had been transformed into the old woman, not to throw away her old chair, for she still came to the house to sit on it. Still another lady visited the Man Mai to ask her deceased female relative whether she wished to be cremated; the Man Mai told her that it was acceptable, but that the two pieces of jade inside the coffin should be removed. This is all very mysterious, but I have heard so many things like this from my customers.

This proprietress was often asked by customers to introduce Man Mai, but she was very cautious, reminding customers of the cost of the service (HK$1,000 or more) and concerned over the trustworthiness of the Man Mai.

> I introduced a widow to this Man Mai. Her husband had asked workers to fix their air-conditioner, but he died before the work could be done. The widow asked the Man Mai to ask her husband if he had anything he wanted to finish, but the air-conditioner was not mentioned. The Man Mai then told the widow that her husband was still paying for their flat and that their son would soon marry. As the son was only sixteen and their mortgage had been fully paid long before, the widow knew that this Man Mai was not telling the truth. As this Man Mai was not reliable, I did not introduce any more customers to her and in fact, do not do this at all any more.

Other shops were more active in assisting customers in need of advice from the next world, providing introductions or addresses if the customer really wanted the information, and if the Man Mai was reliable.

> I have introduced one reliable Man Mai Po to others. Three daughters of a deceased lady went to see her and she [the Man Mai Po speaking in the voice of the deceased] said, "You should not throw away my clothes since there is money inside." The children originally wanted to give the clothes to others, but

they went home and searched their mother's clothing and found $1,000 in the pocket of one jacket. One of the daughters called me and said she should invite me to a restaurant since they had found so much money.

Still other shopkeepers had themselves sought out the services of such women.

I have been to see the Man Mai to ask whether my father could receive the offerings that we offered to him. My father was much older than my mother and when he passed away, my mother, at the age of forty, had eight children to look after. When we talked to my father, he said that he was really unwilling to die, "I died because I met bad luck, running into some 'dirty things.' Don't be so sad. I know it is hard to care for eight children alone, but our children are good. Take good care of them and have patience."

Despite such success, it is not clear that urban worshippers are as keen to seek the services of Man Mai Po as are their New Territories counterparts.

Modern Funeral Offerings

Pitched paper funeral offerings are fabricated in workshops still operating in Hong Kong as independent companies, or as adjoining sections of an established retail shop, many having achieved a reputation for the quality of their items and for courteous and helpful service. The current repertoire of paper funeral offerings, or gifts for the dead, is both various and complex. It includes non-pitched paper materials, mostly of clothing and accessories and various forms of spirit money, and the pitched paper materials, the three-dimensional modeled objects.

The offerings consist of what I have termed (Scott 1997a) the basic set and the items of everyday use. The first category was created early in the research, when I noticed that workshops making funeral offerings all prominently displayed lists of standard items on a sheet of paper, so that customers could make their selections. While there were some variations from workshop to workshop, the trade recognized a basic list of funeral items. The basic set is made up of the pitched models deemed necessary for the successful conduct of the funeral rituals. One master termed them the pitched materials for "listening to the scriptures" (聽經), as scriptures and prayers are recited during the funeral rituals. These items are to assist the soul in transition and to help it escape from the consequences of sin. Standard items include a paper crane and its accompanying willow banner, gold and silver bridges, dragon tablets, a bathing pan, models of servants, and also include the house and the car, although these two items play no part in the funeral rituals themselves.

Some scholars describe these basic offerings in terms of the commemorative services performed at seven-day intervals after death. While Dore recorded a bridge (probably of paper, although he only describes it as of "rough construction"), paper figures (probably the servants), and a paper sedan chair as necessary items for the funeral itself, he also noted that one or two paper houses were burned on the commemorative ceremonies of the forty-ninth day (Dore 1914: 46, 51, 59, 61). Burkhardt lists the offerings for the commemorative services for the seven-times-three ceremonies (the twenty-first day after death) as including golden and black trunks for clothing, replicas of actual gold and silver mines (which he described as "pillar-like structures of flowered paper with a projecting framework on top" and which were trimmed with paper flowers), and an edifice to represent the gate of the City of Hell (1955: 121–2). Ceremonies for the seven-times-five (the thirty-fifth day after death) included another replica of the gate of the City of Hell, this time with paper sedan chairs (1955: 129). A more recent account of the offerings for the thirty-fifth day services describes the following:

> At seven o'clock everyone went up to the roof to burn the addressed, paper trunks, containing paper money, in a steel incinerator. 'Gold' and 'silver bars' were also sent to long dead relatives. In addition effigies, made of coloured paper and cardboard stretched on bamboo or rattan frames, of a maid, a driver, a car (with lucky registration number 888), a house and furniture, and little black mourning strips which had been pinned on jackets, were burned. The names and messages of all donors were also burned so the dead person would know who had sent her presents. (Waters 1991: 122)

The second category, the items of everyday use, are basically three-dimensional models of useful objects, "the real items for the ancestor to enjoy," as one master explained them (the items of the category of "model paper pitching," 模型紮作). The items of everyday use can be offered during the initial ceremonies, at the seven-day commemorative ceremonies, or long after the funeral rituals are over.

The Basic Set

The basic set consists of items that serve in the funeral rituals to assist the deceased in a successful transition to the next world. While the actual number of items in the set varies, there is general agreement among shops on a list of approximately thirteen items. One workshop listed the contents as follows: a Dragon Tablet (龍牌), the Immortal Crane (仙鶴) and its accompanying Willow Banner (柳旛) which actually looks like a white fly whisk, one set of a red and a white banner (紅白旛), one bathing pan, a package of bathing clothes, a pair of mountains in gold and in silver (金銀山), the image of the Breaking out of Prison [Hell] Spirit (破獄神) and a sedan chair (轎). Also included were the platform for observing one's home village (望鄉台), a pair of male and female servants, a pair of bridges (one gold and one silver, for the souls to cross on the way to becoming immortals in heaven), a Chinese-style safe to hold personal items for the deceased, a red cabinet for storing clothing, a car, a Western-style multi-floored house with a garden, an additional pair of storage chests for the Gold and Silver Paper, a television set, and a set consisting of two seven-feet bridges in gold and silver. Some of these items (the servants, the chests) are reminiscent of the objects Wieger observed in 1913.

The male servants are often dressed in Qing or Republican-era costumes; the gray or blue long jackets with stand-up collars, worn with matching trousers, black cloth shoes, and a Western-style hat. Female servants are attired in the side-closing jackets, trimmed with paper rickrack, and trousers, with their hair done up in chignons. Both male and female servants have finely formed faces of papier-mache, neatly painted with distinct features against a rosy, healthy complexion. In such form, they are certainly more lifelike and finer than the "feet slaves" described by De Groot, "made in the roughest possible manner of paper pasted on bamboo splints, are not more than a foot in size" (1892: 24). With the last decade, smaller models of these servants have become available at retail paper shops. The author's collection contained two sets. Twenty-one inches tall, males were dressed in elegantly fashioned Republican-style trouser suits in black or deep blue, with accompanying black snap-brimmed hats and flat "cloth" shoes; real buttons closed the suit jackets. The females were dressed in pant suits of flowered material trimmed with real golden rickrack around the collar, closing and bottom edges; the jackets were closed with tiny golden clasps. The females' hair was cut in stylish bobs with bangs, secured with golden clips. In all such sets, both males and females have hands with finely cut fingers and modeled thumbs, and heads of papier-mache, finely painted with rosy lips and cheeks. The males generally have pink faces and the females, white. No matter whether the original large forms or the newly reduced models, these servants are intended to serve the deceased in the next world.[6]

Many of the items above appear during specific stages in the soul's movement from one state to another, during the sections of the funeral ritual "for the reading of the scriptures." For example, the Immortal Crane with the Willow Banner is the first item burned at the funeral. The crane is white, like a real crane, with a red patch on its head, straight legs, and the willow banner in its beak. The crane's purpose is to fly to where the soul is — the place where death occurred — and call it back so it can be sent on to the next world, borne on the crane itself (Ball 1926: 405, see also Doolittle 1865a: 193). The officiating priest burns the crane, while calling out the name of the deceased. The next items to be burned are the pair of red and white banners that are held by the deceased's son (the red) and the deceased's nephew (the white); those holding these banners must be male. They are also part of the ritual of calling back the soul, for both have the name of the deceased written on them.

Respondents did not always agree on the precise details of the meaning and use (including the burning order) of all items in the basic set. The Chief Dragon Tablet (正龍牌) and the Vice Dragon Tablet (副龍牌), which appear above as simply a Dragon Tablet, consists of elaborate, flower trimmed paper tablets bearing the names of the ancestors. If a married woman dies, the surname of her husband's family is listed on the Chief Dragon Tablet, and the Vice Dragon Tablet contains the surname of her ancestors. A second master said that the Chief Dragon Tablet was for the newly dead, and the Vice Dragon Tablet was for all the ancestors; the meaning of the term "vice" was not "secondary," but represented ancestral depth. These tablets are usually burned third in the sequence. According to the first master, the fourth item to burn is the western house with the garden (for the dead need a home to live in), and the rest of the items can be burned in any order. Not everyone agreed with this; the second master said that all the "pitched items for reading the scriptures" could be burned at the same time, although the bathing pan and clothes should be burned early on, for the dead needed to bathe and change clothes before listening to the scriptures.

Variations in the basic set

Shopkeepers and paper masters all agreed that items in the basic set were important; certain objects were necessary for the proper completion of the funeral rituals, and others were vital to the comfort of the deceased. However, it was understood that families on limited incomes might not be able to afford the full complement, so the content was adjusted. For example, one could save money by purchasing one bridge with one end golden and the other end silver instead of buying two separate gold and silver bridges. Likewise, houses could be purchased without the attached garden in the front. If the family faced serious financial difficulty, shopkeepers would identify items of greatest importance; the Master (to be introduced in Chapter 6) considered the first eight items on the previous list as most significant. Other shopkeepers and paper masters decided on a case-by-case basis, and some adjusted their prices to accommodate a seriously needy customer.[7]

In addition to variations arising from financial constraints, there were differences of opinion among the paper masters as to the content of the basic funeral set. The example of the basic set given at the beginning of this section contains seventeen items (the first eight of which were most important) — a somewhat expansive collection when the average size of a set varies from ten to thirteen objects. However, other shops asserted that there were "many tens of items" to purchase. The workshop producing the seventeen-item set placed the house and the car on the second list of items, although most masters placed these on the first list. Likewise, a paper television set would not be placed on even the second list of most shops, for it is not critical to any part of the funeral ritual, but it is an item that most customers buy. A few shopkeepers preferred a minimal approach, believing that all the dead really needed was a paper chest or two to hold their money and paper clothing.

There are many reasons for these variations. Buddhists are not expected to burn offerings for their dead, although some of them do; I attended a Buddhist funeral in which clothing and Gold and Silver Paper were burned on the first day. Paper masters understand this, and this could account for some of them adopting a minimal approach.

Other masters display the same variations in belief as do the customers, as they too have learned their trade in varying ways, at different times, and with different masters. Finally, items have changed with the passage of time. Very elderly masters may craft the basic set in a very classical fashion, while younger masters have been influenced by subtle changes in individual items. As a comparison of Burkhardt's (1955) and Water's (1991) lists of items suggests, necessary items do change in form and type as time goes by. Finally, variations in the content and design of the basic set category of funeral offerings may also be the result of ethnic differences.

The funeral offerings for Hong Kong's Chaozhou community differ somewhat from those normally used. Their basic set includes the red and white banners, a platform for looking back to the place of origin (which refers to the moment in the next world where the soul is allowed to view his home village, to which he can never return and which he must now forget); an ensemble consisting of a bed, a pillow, and a quilt; a tea set for brewing Iron Guan Yin tea; a water bucket (for male deceased) or a basin for foot washing (for female deceased). Masters could not explain the use of the latter two, other than saying these were for cleansing. Yet another workshop master told of one special item needed for deceased females of Shanghai origin — a cow, which was to drink up the dirty water for the deceased. Unfortunately, the respondent was not so clear about the history of this beast or what was meant by the dirty water, but the nearly life-sized replica took him two days to make and cost "over one thousand" (HK$1,200) dollars. Another Shanghai item is the Assembling Treasure Basin mentioned earlier.

Despite the differences of opinion as to where they belonged in the lists, nearly all customers ordered the models of houses and cars. The paper houses (sometimes referred to as village houses, 鄉村屋) are very lovely examples of crafting. They are mostly made up in the New Territories–style — two or three-storied village houses with flat roofs, front balconies on each floor, tiled outer-walls, and attached front gardens within an enclosing wall. The interiors are carefully done, individual rooms delineated with internal walls, lighting fixtures and outlets, framed pictures on the walls, and complete bathrooms. The furniture may be three-dimensional and free-standing models, very lifelike except for their small size, or printed on flat paper and glued to the walls of each room. The front garden often contains replicas of trees or flowers in pots (the Hong Kong custom), or the enclosing walls may be painted with plants and shrubbery. Many of these homes are accompanied by a suitably attired Sikh watchman, just as are (or were) many real-life Hong Kong establishments; some even contain small replicas of dogs and other pets. Recently, in the same manner as for the pair of servants discussed earlier, smaller and much more portable versions of these houses have appeared for sale in retail paper shops, so customers need not go to funeral workshops to make the order. These models, while much reduced in size, contain the same attention to detail as seen in the workshop versions.[8]

The automobiles may also be very elaborately crafted, which is not surprising given their numbers in Hong Kong and the efforts expended by living residents towards owning the most prestigious models. Paper masters replicated exactly the models customers most ordered: a Mercedes Benz or Rolls Royce, but also Porsches, Jaguars, and other expensive sports cars. "I had an order from the family of a young man who died in his twenties; he owned a Lotus car and the family wanted one made. So, I went to the department store to copy a toy model of one. Everyone said the one I made looked just like the real thing." These cars, often made up in the color blue, most appropriate for the dead, can be equipped with doors that open, steering wheels, seats, headlights, interior finishing — the full complement of interior details — and the expected lucky license plate in multiples of the number eight. Most are crafted in five, seven and nine-feet lengths (models purchased in retail stores are smaller, from six inches to two feet or so in length), but masters will craft them to any desired size. One master known for his perfect car models crafted replicas of Rolls Royce measuring nine feet long. Costing many thousands of dollars, these required many days of labor. He complained that the grill took a long time to master and the workshop had to make special wheels. Modeled cars usually come with a uniformed chauffeur, even if in real life very few citizens can afford such help.

The Items of Everyday Use

In addition to the basic set, there is a second large category which I have termed (Scott 1997a) the items of everyday use. This category includes the daily necessities of life as these are for the living, such as electrical appliances and household goods, clothing, personal items, spirit money, and the special items or extra gifts for the dead. In one sense, basic necessities (other than the forms of spirit money) could be considered as special items, because customers who are not satisfied with retail examples can order any and every item made to specification. However, as many of the smaller objects now available in retail shops are of quite acceptable quality, it is reasonable to separate the truly unique items into the distinct category of special items.

The special items

The group of special items is truly infinite in content, encompassing what the deceased wished to possess in the next world, what he or she actually possessed in life, or what the family of the deceased wished to provide as special gifts. As Wieger observed, "Any figures that one desires are made . . . If other images are asked for, some scenes of comedies are depicted [he likely meant scenes from popular operas], or animals spitting cash" (1913: 567–9). As seen, some individuals plan carefully before death, taking steps to be certain that they will receive what they most desire. Many of these special orders are a form of wish fulfillment, in that the deceased never owned the objects while alive. For example, while cars are usually provided as part of the basic set, orders are generally for the most expensive models (Rolls Royce, Mercedes Benz, Italian sports cars) which most people cannot afford in real life; further, orders can be made for multiple sets of cars, which again, few of the living actually own. A young paper master explained that one family, whose deceased father loved to drive, had ordered an entire fleet of expensive cars: several Rolls Royce, Mercedes Benz, and Lexus. Looking over the models, the family was pleased but concerned, realizing that they had forgotten something. After some thought, they ordered a detailed model of a gas station, so that their father never need worry about fueling all those cars. Buses, motorcycles, and minibuses are also available.

Some of the objects ordered are difficult to explain as other than customers' very personal desires or simple quirks; these are the truly unique or one-of-a-kind items. The family of an avid racing fan requested a huge model of the Heavenly Jockey Club (天堂賽馬會), a racecourse complete with bleachers, electronic scoreboard, and horses. The entire model, larger than the shop, was modeled in sections and assembled at the funeral. The master told us that the only thing missing was the spectators, for he could not possibly craft tens of thousands of them to set within the bleachers. Another master explained how one of his customers ordered a nine-feet replica of a Buddhist pagoda to be offered to a Buddhist relative (even though Buddhists are supposed to be unconcerned with such paper offerings); it took him one week to complete. On the opposite end of the scale of peace and harmony was the order for a set of paper guns, including handguns and machine guns, whose purpose in the next world remained a mystery to the master. As firearms are illegal in Hong Kong and only law enforcement officers (and criminals) own them, one can only speculate about how the deceased was to use them. Perhaps this was a special order for a deceased gang member; offerings of this kind may not be so uncommon in nearby enclaves.[9]

Other special orders reflect cherished everyday activities or habits, including the keeping of animals as pets. Animals are rarely seen among Hong Kong funeral replicas, and are equally rare in the literature. One reference comes from Dard Hunter:

> In Bangkok, where the population is made up of three Chinese to every Siamese, I recall standing before one of these shops for hours watching the construction of the replica of a huge dog, the frame made of thin strips of bamboo . . . Upon asking the Chinese worker how the dog was to be used, I was told that a wealthy Chinese merchant had just died and that this was a representation of his mastiff, the imitation animal had been ordered by the dead man's relatives . . . the master would have his favorite dog with him when he reached the spirit world. (1937: 6–7)

One order placed at a Hong Kong retail shop consisted of a group of racehorses, complete with jockeys and silks, for a man who had been an avid racing fan. A female apprentice jockey, who was killed in a riding accident during Hong Kong's 1999 racing season, was given a large complement of horses and riding accoutrements, as well as a set of horse exercisers (馬伕) (*South China Morning Post*, April 12, 1999). The implication of such a gift was that in the next world she would no longer be a lowly apprentice but a woman of means and the owner of her own stable. Other masters described the replication of especially beloved pets, mostly dogs, sometimes cats, or of an order for a goldfish bowl, complete with fancy goldfish. A more recent and poignant example described a pair of golden paper monkeys.

> Kam Ying used to go everywhere "Monkey Man" Chan Yat-biu went. But the eight-year old rhesus monkey cannot follow her master into the next world. In her place will go two paper

monkeys along with a two-storey house and other ritual offerings at the funeral of the Kowloon City medicine hawker who kept Kam Ying as a pet . . . His son, Chan Yiu-wing, said he had the pair of gold-coloured monkeys made to order as one of the last things he could do for his father. (Cheung 2004)

Customers at retail shops can also order detailed models of birdcages, complete with paper bird seated on the perch, reflecting the pleasure taken by the elderly in the old pastime of keeping songbirds. Despite these examples, the reproduction of pets and other animals is still quite rare, and those who make orders understand that the animals so replicated are not meant to be exact copies of the actual animal, if it is still alive. Nevertheless, most recent offerings have seen the limited appearance of pitched paper models of dogs, notably a small and rather chubby version of a Dalmatian (Chow 2005).

Scholars have amply documented the significance of food offerings for the dead (see, for example, Ahern 1973; Stevens 1997; Thompson 1988). As family members regularly offer real food at the major festivals honoring the dead, it is not necessary to repeat such gifts in paper. About fifteen or so years ago, paper comestibles for the dead were not so common and were custom-made. One workshop owner described with some amusement an order for paper noodles and paper bread buns, while another filled an order for a paper durian (Southeast Asia's famous foul-smelling fruit). By the 1990s, however, retail paper shops had begun to stock increasing amounts of pre-crafted comestibles. Most of these factory-produced examples originally fell into the category of luxury foods, snack foods or other indulgences, and beverages. For example, most commonly available were packages containing bottles of VSOP (a popular type of cognac), Coca Cola, and paper glasses. Realistic cigarettes and cigars (no concerns about lung cancer in the next world) were also sold in different brands, each pack open at the top so that one could see the individual sticks and their filter tips, accompanied by replicas of lighters. Also available were six packs of assorted beers (bottled in Hell), soft drinks, mineral waters, and as time passed, canned sweetened teas.

These original items are still produced, but replicas have become more elaborated and varied. Candy is a popular item with the appearance of a popular Italian chocolate and hazelnut candy, complete in every detail including its distinctive box and individual foil wrappings. Some of these boxes of candy are more deluxe, with the chocolates sharing space with coconut candies — the latter small replicas wrapped in real candy wrappers for authenticity. Other boxes include very realistic models of ice-cream bars and chewing gum. Also of recent manufacture are the packages of true luxury foods: sets of four realistically designed cans of abalone, shark fins, sea cucumbers, and birds' nests, all bearing barcodes of multiples of eight, a lucky number. Some shops carry what are obviously handcrafted examples of special delicacies and health foods such as sharks' fins packed as they are in restaurants and very realistic full-sized, handmade models of superior ginseng roots.

While all these may be seen as true luxury foods, a wonderful variety of paper *dian xin* (點心) have begun to appear in retail shops;[10] one's ancestors can now be treated to that quintessential of all Hong Kong family pleasures, *yin cha* (drink tea, 飲茶). Another family dining treat, the basin meal (食盆) has recently appeared. Labeled as "higher grade basin meal," it is presented in a paper pan much like the real item, its top adorned with realistic models of crab, shrimp, shellfish, scallop, realistic abalone, lobster tail, eel, roasted chicken, roast pork, green onion, and vegetables. Underneath can be seen fibrous threads representing noodles and tofu skin. Much fancier than normal restaurant fare, this version appeared quite popular (for an explanation of a basin meal, see Watson 1987). Along with all the fancy items are increasing amounts of everyday canned foods such as chicken broth, fried fish, cooked pork, longan and fruit cocktail, even the popular black turtle jelly (龜伶膏). One can even purchase packages of five kinds of popular cup noodles. Amidst all these reproductions of processed foods, are the packages of individual, and very realistic, cardboard models of popular species of raw fish, prepared and ready for steaming in the kitchens of the next world.

In short, comestibles, which began as special handmade orders have rapidly become standard items for mass production and a common enough offering for those wishing to comfort the dead. Recent investigations (Scott 2004) suggest, however, that many customers have not yet made up their minds about paper replicas of foods. While all agree that paper offerings are important and that replicas of food are quite appropriate as offerings, there are those who do not purchase them. Some explain that they still prefer traditional items, while others explain that such paper replicas are not necessary. The latter further explain that paper foods cannot be consumed by the family after the ceremonies, thus negating the feeling of sharing with the dead which arises from the use of genuine foodstuffs during these commemorative meals and rituals. Those who do purchase such replicas are quite enthusiastic, stressing the great variety of items and the fact that paper replicas are good ways to provide true luxuries and special foods that the ancestor might not have enjoyed while alive. Further, such items are considered reasonable because offerings must be burned and it is unreasonable to burn genuine food; the paper versions become the real thing in the next world anyway. However, these respondents combine paper replicas with real foodstuffs when they worship. Whatever the individual opinion regarding their use, paper replicas of foodstuffs are increasing in number and variety.

Other special orders provide fascinating glimpses into customers' views of the needs of loved ones in the next world, including their need for recreation. One order, reluctantly refused at one shop we visited, was for a complete eighteen-hole golf course. Travel, now so much a part of the daily life of the living, is catered for by the use of Hell passports and mock-ups of airline tickets from "Hell Airlines,"[11] while travel over shorter distances can now be handled by mock-ups of Hong Kong's own popular Octopus card for public transport, and by tickets for Greyhound-style coach trips. Transportation is, as already seen in the orders for fine cars, another common theme of special orders, although many customers would not order paper cars if the deceased did not know how to drive. If that were the situation, the cost of the car in the basic set would be subtracted from the order. However, the ordering of a car and a driver solves that problem. Much more common now are the models of jet airliners and yachts, which can be purchased in retail shops already made up (planes in roughly one to three feet in length), or in slightly larger, yet still scale, versions by the workshops — no shop has yet managed to craft a full-sized 747. Despite all this expertise, crafting a realistic mode of transport is sometimes just too much.

> Some years ago, a man died in a motorcycle accident. His friend came to us and asked my husband to make a paper pitching of that motorcycle. Although we could have charged $1,200 for it, my husband would have had to go to the center for vehicle surrender to look at it; he refused, as he knew it would be messy [due to the accident] and no longer recognizable and also, he would have to wait a long time before he could get to see it.

All of the shops were prepared as well to make up variations of the Street of the Dead (陰州街), an actual city street made up with all the shops and places necessary for the continuance of everyday life. In addition to a fine home for the deceased, these streets can contain clothing and dry goods stores, grocery stores, motion picture theatres, department stores, wet markets for fresh vegetables and meats, laundries, betting shops, and herbal or Western medicine shops — in short, anything the customer believes the street must contain to ensure that the deceased (now a landlord) will lead a full life in the next world. Each of these shops is individually made, furnished, and given a name, such as the Hell Restaurant (冥通酒樓). Some of these street models are so large (about seven feet high and about twenty feet long, with two sides of the street depicted) that they are crafted in sections and put together at the time of the burning. Families concerned with the comfort of their deceased family members, and possessed of suitable finances, can order absolutely anything they desire to populate this street.

The daily necessities

The more common daily necessities are extremely popular with paper shop customers and a source of great fascination to casual visitors. Most retail paper shops now stock considerable numbers of these replicas purchased from wholesalers in the same manner as the non-pitched items for everyday worship. Many may be burned at the funeral or during the commemorative ceremonies but can also be burned to the deceased during the Qing Ming or Chong Yang holidays.

First, there are the various electrical appliances and gadgets, including fans, rice-cookers, television sets, telephones, VCRs, irons, air-conditioners, computers, calculators, refrigerators, washing machines, DVD players, LCDs and so on. These items can be very elaborately constructed with moving parts, handles and knobs, and are among the most complicated of pitched items. Some masters consider the refrigerator as especially difficult to craft because its modeled door must open and close, and then stay closed. As well, it must contain all the shelves, including the egg trays and door compartments. Also difficult to craft is the compact disc player, which may have a turntable which can revolve and a set of compact discs to insert under a lid that can open and close. Retail shops also sell the paper replicas of the most up-to-date computers, DVD players, Sony Walkmen, kitchen appliances, iPods, and other desired items. Mobile phones are very popular among Hong Kong's living residents, and all paper shops now stock them for use in the next world. When they first became popular, mobile phones looked much like field telephones or walkie-talkies, but they have since become as small and sleek as their ubiquitous real life counterparts.[12] Currently available packages of the latest models of mobile phones come complete with cases, plugs and batteries, all in paper.

Other forms of relaxation and entertainment are not ignored. There are paper tea sets, including the Chaozhou models for the proper serving of the Iron Guan Yin tea they prefer, although for the Chaozhou, the tea set is a necessity, not an extra. Paper mahjong sets, each individual tile made exactly to scale and printed like the real thing, are also available, along with domino sets, and packs of both Chinese-style and Western-style playing cards. Increasingly, shops have stocked models of soccer balls, baseballs and mitts, tennis rackets and paper models of games.

Always popular are the items of personal use — paper clothing (of prefabricated or custom design), underwear, hats, shoes, handbags, and jewelry. Simple clothing for the ancestors can be made of the Five or Seven Colored Paper discussed earlier for the ghosts. Like the ghosts, the ancestors can also use this paper to make their own clothing in the next world. Or, customers can select larger pieces cut in the style of old fashioned robes, also made of Five or Seven Colored Paper and printed with elaborate motives of flowers and geometric shapes. The older shops carry clothing sets of old-fashioned cut, made of somewhat heavier paper in dull colors and printed with tailoring details. However, many customers now prefer the most up-to-date replicas of stylish clothing, and what is considered good clothing for the dead has been changing.[13] These newer items of clothing can be surprisingly well made, with shoes fabricated with shoelaces and stitching details, or if sports shoes, with coloring and designs reminiscent of the most popular brands. High-heeled shoes, sandals, and boots in the height of fashion, and coveted brands of sports shoes (to be used with the replicas of sports equipment above) are offered alongside the classic black kung fu shoes in paper. Custom-made clothing may be full size and fully wearable, and even pre-packaged clothing is becoming more interesting and more reflective of current fashion. Shops sell individually boxed men's shirts in contemporary business-favored pin stripes, accompanied by a tie in tasteful colors, as well as replicas of brand name sports shirts. Suit packages come complete with suit, tie and matching shirt, while other combinations consist of shirt, tie, watch, and upon turning over the package to the back side, pants (including blue jeans), and "leather" belts and wallets. Women's fashions have become more modish, even daring, as seen in recent packages of frilly lingerie sets (bras and underpants) in fetching pastel colors. In short, clothing has increasingly reflected the modern styles that people actually wear every day. There is also a variety of jewelry, mostly rings and bracelets of gold or gold set with jade, but there are also jade pendants and bracelets, ear studs, and rings for women. Sets of personal jewelry for men contain cuff-links, fountain pens, and watches.

Items may reflect the deceased's physical condition in life. Shops have crafted paper wheelchairs or orthopedic shoes so that mobility in the next world would not be affected. Variations on this theme include a full set, uppers and lowers, of realistic pink dentures, crafted so carefully that they could function as night guards for the living. The category of items for personal grooming has also expanded. Retail shops now stock personal hygiene sets composed of a tube of toothpaste (some in a mock-up of the infamous brand of toothpaste no longer available in the world of the living, Darkie — now gentrified to Darlie), a toothbrush, and a replica of a glass cup. Boxes of medicines and Band Aids are made up in actual size. Tiny travel sets of famous brand electrical shavers, complete with plugs and adapters, can be purchased, while other sets contain replicas of soaps and towels, or of combs, brushes, hair oil and hair clips. Ladies conscious of their appearance in this life may continue to use make-up in the next world, for packages of eye shadow, lipstick and lipstick brushes, and powder are available. Before applying such make-up, they can clean their complexions with Pond's vanishing cream or Hazeltine facial foam, and soften their hands with "Paesr" (Pears) hand cream. Hairdryers and curling irons take care of styling needs.

There are also items of personal finance — the check books, savings account books with withdrawal and deposit slips, ATM cards, and credit cards — all made to scale and drawn on the Bank of Hell. Bankbooks, printed in auspicious red with gold embossing, are just like the real thing, with sections for account name and number, and pages marked for the standard machine recording of withdrawals, deposits, and balances. Each one bears an account number with multiples of the lucky numbers of two and eight, the pronunciations of which are homophones with the words for prosperity. Checkbooks are reproduced with the same concern for accuracy. The credit cards, it should be noted, bear the image of the King of Hell, and in colors (greenish blue, white, and black) and design elements are suspiciously similar to the American Express card, providing an otherworldly twist ("Don't leave this world without it") to their advertising slogan. Also available, should one prefer them, are the Master Cards. The currencies popularly known as Hell Money, resplendently printed in full color and of elaborate design, bear the image of the King of Hell. Hell Money is printed in variable sizes but generally comes in huge denominations; notes of one and five hundred million dollars are common. As Cave observed, although such bills "are outside most people's experience . . . the contemporary worshipper feels more at ease offering these high-denomination notes on the Bank of Hell" (Cave 1998: 3). Yet, more recent examples are clearly printed, in English, in one hundred dollar denominations. Currently available forms are designed to resemble various international currencies, such as Renminbi, United States dollars, British pounds, and Hong Kong dollars.

The Hell Money complements the large variety of gold ingots, bars, and coins currently available. The ingots are fashioned from stiff paper covered in gold paper, then stamped with the gold weight mark; coins are stamped out of heavy paper and covered with either silver or gold. A customer can purchase boxes of golden Canadian Maple Leaves or Krugerrands just like the real thing. If in silver, the coins bear an image that resembles Yuan Shikai (袁世凱 1859–1916), the first president of the Republic of China after the 1911 revolution (Schoppa 2000: 178). Shopkeepers said this might be a vague allusion to the thickness or purity of the genuine silver coinage in circulation at that time. As already described, the ancestors also require a large supply of Gold and Silver Paper, each sheet folded into ingot shapes. Customers can purchase these papers pre-folded and boxed for sale at the shop, but most customers prefer to fold their own. Gold and Silver Paper offerings also vary according to ethnicity. Shanghai silver for the ancestors may be purchased in most shops, in thick packages of silver paper (in Shanghai style, the entire sheet is silver — there are no plain paper borders on this form) or in large boxes of pre-folded silver ingots. Packages of unfolded Shanghai silver are also painted at two corners with the green and purple usually found on First Treasure enfolding paper. Overall, a full array of financial and banking services, and an entire complement of funds to place in accounts covered by these services, is available to both residents and entrepreneurs of the next world.

Offerings for children

There are differing scholarly accounts of funerals for children.[14] One recorded by Patrick Hase for the New Territories described the procedures:

Children dying before about the age of five were regarded as inappropriate subjects for funeral rituals up to the end of the War. Where such a child died, the family would quietly inform the elders. The following night the family, particularly the children, would move to another room to sleep, leaving the house unlocked. In the dark before dawn, at about 4 a.m., the elders would quietly come in with a basket. The child would be placed in the basket and carried off and placed at the foot of a large tree in a certain part of the village fung-shui grove and left for the birds and the dogs . . . Children dying between about 5 and 12 years were also denied rites and mourning. (1984: 162–3)

Burkhardt agreed, observing:

It is considered unlucky to bury a chil.d of under three, for fear death striking at another member of the family. Consequently the tiny bodies are often left exposed, sometimes near a public cemetery, and sometimes on the seashore, or consigned to the current of a river . . . The Boat People alone recognise the child to possess a soul which is commemorated after death and make images of their deceased children, the boys mounted on lions, and the girls on white cranes. (1953: 175)

Attitudes have changed since the 1950s and families devotedly care for deceased children as well as adults, including the burning of offerings. Most paper shops sell a particularly poignant group of items for children to use in the next world: school books, satchels, and composition books. Children also require clothing and other personal items, but their clothing packages have been generally of the same style and size as those purchased for adults. Some shopkeepers said that the size of the offering depended on how much time has elapsed since death. "Parents whose sons died may buy smaller sizes; after the child has been dead for several years, however, they will burn a larger size of clothing." Examples of book bags, exercise books, and shoes made just for children are available. One old shop produced clothing specifically for "young boys." Two pieces acquired were very simple old-style jacket and trouser sets, one in grey and one in blue-green printed with indistinct flowers, with collarless V-necked jackets adorned only with three pasted-on blue paper buttons. The accompanying trousers were folded from one sheet of paper, glued at the seams to create the legs, and finished with a white band at the waist. A small selection of toys has gradually appeared in retail shops within the last ten years. Recent examples include Gameboys and other popular items such as the Rubix Cube, toy cars, tops, and bottles of liquid soap, complete with "plastic" wand, for bubble blowing. Even further, children's choices in food have not been neglected, with shops selling packaged replicas of McDonald's happy meals and other burger sets.

The Flexibility of Funeral Offerings

Many items within the basic set of funeral offerings must conform to images enshrined in the performance of funeral rituals and in classical perceptions of the other world, and therefore they are not subject to great changes. They are not expected to modernize. The situation is quite different for the items of everyday use. By being replicated in paper, modern items of technology and contemporary fashions are transformed and provided with a new identity as proper offerings, appropriate grave goods. Ancient categories of offerings such as transportation, clothing, housing, and daily necessities are retained, but their specific contents are kept up to date. Whenever a new item of technology or an improved model appears on the market, it can be fabricated to augment or replace the paper version already available. Replicas of standard desk telephones have given way to mobile phones; as the mobile phones themselves become more compact and intricate, so do their counterparts in paper. The same is true for calculators, which have been replaced by the latest pocket-sized versions, and personal computers (complete with screen, keyboard, and software discs), while old-style stereophonic systems with turntables have been supplanted by working (i.e., containing moving parts) examples of compact disc and DVD players. Television sets, once simple and clumsy in design, have given way to the latest in liquid crystal technology. Even clothing design, which is more conservative, shows the effects of this change; paper shops display stylish high heels and the latest in sports shoes alongside the traditional flat slippers, and modern suits, shirt and tie combinations, blue jeans and sportswear next to Qing-style jacket and trouser sets. The classical appearance of the next world, of Hell, is definitely changing.

Customers see no incongruity in the changes that have occurred, and consider such items acceptable offerings. Although not so common in actual practice, replicas of items of modern technology may be burned to fairly distant ancestors, suggesting that long deceased individuals can accept new items that they had never envisioned when alive as readily as do the recently dead.[15] Many shopkeepers declared that there were no differences between items burned to the genealogically closest ancestors and those further distant, nor between those who died long ago and those who died recently.[16]

Thinking about the size of objects also reflects a capacity to recognize change. Even the Neo-Confucian philosopher Zhu Xi set no absolute rules on this matter, saying only that, "The objects [the grave goods] should resemble those used in real life but be smaller" (Ebrey 1991: 109). Many modern paper funeral offerings are built to correct scale and are usable "as is." This is seen most clearly in the category of the items of the electrical appliances, which are life-sized. Paper money and ingots are also made close to the size they are in the real world. Other items, such as the cars and houses that are part of the basic set, are most often not fully life-sized, however detailed they may be, because they would be exceedingly difficult to craft and to store if they were made to exact scale. Some masters believed that it was better to have everything in life size if possible while others were not so concerned. For many, the prices of small and large objects, like automobiles, are the same, for while the large size requires more material, the smaller size requires more concentration in crafting; the price evens out. However, a minority felt that size was important, for the object cannot change in the next world from its original crafted form. As one funeral master expressed it, changing sizes is illogical. "How can a two-feet long car be enlarged? It is only something symbolic and [for] psychological comfort. I have no idea, but just craft for the customer."

Clothing packages are not always crafted to scale, with handcrafted examples more likely to be life-sized while printed ones somewhat less than life-sized. There are no set rules about this, although there is some difference of opinion over what form these offerings will take in the next world; an example of this was seen above in the discussion of paper offerings for children. Some shopkeepers do not sell the smaller sizes of ancestors' clothing, saying that they seldom give smaller sizes to ancestors anyway. "[After being burned to the ancestors], the clothing will not enlarge. Since these ancestors were adults, if you offer them small clothing, how could they wear it? So, I do not sell the small sizes." Others, such as the shopkeeper who sold the paper clothing for children, believed the sizes could be adjusted to reflect the deceased child's growth in the next world. That such growth and maturation could be a possibility to keep in mind when making offerings is seen in one respondent's dream about her dead child.[17]

This is what happened in my dream. I was walking on the street. I saw there some people performing the rituals for the dead. Because it is not good to watch these, I turned away and looked on the ground. Then I saw someone, a boy of about eleven years old, who stopped and stood next to me. He said, "Mother, I died tragically." Then he disappeared and I woke up. I then thought of my baby, who had died after birth, and after I counted the years that had passed since then, I knew that my baby would have been the same age as the boy in the dream.

Still, such questions of size appear to be of little concern to most shopkeepers or to purchasers, for many believe that all items will reappear in the next world in the proper size. No matter how small or how large the paper replica, the item will assume the correct size to fit the receiver or the purpose. When pressed on this issue, respondents admitted that it was a matter of belief, and in the end, unless someone's relative appeared in a dream and complained to the sender, no one knew for certain. It would appear that complaints about sizes of objects are rare, relatives and ancestors being more concerned about sending and receiving what was needed.

Receiving the Offerings

Assuming a large population of souls in the next world, and an accompanying large quantity of paper offerings being sent for their use, one may ask how worshippers ensure that specific individuals actually receive the offerings targeted for them. There are various means — dreams and the use of divinatory techniques such as asking the Ask Rice Woman — of inquiring or checking on the arrival of goods, and purchasers may also take steps to ensure timely delivery. There are different occasions within the lunar calendar devoted to the care of the dead; these include the Qing Ming and Chong Yang festivals, the Festival of the Hungry Ghosts, and the Fu Jian (附薦) a time when the ancestors can listen to scriptures and receive offerings. The Fu Jian, which lasts for a few days, can be held during the Qing Ming observances and also during July, when it is called the Seventh Month Fu Jian (七月附薦). The Fu Jian appears to be an observance of some antiquity, described in a story (ca. 500) of the underworld travels of a monk who met the goddess Guan Yin in one of the chambers of Hell.

Guan Yin preached to him of the benefits of making offerings on the full moon of the seventh month (Teiser 1988: 133). Doolittle described this event in 1865:

> Some time during the seventh month, generally before or about the fifteenth day, occurs the celebration of a remarkable custom, having a principal reference to the happiness and comfort of the dead. It is generally referred to as the "*burning of paper clothing in the middle of the seventh month.*" Its professed object is to furnish clothing and money for their deceased ancestors. In order to obtain this result, comparatively large quantities of mock-money and and mock-clothing are provided, and burned in a large furnace or censer before the tablets of the ancestors . . . (1865b: 61)

This ritual (also described by Hodous in 1929) has given its name to the Fu Jian Bag (附薦袋), an item which Hunter described as an envelope called a "hua pao-fu" (1937: 42), which is burned on the next to last day of the Fu Jian, filled with money and clothing packages for the ancestors. Sometimes, individuals may burn a Fu Jian Cabinet (附薦槓), which also holds such gifts. All materials are put into the bag (or cabinet), upon which is written the name of the ancestor and the date of the burning, and the bags are sealed with a Label (literally, a "sealing strip" [封條], a yellow slip which closes the bag. Both bags and chests are a neat and tidy way to send a large amount of items, and such bags are burned at all holidays for the dead, to ensure that the dead will be delivered from suffering (Teiser 1988: 134). The contents of these Fu Jian Bags have recently become quite varied. Bags seen being packed during Chong Yang in Hong Kong contained packages of gold coins, clothing packages, four kinds of Hell Money, Money to Live, modeled paper shoes, Seven Voice Incantations, passport and credit card sets, Gold and Silver Paper, boxed paper dress shirts, and White Money. Boxed clothing was removed from its plastic wrapping, and other items were either spread apart in a fan shape before stuffing into the bag or put in one by one. Other pre-packed Fu Jian bags sold by hawkers at the site contained quantities of Gold Paper folded into ingot shapes. Worshippers have also begun showing more individuality in their methods of closing the bag. While most still use the Label for this purpose, Fu Jian bags have been seen sealed with three or four varieties of Hell Money, with the Label plus two or four folded sheets of Gold and Silver Paper, with sets of three (meaning "life") pieces of Money to Live, or with three evenly spaced clusters of White Money. Other families chose to staple shut the bags, but trim them at both upper corners with ingot folded pieces of Gold and Silver Paper.

Some shopkeepers maintained that these bags were actually nothing special, but simply mailing bags (郵包), but others declared them a proper means of sending offerings. Fu Jian Bags used by the Cantonese are grayish cream in color, with the auspicious designs printed in green in the middle; those for the Shanghai community are approximately one-half the size, in deep red, with the design printed to the edge of the item in black. While rare, one was seen recently at a site for Qing Ming observances. Both bear identical auspicious phrases, but decorations on the outer border can vary. More recently, a multicolored version of the Cantonese Fu Jian bag has appeared, in which the background is still grayish cream, but the auspicious designs of dragons, phoenix, cranes, and bats are printed in full color. The printing quality is also very high. While this version is quite attractive and appears to be gaining in popularity, most worshippers still use the older style bag. While the bag (or the cabinet) can be sent at any time, most people burn it during Fu Jian, Qing Ming, or Chong Yang. In any event, what a worshipper burns will go to his or her own ancestor, if the name of that ancestor is written on the bag. If the worshipper burns on behalf of another (helping a friend burn to his or her relatives), then care must be taken that the name of this other recipient is correctly written on the bag.

Another method of ensuring timely delivery is the burning of a Passport (通行證), which contains the name of the deceased and the place where the person was born — of concern if the deceased died in Hong Kong but wished to return to his or her birthplace. But, the Passport also allows movement at the place of death, to allow the dead to travel to other places to receive offerings.

> In the past, Hong Kong relatives would burn this passport to the dead relatives who lived in Mainland China. After the deceased on the Mainland received the passport, they could come to Hong Kong. So, fathers and grandfathers could come here and receive all the offerings being burned here by sons and daughters. Also, if the dead relatives lived abroad, then the address of the place at which they died was written in the language of that place; say, in English or French.

Burning the Passport also enables the dead to enter the other world and then to move about freely. A Passport burned in the funeral home asks the dead relative to come to the funeral home to listen to the scriptures that will ease their pain and allow them to pass serenely into the next world. In all cases, the Passport allows the dead to listen to scriptures and receive paper offerings.

Shopkeepers and workshop masters admitted to not knowing for certain if items burned are actually received. "It is impossible to know whether the dead will receive it or not," one proprietor told us, "I am sure that no one will know whether they will receive it or not. For example, someone told me that Hell Money was not needed, and I asked why he said so, had he been in the underworld?" If there are still doubts, additional steps can be taken to ensure safe arrival. In 1941, Lowe explained that the deceased would be accompanied by an assistant to take care of offerings.

> This honest-looking young man is the person to whom is entrusted the custodianship of gold and silver hoardings. He lives and dies, so to speak, with the cash register and the storehouse key in his hands. Made of paper, as is also the house under whose roof he stands, he stays there rain or sun on duty twenty-four hours a day, a veritable Good Man Friday. (1983 [1941]: 114)

Hunter also noted the Beijing guardians of the chests of white and gold treasury money, figures called treasury officers, who were given food and drink and sheets of mock money tied around them. They were burned with the chests they were assigned to protect (1937: 61). Shopkeepers added that various deities may intervene to ensure a fair distribution, to both ancestors and to hungry ghosts, of needed offerings; this is a proper responsibility for gods. Masters explained that the Earth God could do this, and Guan Yin was often cited. Guan Yin's intervention is particularly invoked during the Festival of the Hungry Ghosts, as she has the authority to see that each of the hungry ghosts receives its share of all the offerings burned at this time. These deities can also ensure timely delivery to ancestors.

Paper offerings for the dead are characterized by elasticity and a capacity to absorb both new elements of material culture and changes in technology. This process is especially marked in the group of items of everyday use, in which obsolete models are regularly replaced by the most up to date examples. If indeed the next world is like this one, an emphasis on objects that are the most current models available, make perfect sense. In 1964, Hugh Baker referred to village funerals in which offerings consisted of incense, candles, paper money, and "a paper sedan chair complete with bearers" (Baker 1964: 36), but the latter are rarely, if ever, crafted now. One elderly paper master explained:

> In the past, the sedan chair was used by the people of the Qing Dynasty, and there were civil sedan chairs (文明轎), but now

there are none. People seldom order these for ceremonies, and vehicles have become popular. In the past, there was the wheeled sedan chairs (轎) pulled by men. But, this is not popular now, as it was before Japan retreated from Hong Kong. Now, cars are burned instead.

One form of an item is replaced by another, as time in the next world passes as it does here. That this capacity for change has long been a characteristic of the industry is suggested in a photograph, originally taken by Sidney D. Gamble in Beijing in 1924.[18] The photo in question depicts an amazingly lifelike and life-sized paper model of a Ford Model A car, complete with what appear to be movable wheels, headlights, doors, steering wheel and horns. The accompanying driver is attired in a Qing-style long gown, but a Western hat. The categories of funeral offerings, and perhaps the deceased themselves, are definitely kept up to date, providing a fascinating glimpse of the other world as it is envisioned by those ordering the materials.

5

The World of Shops and Customers

The Chinese simply call it the Paper Shop . . . Carefully hung on the wall of the shop at the entrance are several thick wax candles, dyed red with hand-moulded dragons in gold in high relief . . . Sticks of incense, varying in thickness from three-inch to a wax vesta, are ranged along the western wall. On the opposite wall are pigeonholes, containing bundles of Bank-notes issued by the HELL BANK, for use of departed spirits in the next world . . . Perhaps the most interesting line of stock is the collection of charms, and talismans in the form of coloured scrolls, which are either burned before the appropriate deity, or are hung to avert evil influences. (Burkhardt 1953: 161–2)

If visiting today, Burkhardt would find Hong Kong's retail paper shops (衣紙舖) little changed from the ones he knew and described in this passage written over fifty years ago. Hong Kong's paper shops still present a feast for the eye, attracting foreign residents and tourists (Anderson 1970: 154)[1] as well as a regular clientele of local worshippers.

Paper shops have been a feature of Chinese villages and towns since the Song (Cave 1998; Qin 1958), and are established features of Hong Kong's urban landscape.

In Hong Kong, those seeking paper offerings for worship can make their purchases in a variety of ways. Not all the sources of offerings are commercial businesses selling to the public from recognizable and fixed spaces; in short, not all entities selling paper offerings can be properly called shops. Paper offerings can be purchased from hawkers, or from temporary businesses such as seasonal stalls. A useful selection of paper offerings, charms, candles, and incense is sold from hawker stalls in the older street markets in Kowloon and Hong Kong Island, such as the markets between Mong Kok and Jordan Roads, or those north of the Kowloon-Canton Railway Station in Hung Hom. While many of these stalls are operated by licensed hawkers on a long-term and fixed-pitch basis, holidays such as the Lunar New Year bring out scores of mobile hawkers near the most popular temples or on any well-traveled sidewalk or street corner. Among these mobile hawkers are indigent elderly who sell paper, incense, and good luck charms at the gates of temples; purchasing from such sellers is also an act of charity.

Regular retail paper shops range in size from small spaces in the shopping arcades or dry markets of public housing estates, to large and airy street-level shops in commercial areas. The retailers account for the largest quantity of items sold to individual worshippers, selling the paper offerings, as well as candles, incense, ceramic and brass lotus lamps, incense burners for the family altars, and the porcelain or wooden images of deities.[2] By the late 1970s, a number of retail shops had expanded their inventory, adding secular forms of paper (including table napkins, tissues, wrapping paper, and stationery), and even school supplies, toys, and Hong Kong's famous red, white and blue striped plastic carrying bags. As a result, a number of shops appear "half and half," with one side devoted to paper offerings and the other side to other forms of paper. Retail paper shops also stock a great variety of seasonal items for the lunar and solar holidays, such as the plastic garlands, cardboard cutouts of auspicious figures and animals, painted or printed forms of good luck couplets (揮春 / 春聯 / 對聯) popular during the Lunar New Year,[3] and paper lanterns for the Mid-Autumn festival. Turning strictly to the paper offerings, the rule of thumb is the larger the shop, the more variety it can stock, and the older the shop (and if it is in an old neighborhood) the better the chances that it will stock the rarer items expected by an elderly clientele.

Some paper shops are retail-workshop combinations. A number of these establishments are found on Canton, Reclamation, and Shanghai Streets in urban Kowloon. These combination shops, which require considerable space for production and storage, are becoming rare in urban Hong Kong, as neighborhoods are redeveloped and old shops disappear. Only the long-established businesses which own their shop spaces can combine operations economically, using one half for selling everyday offerings, and the other half for crafting either funeral offerings or other large items such as Flower Cannons. Customers purchasing everyday offerings may watch the workshop employees as they craft these pitched items; the juxtaposition of different aspects (funeral offerings and everyday items) is not considered unusual. As not all businesses dealing in paper offerings are retail shops, before examining in more detail the life within a typical shop, some attention should be given to these other sources of offerings: the wholesalers, the workshops, the factory flats, and the temples.

The Wholesalers

Hong Kong has a number of wholesalers of paper products,[4] who obtain their supplies from the Mainland or from factories in Southeast Asia. Some of these companies appear exactly like retail shops in their layout and do sell to individual customers, while others are strictly wholesale, with no provision for individual private customers, although they do sell to hawkers. The majority of their business is bulk selling to retail shops and temples, or exporting to markets abroad. The owner of one of the largest companies said: "We supply many stalls, like those at the Wong Tai Sin Temple or those at the street, the mobile hawkers. The scope is very large, and it is very difficult to get statistics for you, but the approximate number is several hundred, about two to three hundred." These businesses require a lot of storage space, and for this reason, some of them have moved to factory areas in the New Territories. For example, the wholesaler speaking above had purchased a huge warehouse space in a new industrial building in the factory area of Fo Tan (火炭), outside Sha Tin. Its clean and well-organized premises, two stories high, were divided into metal shelf storage spaces and custom-made bins for stacking all the everyday items that retail shops need, plus a fair quantity of more unusual items. Orders were taken at the main office, located in a corner of the storage area; customers could easily

scan the shelves to determine paper quality. In addition to the hawkers
and retail shops, this company also served twenty to thirty temples, in
all parts of the Hong Kong SAR. As the owner explained:

> There are usually stalls in a temple. Since the stalls buy the goods
> from us, the temple sends someone to take the offerings from us.
> The hawkers give our telephone number to the temple official,
> the person responsible for conducting the services and also
> responsible for buying the goods. As there are contacts among
> temples, one temple may introduce us to yet another.

The longest established wholesalers do not advertise (although
they are listed in telephone directories) in the manner of other retail
businesses; as their reputations are built on word of mouth. The
wholesaler quoted above managed a family-owned business, and so did
not employ salespeople to go outside and promote their goods. What
he termed the connected way the company did business took care of
new accounts. If a business consistently strove to provide good quality
goods, reliable service and assistance, and reasonable prices, it would be
successful. Due to the fixed prices of most non-pitched offerings and
the regular demand for the same basic items, there is little variation
among supplies, other than quality of manufacture and small variations
in the sizes of items. As a result, there is lessened competition among
wholesalers, although some wholesalers will arrange for their suppliers
on the Mainland to create a special brand of paper using the wholesaler's
name, or to design an eye-catching wrapping. Also, if the wholesale
company stocks smaller pitched items such as Golden Flowers,
Pinwheels, or small funeral offerings, there will be variations in this
handmade inventory. The reputation, and the competitive edge, of the
wholesaler could be affected if these items are poorly made, even if the
other offerings are high quality.

The Workshops

In 1937, Dard Hunter described a Chinese funeral offering workshop
in Bangkok:

> The front of each shop is usually decorated with a number of
> gaily painted mirrors, and the interior takes on the appearance
> of a veritable paper museum, all manner of funeral paraphernalia

hanging from the ceiling rafters, and with shelves, drawers, and cases literally overflowing with every conceivable variety of decorated and coloured paper used in the making of these weird reproductions; quality and workmanship vary to suit both the rich and the lowly, but all alike are destined to be burnt at funerals. (1937: 6)

While recorded nearly seventy years ago, the interest of these paper workshops is the same today in Hong Kong, although none are adorned with "gaily painted mirrors." Hong Kong workshops look a bit different, as seen in this record from field notes, also of a funeral workshop:

At first we could not find the workshop, as it was upstairs from a metal fabricating shop, and the stairs looked quite dark. An elderly man approached and asked us what we wanted and on our answer, told us to follow him up the stairs; the owner had just stepped out. Inside, the workshop is made up of two large rooms along an open corridor which overlooks the tin roofs of the squatter huts on the ground. The ceiling over the corridor is hung with red, yellow, and white willow fans for the cranes. We enter the main workroom, which was light and airy, where on the left a large blue car, nearly completed, was sitting. Hanging from the ceiling was a large cluster of white cranes, while against the wall were a line or three houses for the dead, complete with servants, furniture, and a paper garden with trees and a fountain. In the doorway to the second room, a young man worked on a pile of bamboo strips, making up a frame for yet another house.

Paper offering workshops may be independent businesses under the direction of a famed paper master, or branches of a retail paper business located in a cheaper area to save on rent. The majority supply funeral offerings and are often established, as is the example above, on the upper floors of the pre-Second World War residential buildings (*tang lou* 唐樓) in the older districts. The upper floor location is cheaper to rent than a street-level space. The large objects which cannot be carried down the stairs or in the elevators are simply lowered out the windows; the most elaborate funeral creations, although awkward, are not very heavy and can be handled by one or two men. Those items that are too bulky to be moved out in one piece in any manner, such as houses or The Street of the Dead, are crafted in movable sections; these sections are then assembled outside the shop just before delivery, or at the site of the burning. Other workshops are devoted to the crafting of Flower Cannons, lanterns, Golden Flowers, or Pinwheels.

The Flower Cannon (花炮) workshops require the most space, for the Flower Cannons are towering creations, reaching fifteen feet or more in height. A very few workshops create the elaborate silk and paper lanterns for display in the public parks during the lantern festival following the Lunar New Year. These displays are featured prominently in newspaper and magazine photo essays.[5] At one time, Hong Kong paper offering workshops also made Golden Flowers and their accompanying Spirit Reds, but most have gone out of business, the victims of redevelopment. One of the last, and most skilled, of the masters of handcrafted Golden Flowers left the trade in 1989. During a visit to what was his final small workshop he told us, despairingly, that he had already moved his workshop three times because the buildings in which he rented space had been sold, and then torn down for new high-rises. Exhausted by these moves and losing money in moving expenses, he declared that he was now too old for so many difficulties and had resolved to shut down his business. We placed what was probably the last large order for his creations. By the early 1990s, only one workshop made Golden Flowers and that only occasionally, but a combination retail/workshop in the Yau Ma Tei (油蔴地) area of Kowloon, also famed for its funeral offerings and Flower Cannons, still produced handcrafted Spirit Reds[6] in the original style — that is, hand tufted and stitched in silk.

Factories and Factory Flats

Some Pinwheel manufacturers had established themselves in small units in factory blocks scattered around the urban districts and in the New Territories, while others had set up in the large single residential units or adjoining ground-floor shop spaces of the older public housing estates. Such premises allowed sufficient space to set up the machines to punch out the trimmings, print the attached lucky phrases and help shape the metal frames. In addition to officially rented spaces, Pinwheel makers we interviewed often used the public space in front of or adjoining the shop space. One Pinwheel master regularly worked in front of his factory, enjoying the breeze and chatting with passers-by and estate residents while he shaped the frames of his Pinwheels on a workbench he had made himself. These public housing estate units were very supportive to the trade; rents were reasonable and it was possible to rent enough space both to work and to store the finished items until sold. Still other

Pinwheel manufacturers had set up shop in rented units of formal factory blocks, where their completed creations could be seen stacked in the common balcony corridor running along the entrance.

In the early 1990s, four masters continued to craft Pinwheels at home, creating the old-fashioned varieties from bamboo and paper, using no machines, and storing all raw materials and finished products in their homes. This manner of manufacture had become increasingly difficult to maintain, given increased restrictions on the use of flats and the lack of space in the small public housing units. One home workshop we visited was filled from floor to ceiling with stacked boxes of completed Pinwheels and the raw components for manufacture, while the remaining floor and worktables were covered with Pinwheels in all stages of completion; the family lived in one bedroom. One famed Pinwheel master enjoyed long-term and inexpensive rent on a two-storied village house in a tiny urban cottage area still surviving near a major temple. He had (barely) enough space to craft and store the elaborate Pinwheels he sold at the temple during the major holidays. Another craftsman had moved his workshop to a space adjoining his village home near the border with Shenzhen; he said that was the only way he had enough affordable space for both his family and his business. While we could understand the practical reasons for his decision to move, walking to his factory in the heat and humidity of a Hong Kong summer, along a road filled bumper to bumper with exhaust-spewing container trucks, sorely tested our research enthusiasm.

The ever-present concern with space restrictions seemed not to have affected the sizes of the Pinwheels, however, for those masters operating in the small housing converted-to-workshop spaces regularly produced quantities of quite large specimens, while the manufacturers set up in the units of factory blocks tended to produce large quantities of the smaller varieties. Pinwheel makers using machines sold directly to a few selected retail shops, or to hawkers for selling at temples during the New Year. The four craftsmen who continued to hand-fashion all their Pinwheels (three have since retired) sold them in person, or with the assistance of children and other family members, at the temples, or sold very limited quantities to hawkers they knew.

At the Temples

Finally, paper offerings may be obtained at most Hong Kong temples. The Wong Tai Sin and Tian Hou Temples in Kowloon, the Man Mo Temple on Hollywood Road on Hong Kong Island, and the Che Gong Temple in Sha Tin, New Territories, are notable examples. An area of the temple is set aside for selling everyday offerings, plus incense and candles. During major holidays, additional areas of the temple grounds may be set aside to accommodate both the increased sales overall and the appearance and sale of seasonal paper items such as the Pinwheels (actually, available during other holidays) or papier-mache chickens (at the birthday of Tian Hou), which are prominently displayed at the offerings counter or near the entrance. The temple shops sell nearly all of the most commonly used items, including oils and incense, but with a heavy focus on religious souvenirs, they do not stock the great variety of paper items that a regular retail shop has available.

Temples account for a smaller percentage of sales of everyday paper offerings except during festivals, for most worshippers arrive well provisioned, having visited their favorite shop beforehand. Certain temples, such as Wong Tai Sin in Kowloon and Che Gong in Tai Wai (大圍), are widely recognized as places to buy Pinwheels. A separate structure on the Wong Tai Sin temple grounds, on the outer perimeter near the building housing the fortune-tellers (for which the temple is also famous), also houses a number of small establishments selling the necessities of worship.[7] Before the area around the temple was cleared in the mid-1980s,[8] this outer perimeter was home to an even larger number of small wood and tin-sheeted shops and hawker stalls, all arranged along a winding path to the temple entrance and each selling Pinwheels, everyday offerings and the religious souvenirs for which the temple was (and still is) noted. During the Lunar New Year, and especially on New Year's Eve, this path was thronged with crowds of devout worshippers and celebrants, all moving slowly forward amidst the brightly lit stalls towards the temple, itself ablaze with lights and candles, and thick with floating bits of burned offerings and the smoke from countless sticks of incense. While the stalls (and much of the festive atmosphere) were swept away when the outer perimeter and the path were redesigned, the original excitement is regained at the birthday of Wong Tai Sin and at every Lunar New Year, when craftsmen and hawkers set up temporary stalls to sell offerings, and dozens of itinerant hawkers and elderly sellers of incense and paper congregate at the temple gates.

Che Gong Temple (車公廟) in Tai Wai is also justly famed for its Pinwheels; everyone in Hong Kong knows that Che Gong is a good place to purchase the most beautiful and auspicious examples of the craft. Approximately a week before Lunar New Year's Eve the Pinwheel stalls are set up along the lanes outside and within the temple grounds. Before the Che Gong Temple was renovated, the Pinwheel stalls were set up along the sidewalks and original designated paths leading into the temple a few days before the holiday. As with the Wong Tai Sin Temple, there was only one official entrance path along which thousands of worshippers would only slowly make their way into the temple grounds. Pinwheel sellers took advantage of this to hawk their wares to worshippers as they moved along the path, while other sellers took places along the outer walls, on the lanes leading away from the temple, to sell to people leaving the temple.

Even at monasteries, such as Bo Lin (寶蓮寺) on Lantau Island (大嶼山), one may purchase paper offerings. Business is done at the monastery gates, where hawkers set up booths for Pinwheels and other religious souvenirs. It is understood that retail shops selling the staples of Buddhist worship do not normally sell paper offerings. Despite this understanding, a number of these shops (for example, certain of the retailers on Shanghai Street in Kowloon which have been established within the last ten to fifteen years) originally stocked a limited supply of the basic elements of everyday worship, believers being loath to completely abandon the practice. At holidays honoring the dead even religious establishments offer such items for sale. The small sales counter within the main hall of Sha Tin's Temple of the Ten Thousand Buddhas (萬佛寺) not only sells numerous varieties of temple souvenirs and Buddhist pamphlets and tracts, but also paper offerings for the dead, including Fate Changers, Longevity Gold, Gold and Silver Paper, First Treasure, and assemblages of offerings for the ancestors.

The Retail Outlets

Retail paper offering shops can be found in nearly all of Hong Kong's neighborhoods, but are particularly characteristic of the older districts away from the more tourist-oriented areas. Within the last decade or so, Shanghai Street in Kowloon has become an even greater attraction for both worshippers and those interested in religious affairs, as it has experienced a notable increase in the number of shops devoted to religion-related supplies and materials, particularly those for Buddhist worship. The streets of the Eastern and Sai Ying Poon (西營盤) Districts on Hong Kong Island are also excellent locations to look for traditional paper shops.

The establishment of paper offering shops in older public housing estates is a long-accepted practice, although the newer estates (built from the 1980s onward) are perhaps less accommodating to this traditional trade. The shops are generally on the ground floors, sometimes inside the block as in the original blocks of Tze Wan Shan Estate (慈雲山邨) in north Kowloon, but more usually as part of the commercial arcade encircling the block along the outside of the ground floor. Until recently, a good example of this kind of shop arrangement was the multiple paper shops occupying the ground floor spaces of the blocks of the Wong Tai Sin Estate surrounding the Wong Tai Sin Temple in Kowloon; as these blocks have been torn down, the shops have been forced to relocate. While so many shops made worship very convenient for estate residents and Wong Tai Sin's devotees, this was a unique arrangement, probably made possible by the great popularity of this temple and the accompanying demand for offerings. Worship at the temple was always at such a volume that, despite obvious competition, a number of shops could do reasonable business. If, as in the newer housing complexes, there are no commercial spaces available within the arcades inside the blocks themselves, then paper shops are established in the dry markets which accompany all public housing estates — shopping for offerings is easily accomplished while purchasing other daily necessities.

Paper shops and their contents have remained identifiable over time. In 1927, Clarence Day recorded his view of a small offering shop in Haining, Zhejiang.

> But paper gods were not the only stock in trade of this busy corner dealer in objects of religious practice. As do most shops of his kind, this one also carried a stock of those other 'indispensables'; namely, strings and bunches of 'yuan pao' (paper money, sometimes called idol paper); candles, red, white, and green; incense sticks packed in convenient packets wrapped in red or green paper; . . . In the showcase were little boxes of dollars stamped out of silvered cardboard, for burning in front of graves. (1927: 279)

A typical paper shop is crammed from floor to ceiling with a great variety of items, often elegantly designed and crafted, always colorful.

While casual visitors are attracted by the sheer beauty of the items on display, the beauty of the offerings, while definitely noticed by believers, is secondary to their primary purpose as vital components of domestic rituals and temple worship. Yet, to those well acquainted with the industry, the attractiveness of the shop cannot be denied, as the contents are both enticing and irresistible. Many long-established paper shops have the front open to the sidewalk or street, allowing ease of access and an unobstructed view of the contents, making it easier to attract business. Floor-to-ceiling shelves line the three inside walls, the shelves often subdivided into the pigeonholes that Burkhardt described, filled with stacks of different varieties of paper offerings arranged according to the festival or occasion in which they are used. The floor space in front of these shelves usually accommodates even larger stacks of pre-packed and hand-assembled packages, or open bins or cardboard boxes overflowing with bulkier items.

Retail shops come in all sizes, including tiny units approximately ten feet by six feet located in the markets of old estates, or squeezed into the spaces within the stairwells of private buildings. The typical size of shops operating within the arcades of more modern public housing blocks ranges from 300 to 500 square feet. Larger shops operating in the spaces in the ground floor of private housing towers are somewhat larger; the size of the shop depends on the rent to be paid. Some shops have additional spaces behind the main room, for storage or even for cooking meals, and in a few old shops built according to now-rare building plans, a toilet may be included, as well as a tiny stair to a loft space for more storage. One shopkeeper owning a shop in a public housing estate joked that if he had a shop of 1,000 square feet, he could certainly fill it with paper; such remarks are common among shopkeepers, all of them wanting more space. Every inch must be used. Most shops have a counter with the cash register, often glass enclosed so that still more items can be displayed; usually the countertop itself doubles as a display space stacked with offerings. Even the ceiling is festooned with the metal hooks and bamboo poles used to hang bundles of paper clothing, plastic bags filled with painted trim, circular Lucky Basins edged with Honorable People Papers, clothing packages for the gods, and paper replicas of clothing, household goods, or small electrical gadgets burned for the dead. During the weeks preceding the Lunar New Year, the ceiling display changes, the regular items set aside to support the dazzling array of Golden Flowers, and their accompanying red cotton or silk Spirit Reds. Taking care of the spiritual needs of customers does not preclude shops taking care of their own; retail shops have their own wooden altars, in a variety of sizes, placed somewhere within the shop, usually on a back wall. There, in addition to the images of the deities (such as Guan Di and Guan Yin), the owner places a fine set of Golden Flowers and Spirit Reds, vases of flowers, red electric or wax candles, and offerings of fruit and incense.

First-time visitors or those unfamiliar with paper offerings may find the contents of the average shop confusing, even if the colors and atmosphere are enticing. To the uninitiated, the sheer variety and quantity of paper offerings is bewildering and seemingly without order. As already explained, there are a number of overlapping classification schemes that professionals in the trade use to organize (or not organize, as the case may be) the materials they craft or sell: the distinction between pitched and non-pitched objects, the items grouped according to the recipient (gods, ghosts, ancestors) and items grouped according to their ritual purpose. However, these schemes are not reliable guides to predicting what is placed where in shops, for there are no rules regulating the placement of paper offerings relative to each other. Shopkeepers explained that different offerings are not in conflict and do not affect each other's ritual efficacy, so pitched items for the dead can be hung near Lucky Basins, and clothing for the ancestors near that for the ghosts. But, for convenience many shopkeepers will set near to each other the items that are commonly used together, such as those for a festival or ritual occasion, or for problem solving. Each item has its own space, although by the end of a busy day, these spaces can messily overlap. It is also common to find items of one kind, such as currency, placed close together, so shopkeepers group the Hell Money near to the Gold and Silver Paper and the Longevity Gold. The everyday offerings are given the most space because they are sold in greatest quantities. These include the paper currencies, First Treasure, Solving of 100 Problems, Money to Live, Honorable People Papers, paper clothing, Five Treasures Document, and pre-packed assemblages. Given the great variation in the sizes of retail paper shops, shopkeepers must be ingenious if they are to make maximum use of what space they have. Although the subject will be discussed further in the next chapter, the issue of taboos or internal restrictions could be mentioned here. Respondents explained that taboos concerning feminine pollution were not serious issues in their shops, including the workshops for funeral offerings. While others have suggested that certain precautions do apply to retail shops, as these shops deal with both extremes of otherworldly entities, the gods and the ghosts (Lee and Leung 1994), our respondents did not mention such precautions.

All retail paper shops sell incense, a vital component of worship, which is kept in its own section, organized according to type or manufacturer, package size, or the price; it is further identified by labels pasted onto the shelves. Paper shops stock a wide variety of incense, and sometimes one entire wall of a shop is devoted to it alone. Of course, many households continue to buy incense, and other items made of aromatic woods and compounds, at the few retail shops still specializing in this product — a number of these can be found in the older streets and districts. Retail paper shops and other establishments selling paper offerings purchase their stock either direct from the factory or from Hong Kong wholesalers; in either event, the source of the majority of materials is the factories in Mainland China.[9] The majority of Hong Kong factories that once produced paper offerings, such as the famous makers of Golden Flowers, have long ceased production, victims of ever-increasing rents, the loss of space, and labor costs. The only resistance to this dismal process comes from the few Pinwheel makers who are still surviving, but facing increasing pressure. The small pitched funeral items are imported from Southeast Asia, notably Indonesia and Thailand, where they are made in factories established by Chinese emigrants of Chaozhou origin. A few shopkeepers stock the Gold and Silver Paper manufactured in Taiwan.

Daily operation and shop life

Retail paper shops in Hong Kong are open seven days a week, from around 9 a.m. to 7 or 8 p.m., so even customers who work long hours are able to stop after work to buy supplies. These long hours are hard on the shopkeepers.

> This trade is just too time-consuming. I open the shop at 9 a.m. and close it at 8 p.m. I work nearly twelve hours and maybe longer. We work longer during the festivals, and usually close the shop later, at 9 p.m. You need to work longer during festival because the housewives or the factory workers must buy after they get off work. This trade is too hard.

Most morning customers are the housewives, who worship early in the day. The afternoon customers visit during the day's second round of grocery shopping. Despite the turnover of customers, the long hours can be monotonous for the shopkeeper. "Doing this job is quite time consuming, because you must sit from morning to night. You would be lively when someone comes in and talks to you, but sleepy when no one comes in."

During the major religious holidays the number of customers increases dramatically, for the occasional worshippers wish to catch up on their devotions and so join the often hundreds of regular customers who throng the shops to purchase. Shopkeepers said that they were busiest in the autumn, winter, and spring due to the number of religious observances during these periods. The very busiest times are the Lunar New Year, when customers buy the special items to insure safe passage for the family, and the Qing Ming Festival to honor the dead, when the shops are packed with customers buying gifts for the ancestors. As the overworked owner of one very successful shop explained it:

> Many shopkeepers complain that this is hard work and they just can't stand it. Paper shops are difficult to operate, as the space is limited but customers come in and out all day. Yesterday, for example, we had to work for so long that we ached all over. When the festivals arrive, we have no time to eat, even no time to eat breakfast. The hardest time is at the end of the year, when we have no time to help the children with their homework — in fact, we don't have time to take care of them.

We then asked, "Since many customers want to purchase the already packed assemblages for their worship of the deities, is it possible to assemble these packages during your free time before the holidays, so that the customers can just pick up the packages they want when they arrive?"

> In principle, yes, but in actual fact, there are so many customers during busy times that it is just impossible to keep up with the demand, even if we pack continuously. Just look at this package [the respondent was referring to an assemblage for the sage Wong Tai Sin]. Every customer buys four to five packages at a time, so how can you keep up? At the end of the year, each person buys thirty to forty packages, because each god requires his own package. If a customer has six to seven altars to serve, each with the god, and she worships five times at the end of the year, that is seven times five and that is thirty-five packages. And these are just the clothing and general worshipping packages, not the special items.

On a typical day, a shop opens for business and the first few customers come to buy. As many are old customers from the neighborhood, they stay for a while, setting their purchases from the market on the floor, and share a cup of tea, chatting with the shopkeeper about this or that, telling them small matters about their families, or asking advice for which papers to buy. Many select and arrange their own offerings, or ask about special orders for the next holiday. At odd moments, the shop cat makes an appearance. Resident cats are common features of more traditional Hong Kong retail establishments, and older paper shops have a special need for them, as the inventory of a shop or a factory can suffer from unchecked rodent appetites.[10] As shopkeepers say, "Rats love paper, but cats love rats." Cats greet customers (or researchers) at the entry, doze atop the counter, or daintily pick their way among the piles of offerings.

In the periods between customers, the shopkeeper is hardly idle. While those managing smaller shops may confess to periods of boredom, owners of large shops have many more responsibilities related to their larger inventory. While occasionally stopping for a cup of tea or for lunch (if this is not a holiday period), the owner unpacks recently arrived boxes of paper goods, stacks or rearranges the offerings, dusts the shelves, or cleans the floor. On occasion, salespeople selling paper or miscellaneous items stop in to chat, as do employees of neighboring shops. As most shops have a small worktable for making small offerings, at some time the shopkeeper will sit down and begin folding the Gold and Silver Paper into a variety of ingot shapes for burning. A number of shops create their own special clothing for the gods, and so the shopkeeper will be kept busy cutting and painting the paper gowns, crafting the accompanying small shoes or boots, and packing the set in paper wrappers. As described earlier, some will try to keep ahead of demand by assembling packages of offerings. Those shopkeepers who know how to craft the smaller of the pitched items, such as the Lucky Basins made for birthdays, will also be busy making them.

Like many other aspects of the trade, the personnel of the paper shop vary in number and in kind. During our visits, roughly half the shops had been established as family businesses, some of them for well over half a century. By this, it was explained that a close relative had begun the business, or had taken it over from yet another relative, and the current owner or manager was related to that person, usually a father or grandfather. This was true of both retail shops and of workshops. For both workshops and retail outlets, family labor is still an important component of operation, for all businesses need to save on expenses, and those dealing in paper offerings are no exceptions. In a typical shop, the workforce might consist of a husband and wife team, with some of the children coming in to help during the holidays or for a few hours each day. During the time of our visits, this pattern was already becoming more difficult to maintain, for the demands of higher education meant that children were absorbed by homework and school-related activities and had less time for the shop — a situation characterizing many retail businesses. For the same reason, more shops were being taken over by friends or strangers interested in the business when the original proprietor retired, younger members of the family having moved into other professions. Smaller shops generally made do with only one person during both holiday and non-holiday periods, who could be either a male or female. In the workshops, the master's family helped out with the construction as often as needed, and it was clear from discussions that even the younger members of the family had considerable knowledge and experience in crafting the items. These workshops also hire a fair number of non-related workers, as many as six to eight in the workshops crafting funeral offerings. One combination workshop we visited employed, in addition to the owner, four workers crafting pitched paper items and two ladies manning the retail half. Another master of funeral offerings worked with his wife and with two other non-related workers; his daughter, whose skill in crafting he praised, only worked from time to time.

It is not unusual to see an elderly woman or two coming in for a few hours of work for the shop, sitting on a low stool and assembling the more complicated of the pre-packed papers. These women are available for comments and advice, solicited or not, to be given to younger customers who appear unsure of what to buy. If the shop in question is a combination of workshop and retail outlet, the other workers will be busily crafting the larger pitched items like the houses and gardens for the dead, or tending to the retail sales. All will be simultaneously listening to the radio or watching television, chatting among themselves, drinking tea, snacking, and talking to the customers. The end result — combined with telephone calls, the sounds of pagers and mobile phones, and the cacophony of street noise — makes for an atmosphere as colorful in sound as the paper offerings are visually.

Shops and Customers

These shops, whether established within a housing estate or long resident on a street in an old district, are vital components of their neighborhoods. They do not only provide a commodity critical to the performance of the rituals of everyday life, but also a variety of services for their customers, including helpful, even comforting, advice about religious matters. As well as advising those customers who are unsure of which offerings to buy, some shopkeepers assist customers in locating ritual specialists, such as the Ask Rice Women, who can aid them in communicating with their deceased relatives (see Chapter 4). The shops doubling as workshops can provide still more services. Customers who are ordering funeral items may ask about vegetarian halls (for funeral meals), or where to purchase flower arrangements, or clothing for the deceased. For these services, the shops do not act as middlemen in the strict sense of the term and do not collect fees, but, as many maintain cordial relationships with professionals in related trades, they quite willingly share information.

In addition, the shops are a place to meet and chat, a regular part of the daily routine of the worshipper. While paper shops are not social centers (in the same sense as the Mutual Aid Committee offices in the public housing estates, which are safe and convenient places for elderly residents to congregate),[11] they are familiar locations. Some shopkeepers spoke of old customers occasionally meeting at the shop for tea, or for mahjong sessions. While not all retail paper shops operate in this manner, all are part of the normal rhythm of life in the neighborhood, and as such, are viewed as part of "how things should be."

Paper Shop Customers

Hong Kong's paper shops serve a regular clientele, providing for both daily worship and the special celebrations highlighting the yearly ritual cycle, with customers drawn mostly from the immediate neighborhood. If the shop is near a temple it will attract a larger number of "drop-in" purchasers, especially during festivals. Some shops near the tourist areas have even reported increasing numbers of foreign visitors. There is always some client turnover as residents move in and out, partly due to the continuous redevelopment of Hong Kong's pre-Second World War urban districts. Despite this, loyalty to a shop is quite common and old customers who have moved to other districts, even those quite far away, frequently return to the old neighborhood to make their purchases.

Maintaining good relations

The relationship of shopkeeper or paper master to customer is fostered over years of interaction. Shopkeepers took pains to explain how important it was to always treat the customer with respect and politeness.

> If you are impolite to the neighbors, saying 'I don't care if you buy or not, take the things yourself,' then they would not buy for the second time after they had purchased from you the first time. They will say, 'He is so bad . . . don't buy from him.' They will transfer only your bad things to other potential customers and the harmonious combination of heaven, earth and customers will be broken.

Honesty about offerings and ritual procedures is also a critical factor in customer satisfaction.

> I do not know how the other shops do business. I only know the reason why our shop's business is so good; it is because we are honest. Some customers will come to ask us, 'Should we worship on this occasion?' For example, yesterday there was a customer who came to ask me, since her daughter had a back problem and she wanted to worship on her behalf. The worshipping package I selected for her cost only a few dollars, but I told her that she should take her daughter to a doctor. I applied a scientific approach to the matter. The customer agreed and did not buy the package. Some shops are bad, for they will pick unnecessary items to give to customers because they want to earn more money. Or, they will overcharge for a normally less expensive item.

Sometimes, suggesting "too many" items for a situation may be due to shopkeepers' conservatism, or their recognition that elderly practitioners feel more secure when using more items. Also, some very old items are now rare and little understood, and continuing to include them in assemblages may appear excessive when it is simply a following of old practice. Given the excellent public transportation system in Hong Kong, customers can travel from shop to shop, comparing prices and inventory; it would be rather difficult to cheat them for a long period. Retail paper shop owners are fair and careful when dealing with customers, and are quite engaging as businesspeople.

Customers are budget-conscious and price is a concern, which shopkeepers readily admit; this has become even more recognized in light of Hong Kong's recent economic downturn. "People in the past were different from now, in that they would continue to buy from you even if the goods were expensive. Now, people buy at a shop where the goods are cheaper." At the same time, customers want to purchase items of good quality, and will trust only those shopkeepers who sell reliable goods.

> Referring to incense, you must know that Chinese are very superstitious. For example, if the customer cannot light up the incense after trying for several times, she will feel it is unlucky. So, she comes in and tells me about it. I generally exchange the package for a new one for her. That may be enough. But, if I suggest another brand, and it also has a problem, then she may not trust me. In other words, if it happens again, she may suspect me.

Customers are also willing to pay more for handmade items, especially when the crafter is particularly skilled. Good quality also means the pre-packed paper offerings contain the correct amounts of paper, although some shopkeepers may accept a certain amount of slippage. One shopkeeper frankly admitted, "To avoid excessive loss, if a package of paper money is made up in ten pieces, and if one is wrinkled, I may just pull out the wrinkled sheet[12] and sell the package to the customers with nine sheets instead!"

Customer trust is also earned through scrupulous attention to the details of good quality paper, such as using finer paper rather than coarse, and paying attention to proper size and proportion of the items, especially in the generous use of metal. Gold and Silver Paper comes in a variety of sizes, and it is important that one size is not passed off as another and that the amount of gold and silver[13] is correct. Shops either sell a variety of sizes, or make decisions to offer only a certain range.

> The metal on some gold and silver paper is less than two inches in width but some shops still sell it as two inches; some even sell paper with only 1.3 inches of metal, passing it off as 1.8 inches. The gold and silver paper we sell has a metal width of 2.4 inches, so it is of much higher quality.

In addition, paper shops must protect their products from dirt and damage while they are on display. For some shops, rapid turnover and heavy sales solve this problem automatically, but shops with fewer customers need to be especially careful that their products remain clean and fresh looking.

Shops that do not provide consistently high quality goods at reasonable prices, nor maintain a generous attitude towards making things right, will find it difficult to continue, no matter how convenient their location. The result of professionalism, itself a complex mixture of politeness, knowledgeability, honesty, and helpfulness, is a trust between customer and shop that can last for decades. Customers who continue purchasing from a particular shop say that purchasing from the same shop helps to "make life smooth" (順景). By this they mean that everyday events go well, no unusual or distressing events occur, and they feel confident that the results of their worship will be satisfactory. In short, the customer feels an association between buying at a particular paper shop and feeling spiritually secure.

Customers may feel that they have prospered very directly by purchasing from one shop. One young shopkeeper told us, "We have one customer who spends several thousands of dollars at our shop every year because he once purchased an image of Guan Di from us, and then was able to open a factory. After that, his business got better and he opened a second factory. Now, he buys only from us." Other customers, while not as successful as this businessman, nevertheless continue to purchase their everyday offerings, or perhaps more importantly, the special items for the New Year worship, from the same shop, to ensure continuity and the easing of affairs. Still other customers, having bad experiences after purchasing at other shops selling cheaper goods, return to the original shop. For most customers, a long acquaintance with the shop and the good relationship with the shopkeeper are vital to their feeling of security. If a shop is forced to move to a new address, many old customers will travel to the new location, at least for a while, even if the new location is a considerable distance away. Customers do this on the strength of their belief that the link with the shop must be maintained, so that their lives and everyday activities will continue to be smooth and trouble-free.

That this desire for security extends further than the retail arm of the trade is suggested by the opinion of a famed Pinwheel master, who explained:

Most people want to have stable and peaceful lives. They will be content with these stable lives, won't they? Some people like to buy the Pinwheels from the same stall every year. Some people have been buying Pinwheels from the same stall for more than ten years. I have seen one old purchaser who bought her sons and daughter-in-law to my stall and purchased the Pinwheel. Customers have been buying the Pinwheels from my stall for many years. Maybe their lives keep smooth, so they come back and buy the Pinwheels from me every year. This may be based on their belief that they can keep their lives smooth by buying from me.

6

Learning the Trade, Learning to Craft

A master of funeral offerings summarized his experience by telling us:

> When I first came to Hong Kong, I came across the paper shops.
> I thought that paper pitching was so beautiful and I thought
> that it was not just a superstition, but an art. You have to make
> whatever the customers want, so my interests developed. I went
> to the shops and stood in front of the doors to observe, when the
> people finished [making] an object, I used a ruler to measure.
> I learned by myself, and not from a master. When I opened a
> shop, I continued the practice. I copied how other people made
> things, only the objects I made were better, because others
> would not like to change the pattern. They did not know how,
> or were stubborn, or did not like to create [something new].
> Nowadays, making objects requires creativity. I remember that
> I had made a house for a rich man. The customer required me
> to craft a paper building which was the same as the one they
> were living in. Although they provided photos, I had to go to
> the house to look at it, to see it and the car park and the street

lamps, before I could finish the order. Doing this work takes talent and initiative.

Although being completely self-taught is a bit unusual, this master's comments encompass what is expected in the trade — self-reliance, innovation, creativity, and love of learning — characteristics not acquired as a matter of chance, but built into the learning process.

Crafting the Non-Pitched Offerings

Hong Kong masters still crafting (or who had once crafted) non-pitched materials acquired their skills in a variety of ways. Many learned from parents, siblings, or friends who were already in the trade, while others were apprenticed at an early age to support their families. However the skills were acquired, crafting these everyday paper offerings was time-consuming and exacting, demanding the mastery of many techniques and an understanding of paper. Most of the older masters interviewed no longer handcrafted the non-pitched everyday offerings, although they still had the skills and the tools to do so, and could explain in detail how it was done.

The majority of non-pitched paper items sold now in Hong Kong are manufactured in Mainland-based factories. Shopkeepers explained that supplies from the Mainland have varied in accordance with the numerous PRC campaigns against superstition (see, for example Chan, Madsen and Unger 1984) but even without official campaigns, the Communist government has been ambivalent about religious practices and festivals. During the Cultural Revolution, for instance, more offerings were made in Hong Kong because Mainland factories had been forced to close down or limit production. When the Cultural Revolution ended, these factories resumed production and, because both labor and space were far cheaper in Mainland China, their products soon replaced locally made items. With the more open policies of the Reform Period, materials used in worship are more available on the Mainland (Ikels 1996: 256, 258; 2004).

Traditional papermaking in China involved a long series of labor intensive steps (for an extended discussion of papermaking, see, for example Cave 1998; Hunter 1937, 1943; McClure 1986), and even more work was needed to turn the handmade paper into an offering for gods, ancestors, or ghosts. For instance, spirit money (or mock money) needed the addition of tin to simulate gold and silver. The tin had to be beaten by hand into thin sheets, rolled onto the paper, and carefully polished. The paper and the tin were then colored (if the tin had to resemble gold) and the paper further hand-printed with the appropriate elements, auspicious characters, and phrases. Finally the finished product was trimmed and bound into bundles for distribution (Cave 1998). Hong Kong paper masters' descriptions of the making of non-pitched offerings agreed with Cave's depiction. Elderly craftsmen who had once worked in shops making the everyday Gold and Silver Paper, explained how the base paper was rolled out, then embossed with the thin sheets of "gold" or "silver," applied with handheld rollers. If the base paper was not already the correct size, each sheet was then cut and trimmed by hand. Finally, the individual sheets were counted and bound into packages, then tied with string made of paper or twisted grass. Even more complexity was involved in the crafting of other everyday offerings.

One elderly shopkeeper, who specialized in paper offerings for the Chaozhou community, was well experienced in the complexities of these "simple" everyday papers other than the gold and silver. Chaozhou speakers use a distinctive, parallel set of everyday offerings that are more elaborate than those used by Cantonese from other parts of south China. For example, there is the Big Gold (大金) paper for worshipping powerful deities like Tian Hou and Guan Di, as well as Di Zhu and Men Kou, the domestic gods of earth and door. Big Gold is composed of an outer sheet colored, by hand in the best examples, with a watercolor wash in peanut color. On this is superimposed a large rectangle (about twelve by seven and one-quarter inches) of high quality gold. This outer sheet enfolds four additional sheets of the same design (gold on peanut colored paper) in progressively smaller sizes, to the smallest with a gold size of four by three inches. Big Gold is used by the Chaozhou in place of the standard Longevity Gold other Cantonese use to worship the gods, although some shopkeepers explained that it could also be substituted for Gold and Silver Paper for the ancestors. Mr Chan explained the steps needed in the production of the Chaozhou Big Gold:

> I'll say each item is complicated to make, since you must know how to distinguish the top of the paper sheet from the bottom. You also must know which is the back side and which is the front, for you cannot use the wrong side — the color will not stick if you do. Some items require many steps to make. For example, making the Chaozhou Big Gold paper takes thirteen separate

steps, including cutting, measuring the color, drying the paper, collecting the sheets, and adding the yellow — all steps repeated several times. Sometimes I feel unhappy, since the customers may not be satisfied with the items we make. They think that the making of paper is so simple and they don't understand the time and energy spent and the difficulty of handling the materials involved.

In addition, offerings such as the Heart of Money (錢心), used to thank the major deities, and the Peaceful Money (平安錢), also for worshipping the gods require cutting and assembling. The Heart of Money and the Peaceful Money are crafted in layers, in which the designs on the top layer (combinations of auspicious characters and flower shapes) are carefully cut out, in the manner of the decorative paper cuts which these offerings closely resemble. When the layers are assembled, the color of the second sheet appears through the cut-out, lace-like design of the first; the effect is both delicate and beautiful. Turning first to the Peaceful Money, the top sheet may bear the characters for prosperity or for long life in the center, and in the lower cut-out line is often found the phrase, "Peaceful family, honorable people seek and assist" (家門平安, 貴人求助). Also included as cutouts are stylized versions of the character for double happiness (囍) and an assortment of flower and butterfly shapes. An additional overlay of rolled-on fine gold squares complete the item with the cut-out top sheet attached to the red backing sheet with two strips of green paper.

The Chaozhou Heart of Money is among the most beautiful of non-pitched offerings in the total repertoire. The lacey top sheet is made of thin buff parchment paper, color washed in a peanut color which is brushed over the rows (from one to four) of cut-out motifs. Cave identified this wash as a yellow dye made from pagoda tree flowers (1998: 35). Gold embellishments are added, often to the central flower of the top row of cutouts. These cut-outs take up from one-half to two-thirds of the buff top sheet; showing through is the rose backing paper. According to the older shopkeepers, the motives that are cut out — such as the star of longevity, the gold coin motif, or the peach of long life — depend on the masters' choice. The Heart of Money may be purchased in small, medium, and large sizes. The small sizes bear two rows of cut-out design at the top; the medium, four rows of small or three lines of proportionally larger cut-outs, and the largest bears three rows of very large cut-outs. Some Chaozhou shops, such as that operated by the master speaking above, Mr Chan, are very careful of the old ways. They sell the Heart of Money in three pieces, all three enclosed in a single or multiple sheet termed a Money Ingot (錢錠), made of a single sheet of buff paper folded in half, with one side bearing a rectangle of gold and the other, a rectangle of silver, and three red paper triangles attached at the fold line.

A huge amount of hand labor is involved in crafting these non-pitched offerings. Chaozhou items are elaborate in still other ways, for in addition to the cutting and rolling techniques, extra gold or silver paper is attached as trim. The Cake Money (糕錢) or Bamboo Carrying Pole Money (竿錢), burned to the gods at the Lunar New Year, consists of bundles of thin yellow or gray rectangular paper cut through at the ends with crescents in the manner of the more ordinary White Money. However, this plain interior is elaborately decorated with a cover of gold sheets on red paper, further trimmed with gaily painted metallic paper elaborately cut out in flower shapes, roundels bearing the character for long life and long strips of flowers and coins.

Other fine examples of hand-cutting, this time from the everyday Cantonese offerings, consist of the special order paper gowns for the gods, which are actually a form of tailoring with paper. The paper master must first cut the base paper according to a pattern, generally larger than life-size to reflect the greatness of the deity, and then glue the pieces together to make the gown, sometimes adding a separate lining in a contrasting color. The special trimmings are painstakingly attached: colored fringe at the hem (sometimes edging the sleeves as well), sleeve extensions of fine white paper,[1] and a variety of painted metallic cutouts. Due to the time needed to complete all these steps, handcrafted clothing for the gods is available only though special order, except at the Lunar New Year and for a few days preceding the deities' birthdays. In anticipation of the demand at these times, the shop will craft in advance many sets of clothing for each deity.

The gods are not the only ones to receive special gifts of clothing, for handcrafted paper apparel for the ancestors may be ordered at the shop. When crafted by highly skilled paper masters, such paper clothing can be amazingly detailed. One woman shopkeeper, who had inherited an old retail shop from a friend, was justly proud of her meticulously crafted clothing offerings. For example, a jacket from her shop, made of colorful wrapping paper and fully lined, had workable toggle clasps, a high collar, usable pockets and fold-back sleeve cuffs; it was so fine that it could be worn by the living. Other items of clothing may have buttonholes with functional buttons, and dresses may have side openings with "zippers" of printed paper. Shoes are fashioned with shoelaces of string or, if replicating the old-fashioned cloth shoes lined in white cotton, they are lined with white paper. Even the most up-do-date sports shoes, complete with modified logos and shoelaces, are crafted. One shop known for its paper offerings for Hong Kong's fishermen made a particular kind of clothing for fishermen's ancestors using brightly printed cloth — not paper — cut in the shape of gowns. The maker called these Ancestors' Clothing (祖先衣). The shop was regularly given small amounts of unused fabric from tailor shops which was used for the gowns, and small black paper shoes were attached to the bottom to suggest the feet.[2]

In all these, as well as other examples of hand-cutting, the paper master must be dexterous and careful, avoiding both crooked and indistinct cutting (which wastes time and materials), and being careful not to tear the very thin sheets of paper. While elderly craftsmen still try to craft with the old ways of hand-cutting, machines are used for many items nowadays. Very common items such as Gold and Silver Paper, Longevity Gold, and Money to Live are machine-made (if lucky, one can find the original wooden printing blocks for the last item in antique stores), and the packaged clothing for ancestors and gods are machine-cut and printed. Some of the Chaozhou items already described have also changed; recent examples of Peaceful Money are made with thicker top sheets of gold which appears to be machine-cut.

Non-pitched paper offerings may also be hand-painted, a technique most often used on special-order clothing for the gods and ancestors. Clothing for the big gods is commonly finished with a wide band at the hem, painted in lines of color in the "mountain peaks and clouds" motif, a design that was embroidered on silk jackets and shoes during the late 1800s, and symbolized long life and happiness (Roberts and Steele 1997: 70). Also favored as clothing decorations are the elaborate depictions of painted dragons and flowers. The special clothing for the ancestors may have tailoring details (such as buttons and pockets) hand-painted on the surface. The decoration on the metallic paper cut-outs affixed to special clothing, on Lunar New Year offerings made by the Chaozhou (as described above for the Cake Money), and on the New Year Pinwheels are hand-painted. These cut-outs are first cut (now most often by machines) in the shapes of small flowers, auspicious animals such as phoenix, dragons, or carp; scepters (如意), or stylized depictions of characters such as those for prosperity, double happiness, or long life. Then they are accented with painted overlays of pink, green, blue, orange, yellow or gold. Whenever a paper master has the time and wishes to craft the offerings in the old way, he or she will embellish them with as many finishing details as possible.

Apprenticeship and Learning to Craft the Funeral Offerings

A man with nearly sixty years of experience by the time I met him, and an acclaimed master craftsman of funeral offerings, had this to say about entering the trade:

> About thirty years ago, I saw a child of about twelve years old. The mother was dragging the child, her son, holding a quilt and a rattan basket, up the street. Stopping at a small shop, she said to her son, ' This is the shop. Go in and work hard. Be obedient.' At that time, I thought that child must come from a poor family. The family wanted its child to work so as to lessen the burden in providing food. My childhood was similar to this, and I felt pangs of pity and sympathy for the child.

My assistant and I enjoyed talking with this craftsman about his experiences in the trade, and referred to him as The Master. His second-floor workshop, in the Yau Ma Tei District of Kowloon, despite being packed full of items in various states of completion, was always orderly, and his skill was obvious in the finished products. He recounted his experiences:

> I have studied with an uncountable number of masters. I learned my skills as a paper pitcher here in Hong Kong, for I was born and grew up here. My father engaged in this field and it could be said that I inherited the business from him. Actually, you could not say learning, that is, actual studying of the business, for I just observed him. However, my family's luck was not good, for my parents died when I was only ten years old and I had to work. My uncle gave me a job, and jobs were very difficult to get at that time. He said to me, 'La, come and work at my shop' and so I worked from that day onwards. I am now sixty-nine years old and have worked in this trade for nearly sixty years.

Another respondent, in his seventies at the time of the interviews, provided a similar account of his own apprenticeship in the 1930s in Hong Kong.

My uncle owned a large paper shop and asked me to come and learn the trade. It took three years to complete the training. In the first year, the wage was only two dollars a month. In the second year, the wage of an apprentice was three dollars, increasing in the third year to four or five dollars. There was about eight to ten apprentices there at the time, and over ten paper craftsmen, each specializing in his own field. In the first year, an apprentice had to do housework and did not receive much training, but as I was hardworking, I learned the skills after working for one year. The craftsmen then received one dollar a day, and the master craftsmen received forty dollars a month.

When explaining his training to us, The Master added a caution about the proper terminology, saying that paper masters ". . . do not use the formal term 'apprentice', but we call those in this position by the term 'young workers' (童工), or 'kids'. We don't actually have an apprenticeship system such as you can see in the construction trades." The terminology of Hong Kong's Apprenticeship Ordinance,[3] defines a "young person," the target of the Ordinance, " . . . as one of or over the age of 14 and under 19 years" (1976: 3).

Young workers usually enter the funeral pitching shops through family connections, or through the system of introduction and guarantor long established for other trades (Chu and Blaisdell 1924; Cooper 1980: 25). The Master also took in outsiders after interviewing them, but only rarely:

If I want to recruit a new member of the staff, I can't judge completely by his appearance . . . You really cannot accept some people if you had to just accept them on sight . . . because they are messy in appearance or have a strange smile. A general conclusion cannot be drawn on appearance alone. But, I can have confidence if recruitment involves an acquaintance.

Once a worker is accepted, the learning process begins. The young workers first learn how to handle the raw materials, which requires dexterity for even the simplest, most basic tasks.

The worker doesn't know anything when he first comes; he can't even divide the bamboo with a knife. La, just like this, I can divide the bamboo into three or four strips as I like. But, if he doesn't know the technique, he can't even divide it in two. The bamboo he cuts will look like a mouse tail, with one end wide and one end narrow.

The Master then astounded us by rapidly cutting, without even glancing at the bamboo, a series of perfectly long and regular, identical strips.

While the young worker is mastering the techniques of cutting and handling bamboo, he or she is also learning how to handle the paper. Bamboo strips are used to make the frame shaping the pitched offering, and are tied together with glued paper strips that function as twine. If these small paper strips are not cut and glued properly, the finished object will not be smooth and attractive looking, nor will it be stable. In some shops, young workers also had to learn to mix and boil the glue. The young worker must avoid waste by learning to estimate the amount of paper needed to both cover and trim the object. He or she must learn how to select the right kind of paper for the object, how to cut and shape different varieties and thicknesses of paper without tearing, and how to avoid damaging the paper (with small holes or tears at the seams, or smears and spots) with the glue and water. Many hours of practice precede the acquisition of these "simple" skills.

When the worker has become skilled in handling the raw materials, he or she is asked to make small, simple items (the definition of simple, like that of difficult, varies from master to master). The item will not be considered good if it is out of balance, leans to one side, or is prone to falling over. Such ill-constructed items are aesthetically unpleasing, and no one would buy them. Having mastered a simple item, the worker can then go on to more difficult creations, those that are either very large or have moving parts and special details. One young master said that refrigerators were the most complicated item he made due to the difficulty of crafting the door shelves, including the egg container, and assuring that the door itself would open and close like a real one. Another master considered compact disc players the most troublesome, as it was difficult to set in the discs.

Another item difficult to craft is the house with garden, an important item in all lists of basic items. The bamboo frame is first constructed with the four walls and a base, after which the first and second floors and the roof strips are set in place. Once the framework is completed, the worker pastes on the paper for the walls, floors, and the ceiling, and attaches the roof and then the fencing to the front extension that makes up the garden. Doors and windows are cut into the paper and finished off as desired with shutters, "glass" made of plastic or cellophane, and other details. To properly finish the house, a full set of furniture is added, either printed on the paper forming the walls or as actual modeled items set in one by one. These exact-scale furniture replicas are themselves interesting examples of paper crafting, for they are fashioned to closely match genuine wood furniture, especially the desirable pieces created during the Ming and the Qing dynasties. For example, one set of miniature paper furniture in the author's collection echoed a classic late Qing ensemble consisting of a daybed and matching chairs. Fashioned from fine paper of medium thickness and colored to resemble blackwood (酸枝), each piece was finished off with printed inserts echoing the complicated patterns of the genuine stone panels found in fine old furniture. Finally, some shops add paper trees to the garden and a cut-out model of the watchman — often a Sikh guard, identifiable by his turban, beard, and uniform. More recently, smaller versions of houses (small and light enough to be carried by the elderly) have appeared in retail shops. Made of heavy cardboard or thick paper (and as such, identified as non-pitched items), they are fully equipped with furniture and servants, and are professionally finished at the factory.

Watching the paper crafters in the workshops is a fascinating experience; all are busily cutting bamboo and paper, fashioning the strips of cut bamboo into frames with the paper strings attached to their wrists, adjusting the frames as needed, or rapidly attaching sheet after sheet of paper, using paste held in the space between their thumb and forefinger. Previous descriptions of workshops suggest that certain techniques of fabrication have not changed: ". . . we watched him fashioning the ornaments out of thin bamboo strips dabbed with paste carried on his left thumb, when touched with Japanese 'crepe paper' — amazingly strong if left dry — which in turn is twisted into string to form all kinds of shapes" (Osgood 1975: 891).

Making the Golden Flowers and Pinwheels

While available all through the year, the Golden Flowers and the Pinwheels are purchased in greatest numbers during the Lunar New Year, by those believers wishing to honor the gods, and ensure their family's passing into a safe and prosperous new year.

Golden Flowers

The magnificent Golden Flowers were described by Isabella Bird in 1896, in her account of New Year celebrations in the city of Kuei Fu, Szechuan (now Sichuan). "Every shop is brilliant with . . . kin hwa, or 'golden flowers', much made in Shao Hsing, being artificial flowers and leaves often of great size, of yellow tinsel on wires, making a goodly show" (1899: 157). Ms Bird would have no trouble identifying modern specimens, whose appearance, according to their craftsmen, has changed little over time.

Golden Flowers are bought in pairs to be set on either side of an altar, and connected with a red silk ribbon with a metal rosette in the center — the Spirit Reds. Golden Flowers and Spirit Reds may be obtained anywhere that paper offerings are sold. While the greatest varieties are available just before the Lunar New Year, they are purchased any time in the year when setting up a new altar, moving into a new home, or opening a business. Golden Flowers, or Spirit Flowers (神花), do not look like real flowers; they are formed in triangular or elongated inverted kite shapes. Ranging in length from three inches to nearly four feet, they are built up in depth by layers of thin sheets of golden foil, embossed with delicate traceries. These layers are assembled with wires and separated one from another through the use of tubular cardboard rolls or bamboo spacers. The smallest examples are little more than a single sheet of embossed foil, mounted on a stick and trimmed with painted dots or tiny bits of dyed feather. In the larger examples, there can be three or more foil layers, each mounted and stiffened with strips of bamboo. At the back, a sturdy stick of bamboo is attached so that the flower can be easily mounted. The Spirit Red is fixed behind the pair of Golden Flowers. Its central rosette sits between the two flowers, and the two strips of ribbon are attached one behind each flower; the ends of the ribbon hang down along the sides. When in place, the pair of Golden Flowers appears to be holding up the two ends of the ribbon.

The trimmings demonstrate the skills of the master craftsman. The larger Golden Flowers are made with borders composed of one to three rows of colored pompoms, silk or paper flowers, or tightly rolled whorls of crepe paper or plastic resembling wood. The bottom is adorned by a multicolored silk fringe. The center section of the flower contains representations of various deities, usually the God of Wealth. Nowadays, these representations are mostly made of molded white plastic with cursorily painted features, wearing hats and simple, but still hand-cut, versions of long sleeved classical robes in red, orange, or green paper. At one time, the larger and more expensive Golden Flowers held handmade images, shaped from high-quality white wax with delicate, painted-on features (red lips and fine black eyes and eyebrows). These images were dressed in colorful clothing trimmed with strips of metallic paper to suggest cuffs, collars, and belts. Female figures wore metallic paper aprons over their robes, and their hair in dual chignons on either side of the head. The males wore cloth or paper hats like old-fashioned officials' hats with extended side wings, and elderly figures sported long white beards made of fine cotton threads or finely cut white paper. All the figures had hands of white paper, finely cut with delicate individual fingers. By the early 1990s, manufacturers had begun to include more plastic materials on the Golden Flowers, and even more recently, some have been produced with small machine-embossed cardboard representations of dragons, which had not previously been included in the range of trimmings.

Smaller modern Golden Flowers are adorned with paper or silk flowers, large pompoms, and delicate, tiny butterflies in paper or silk, although plastic flowers in garish colors have been featured since the early 1990s. Craftsmen declared that the number of elements on a Golden Flower depends on the size of the frame: the larger the flower, the more auspicious items it can contain. For example, many flowers are finished with pairs of peacock feathers placed along the sides — the number of pairs determined by the size of the flower, so that as many as eight to ten individual feathers may be used on each flower. A pair of Golden Flowers can take more than a day to complete, and is the specialty of a select few paper masters.

Craftsmen did not agree when asked if there was such a thing as an "ideal" Golden Flower; some craftsmen asserted that the metallic paper triangle that formed the body was the defining element of the Golden Flower, and everything else could be eliminated with no loss of spiritual significance, while other masters believed that nothing could be omitted. Others took a middle view, believing that certain elements must appear. One explained, "It is important to have the gold body, the images of the gods, and the peacock feathers." All these diverse opinions were acceptable among the masters. When mounted with their accompanying red silk rosette and ribbon, the gorgeous colors and trims of the Golden Flowers shimmer and glow in the flickering light of the temples.

Pinwheels

Pinwheels are purchased at temples (or at certain monasteries), most notably Che Gong Temple in Sha Tin and Wong Tai Sin Temple in Kowloon.[4] Paper masters say that at these two temples, in the years following Second World War and through processes no longer fully remembered, craftsmen began to sell Pinwheels as temple souvenirs. As Pinwheels have grown enormously in popularity, most of the larger temples now offer them. Pinwheels are sold in huge quantities during the Lunar New Year, to support supplications to the gods for good fortune and family protection during the coming year.

Originally, the frames of the Pinwheels were made in round or gourd shape because these forms expressed the auspicious meanings of "completeness/never-ending" (the round) and "protection from evil" (the gourd). These shapes are still preferred, although new forms such as stars, hearts, and three-dimensional globes have appeared. Pinwheels range in height from roughly six inches to six feet. If crafting the older designs, masters still use bamboo, bending the strips into shape, securing them with wire, and covering the frame in fringed crepe paper (modern specimens have frames of brightly colored plastic or plastic-covered wire), before attaching the pinwheels, which have been cut and folded from brightly colored cellophane (the very earliest examples were made of paper). Each Pinwheel is secured with a distinctive metal pin through its center, and is finished off with the placement of other auspicious elements (see Chapter 7). A thick bamboo stick (actually, a pole in the largest examples) is affixed to the back for mounting or carrying. As with the Golden Flowers, the larger the frame of the Pinwheel, the more auspicious elements it can contain; many are chosen to reflect the personal inspiration of the crafter, because Pinwheels (along with the Flower Cannons) allow considerable personal expression on the part of the master.

Many of the skills involved in crafting pitched objects are the same no matter what is being made — bamboo is cut into strips, shaped into a frame, and covered with paper or decorated with auspicious elements. But as seen, each item requires a number of specialized techniques. To take just one example, to make the Pinwheels the cellophane or plastic must be cut, painted, and folded, the individual pinwheels secured with a pin in such a way that allows them to revolve, and the accompanying lucky phrases (meaning/wish head, 意頭) require some skill at calligraphy. The Golden Flower makers of the old school need to know how to mold and paint the wax figures, and construct their fabric clothing and headdresses, while masters of funeral offerings need to keep abreast of trends and continually learn to make new items. Hence, masters of pitched paper offerings usually craft only one kind of pitched offerings, such as funeral offerings, Golden Flowers, Flower Cannons, or Pinwheels, even if they are knowledgeable about the others. While the less complicated pitched items such as the Lucky Basins can be crafted by most shopkeepers, the pitched items made by masters require special techniques. Yet, learning the techniques is only the first step in becoming a master — using one's creativity involves a lifetime.

Gender and Paper Crafting

In 1886, D. J. Macgowan, writing about Chinese guilds, observed that, "Some, as goldbeaters at Wenchow, allow none but sons and nephews of workmen or masters to learn the trade. The unutterable meanness that moves pseudo-civilized men in the West to debar women from occupations for which they are competent is, as might be expected, rampant in China" (1886: 178–9). In their later study in Beijing, Gamble and Burgess provide little information about women in guilds, other than a reference to a few women attending one of the meetings of the Guild of the Blind, at which the women ". . . visited among themselves or listened to the business being transacted, but did not mingle with the men" (1921: 172).

Men and women both work in the modern paper offering trade. Masters of funeral offerings asserted that there were never any hard divisions between males and females when it came to taking apprentices, even in their youth, although before the 1940s or 1950s very few women were actually accepted into shops run by strangers. As The Master explained:

> Females rarely went to work as apprentices. However, in the past, if a girl wanted to learn the trade and if her father and brothers were already engaged in the paper business, as a family business, then she would know how to make things. She would not be working outside, but would work for her father. Now, we have females learning how to make the frames of these objects. My own daughter over there knows how to do these things; do you think she doesn't know? Of course she does.

Another elderly crafter of Golden Flowers explained that, before the

1950s, women were not allowed to make the elaborate foil background and trim for the flowers, because of men's "fear of competition from women," since women were more nimble-fingered and careful in their work. He was alone in mentioning such attitudes, however.

At present, a large number of women are employed in the combination retail outlets and workshops that craft paper funeral offerings.[5] Personal observation at the largest of these revealed a number of women working on the bamboo frames for houses and cars, as well as assembling smaller items. Some of these women had been hired as relative strangers, while others had learned the trade from a family member — usually a father — who ran the business. In at least three of these combination businesses, the owners' daughters were active members of the workforce; one was especially praised by her proud parents as someone who "knew how to make anything the customer wanted." This woman was much in demand, and, along with her father, crafted all of the funeral offerings in the shop. While exact figures are impossible to obtain, women play an important part in the fabricating of all varieties of pitched paper offerings; an estimated 40 to 50 percent of workers in the trade are female. Visits to shops illustrate the roughly equal numbers of men and women who own, rent, or operate retail paper shops. Anyone with sufficient interest, experience, and financing can set up a shop. Customers do not frequent a store because of the proprietor's gender, but because of the proprietor's helpfulness and knowledge. While some shopkeepers know more than others, this has little to do with gender. Women also have taken leading positions in the wholesale arm of the business; in the early 1990s over half the existing wholesale businesses were owned or managed by women.

Another aspect of the paper offerings trade which should be mentioned is the potential for pollution from menstruating women (see, for example, Ahern 1975; or, on Chinese women and religion, Black 1986; or Harrell 1986). In the views of some of the shopkeepers, there is no problem with pollution in domestic worship, only outside the home.

> Since the god in one's house must be served by that woman [the housewife], and since it is natural for a women to menstruate, if she does not worship during her period, there would be no one to give the gods something to eat [offerings] — that would be unreasonable. However, when she goes to the temple to worship she must tie-shut her trouser legs, or just not go. As there are many worshippers in the temple, the god will not suffer if one woman does not come to worship.

The respondent went on to say that after a birth or an abortion, however, the woman could not worship, even at home, for at least one month, as the birth pollution would cause too many problems, even to a domestic god. In the interval, she could have her husband conduct the worship instead. Other shopkeepers agreed with this more traditional approach for the shops. If a female worker is menstruating, either she doesn't work until her menstrual cycle is finished, or she wears double trousers and ties the ends closed; this prevents the escape of any bad air that would adversely affect the offerings. Another shopkeeper explained how menstruating women must not set the new Golden Flowers on the family altar during the Lunar New Year. This form of dirt, which cannot be cleansed by ritual washing (such as using water infused with the petals of flowers of seven different colors or with pomelo leaves),[6] would adversely affect her family for the entire year. This particular shopkeeper did not, however, mention menstruation as affecting any other item of paper offering.

According to the majority of shopkeepers of retail paper shops and wholesalers, there are no taboos against women workers handling or packing or crafting the offerings during their periods. As one shopkeeper told us, "After all, if you get dirty, just wash your hands." Of course, what he referred to was everyday dirt, not the form resulting in spiritual pollution, but what he meant was that dirt of any kind could be dealt with easily. Most worshippers agreed with this point of view, that menstruation has little or no adverse effect on paper offerings. Some people did add that if a worker or worshipper was concerned about the matter, she could always tie-shut the ends of her trouser legs or, she could ask another person to handle the paper objects she wished to buy. Still others said that young women no longer believed in the bad effects of menstruation, even if the older generation did. In any case, it was more a matter for individual customers to decide. Paper masters also appeared to be unconcerned. As The Master explained it, "There are no taboos that we observe in this business, including that concerning women when they are menstruating. I am a master of paper offerings and I will welcome anyone as a guest."

The Importance of Initiative

Masters of the funeral offerings recognized the need for proper training and explained what attributes a young worker should possess. First, the young worker needed to pay attention and observe shop procedures carefully. "In my native place, you learned by observation. If you were clever you learned fast and well, the cleverer the better. It depended on your [ability to] observe and whether or not you were smart." Paper shop masters did not regularly demonstrate how things were done, or conduct classes, so the young worker had to watch and then try to replicate the procedures.

One master had this to say about training a young worker:

> If I show you how to make it, and do it for you, you no longer need to do it! For example, you have made the frame and brought it to me. After checking and measuring, I'll make a mark on it if it is made correctly. Then I stop and you have to make the next part; if I do all the tasks for you, then you no longer need to do it. In the past, the masters did not make samples to show. Objects which were [and are now] not made correctly were destroyed immediately, as there was no space to keep them. The master would tell you when you made a mistake, but he didn't tell you in advance what to avoid; you knew after you had made mistakes.

Gamble and Burgess' pioneering studies of work and labor in the early 1920s in Beijing note the importance of personal initiative in cultivating the master/apprenticeship relationship. They recorded a set of "Maxims and Rules for Apprentices" for workers in the retail trades. Rule Number Eleven stated clearly, "You apprentices should not be afraid to ask questions. If there is something that you do not fully understand, about judging money, doing arithmetic, writing letters, talking business or acting courteously, you should ask some older man to tell you about it. You should not keep your mouth shut like a wooden image!" (1921: 442). Young workers in the funeral offering trade also learned the value of cultivating a good relationship with the master.

> I did want to do one thing which the master was doing. I really wanted to do that thing. So, I looked at him all the time, in order to let him know I admired him for making the object so beautiful. This led to the master saying, 'You want to make this? La, let me tell you, you should make it this way.' It did not cost me anything to give him appreciation and he taught me special techniques.

It is clear from these informants that the ability to observe and remember, and a willingness to take the initiative and learn independently are necessary traits for a young worker in the funeral offerings industry. But are these characteristics explainable by the restriction of knowledge within the trade? That is, are they strategies necessitated by, and the direct result of, the masters' jealous guarding of trade secrets? Many accounts of traditional Chinese apprenticeship stress this guarding of knowledge and the deliberate concealing of techniques from apprentices (Cooper 1980: 24; Coy 1989; Zhang 1997).

> For a great part of the time the boy is little more than a slave who does the odds and ends of any sort of work his master wants done, and during that time he must be a clever boy or have an exceptional master, or be apprenticed to a relative if he is to learn anything of the trade whatever. It is not until pretty close to the end of his course that the boy is shown how to do things connected with the trade, and even then he is often not taught in any complete way but is kept in ignorance to any possible extent, for fear he will become a real competitor of the master. (Dean 1924: 119)

This passage, from a study of industrial education in pre-Second World War China (published in Beijing), was written at a time when the traditional system was breaking down. Nevertheless, it reflects a common belief that the masters protected their knowledge and restricted valuable information.

Liao T'ai-ch'u gave a similar account in 1946. Speaking of the apprenticeship situation in Chengdu, he observed:

> In a workshop the situation is quite different; he may be able to learn the things that he is given a chance to observe, but there are certain parts that the shih fu intends to keep secret from all outsiders . . . The keeping of secrets by the *shih fu* was especially true in the teaching of Chinese boxing in the older days; for the *shih fu* to teach an apprentice everything meant that he himself might eventually be knocked down. (Liao 1948: 96)

The protection of trade secrets is still of concern. Hong Kong's current Apprenticeship Ordinance states that, "The apprentice also undertakes that he/she will keep the secrets of his/her employer and will not divulge any matters relating to the business or interests of the employer to any unauthorized person" (1976: 12).

The Master's experiences suggest that guarding information was not a major concern of the funeral offerings industry as a whole, and in this practice the industry, which is as old as any other trade, diverges from tradition (see, for example, Golas 1977). The Master was able to cultivate his relationship with his masters and to learn special techniques, but what he learned was not dependent solely on his skills at social interaction. Other craftsmen similarly encountered few obstacles in obtaining information (or in visiting other workshops to see what they were producing). "No, the master did not avoid telling anything that he knew. The master would not keep secrets [of manufacture] that he would not intend to teach to apprentices. No such case. La, sometimes . . . it is impossible not to show your skills." Of course, each learning situation depended on the attitude of the particular master. "In the past, some masters did not care. Some [masters] aimed at finding kids to do trivial tasks for them, someone to sweep the floor, to cook and to do miscellaneous jobs. They didn't care whether you had really learned things."

This suggests that what the young worker learned depended less on a perception that privileged information must be protected, and more on the willingness of the master to teach and to be actively concerned with training the young. The Master has himself trained a number of young people, many of whom now run their own shops and workshops.

> I have taught many people. My purpose of teaching is that they will help me after I teach them. It is true that a few people thought I should not do this, but I told them, you must teach them, otherwise why do you employ them? They'll become useless persons if I just employ them and don't teach them. This is my principle; my aim is to let them help me earn money.

In a way, the issue of teaching or hiding trade secrets is rendered moot by the physical layout of most paper workshops — a large open space — which makes it difficult to hide the procedures for modeling a particular object. Any worker can easily observe what is going on and learn the master's techniques. Furthermore, the larger workshops have quantities of models on hand, stacked in corners or hanging from the ceiling, and a young worker can easily examine them to see how they have been assembled.

As well, there are too many different kinds of funeral offerings (see Chapter 4), for any master to know all there is to know and keep the information to himself. As explained earlier, funeral offerings consist of a traditional basic set for the funeral ritual, and a second set of everyday items that are offered at various times after death. Fabricating the traditional items is more easily taught and learned, for these items are resistant to change; it is more difficult for masters to invent radical new strategies for crafting them, if doing so changes their appearance. However, the mourners' desires to ensure that the departed have a comfortable existence in the next world — at least as comfortable as the one they had while living — means that the additional, everyday items that are burned and sent to the departed will change continuously to reflect contemporary lifestyles and fashions. The ever-changing content of this category places a high premium on flexibility and innovation. As The Master said:

> The followers had to learn by themselves, they had to think about the paper pitching to see if there were other ways to make it better. The master could not teach you this talent, not the creation and changes. Like me, making a model of a laser disc player. I can make one like a real one with a movable disc but my master could not teach me that when I was young. You know, nowadays, there are many objects needed, like rice cookers, refrigerators, aircraft, yachts, and even speedboats. So, making these kinds of items needs one's creativity.

Recognized and successful masters are noted for their ability to create new things, while maintaining the integrity of the older designs. For this reason, the learning process is itself an ongoing and vibrant process.

> As I have said before, there is no end of learning in our field. What is the end? You can't say there are thirty-six roads (三十六道) and I have taught you all. If you want the master to teach you, you will just learn half the skills. The followers had to learn by themselves, they had to think about the paper pitching to see if there were ways to make it better. The master could not teach you this, the master could only teach you some basic things and the follower could never learn 100% because of changes.

The most skilled masters never cease their considerable efforts to expand their capabilities. Special orders require that the Hong Kong craftsman familiarize himself with new items and technologies. If the order is for the latest gadget or bit of technology, the master may need to solve the crafting problem by leaving the workshop and studying the item in situ, visiting retail shops or showrooms to examine the products, or even attending trade fairs to keep up. Cave included an account of a Singaporean manufacturer of funeral items for whose commission a relative of the deceased traveled to London to collect a model and other information on a Rolls-Royce, so that the master could make an exact copy in paper (Cave 1998: 49). Young workers are also encouraged to visit other shops and see what is being crafted, and even to cultivate relationships with employees in these shops. The same diligence applies to more classical forms of knowledge. While the paper masters could not be described as well-educated in a formal sense (although all visited were literate), these gentlemen were knowledgeable about Chinese history and folklore, and quite familiar with the various images of deities, fairies and spirits, and famous heroes, not to mention the repertoire of animal and plant images so popular in classical and popular literature. The trade demanded this knowledge, because paper masters have to be accurate in the design and decoration of the items they craft, at least in terms of popular wisdom. The Master, who once received an order to craft a set of the Eight Immortals (八仙), explained how he went to the library in search of books illustrating how these deities were commonly represented, from clothing and stance to the associated symbolic accoutrements, so that he made no mistakes when he modeled them. With some pride, he showed us some of the books he had purchased on the subject.

It is a common practice in funeral offering workshops to have a number of photo albums of items the workshop has made. These photo albums allow the customer to become familiar with what is available, provide a means of assessing the quality and the level of craftsmanship at the workshop, and are perhaps a subtle encouragement for the concerned relative to provide for the deceased in a manner comparable to that ordered by previous customers. It is both fascinating and instructive to look through these albums, containing as they do a visual record of the feelings of families and the personalities of the deceased, for only in such review can the enormous range of possible gifts to the dead, from furniture to appliances to cars, be fully appreciated. These photo albums have another purpose in that they give the young worker an opportunity to become familiar with the range of items that can be crafted, and how each item should look when completed. As such, they exemplify a standard of craftsmanship to attain.

Masters of the everyday offerings to the dead must be both flexible and innovative. They cannot be routine workers or passive crafters, waiting for someone else to provide information and instruction, but must take the initiative in learning throughout their working life. Those who become masters display creativity, imagination, and a painstaking attention to detail. Their customers, who are anxious to provide their ancestors with a comfortable existence in the next world, expect no less of them. But, while consumer expectation cannot be denied as an influence, it is a supporting rather than a dominating influence. The trade's emphasis is on hard work and creativity, and many masters consider their craft a form of art. "The shape of the paper servant that you make should be like a human. The proportion is very important; if the proportion is wrong, it is not acceptable. The color must be correct. In Hong Kong there are just a few persons who can reach such a level, for people had to make good frames first or else the other parts would not be good [balanced]."

While the examples in this chapter have emphasized the funeral offerings, masters of other pitched items such as Pinwheels and Flower Cannons demonstrate a similar professional commitment and desire to constantly rethink their creations. One respondent who regularly designed his own Pinwheels found inspiration from looking at traditional Chinese paintings and carvings. He visited older Hong Kong neighborhoods such as Yau Ma Tei[7] in search of antiques, or went to the Chinese product emporiums to look over their merchandise (modern reproductions of old-style crafts). Once he had an inspiration, he would draw up a design or ask friends in advertising companies to help him draft a pattern. He also modified some of the auspicious elements by matching them with the year of the Chinese calendar; if the year of the horse was coming, he would select more horses (auspicious symbols at any time) to place on his creations. Another Pinwheel master, probably the finest craftsman of all, experimented with various auspicious elements, combining and recombining them until he saw a pattern or until the gods sent him an inspiration.

The Not-So-Anonymous Master

The emphasis on personal initiative, in acquiring and sharpening a wide range of technical skills, and on creative growth, resulted in craftsmen very proud of their skills, the results of which could be seen in the finished object, a beautifully made paper offering. Some masters considered themselves artists as well as crafters. Given this, can masters be identified? Max Loehr has remarked that:

> Of the various art forms in which they achieved excellence, the Chinese themselves recognized only two as truly artistically significant, namely, calligraphy and painting. Other art forms (architecture, sculpture, lacquer work, bronze casting, ceramics) are considered the work of craftsmen, and their names and lives are rarely recorded. No matter how exquisite their creations be, it

is not possible to distinguish individual craftsmen and appraise their specific contributions. (1961: 147)

Non-pitched paper offerings that are factory produced are anonymous items, in that individual designers are not known to the purchaser and probably not to the wholesaler or shopkeeper either. The situation for handcrafted items is less clear. For example, Tseng (1977) recorded items that she termed "funeral paper garment," very finely crafted, and both hand-painted and woodblock printed. These items appear to be handcrafted clothing for the ancestors, not actual clothing for the corpse. Some of these bore the name of the paper master who had crafted them (1977: 145). It is also possible that handmade examples of everyday offerings (such as those for the Chaozhou community) might be known as the work of a particular master if the shop had long employed that person and his reputation had grown among customers. The same could be true for shopkeepers who crafted their own items; shopkeepers are aware of acclaimed masters in other shops or workshops. But in general anonymity is the norm. The crafters of pitched paper offerings are recognized only by their circle of regular customers. Of course, within the trade itself, highly skilled craftsmen are recognized; Pinwheel masters know about other Pinwheel masters, and so on.

For someone familiar with the trade, the identities of individual masters can be discerned through their characteristic styles and their fondness for certain finishing details, especially in the making of pitched offerings. For example, at the time of the interviews, there were only a few elderly masters (no more than five, and one of these has recently retired) who continued to craft Pinwheels entirely by hand. These handmade Pinwheels were instantly recognizable through their use of colored crepe paper, fine cellophane pinwheels, bamboo mountings, and their near-total avoidance of plastic frames. Hence, if the Pinwheel was handmade, then one could be sure it was made by only one of a few men or families. More specific clues may be seen in the finishing techniques. Each pinwheel is secured and enabled to spin by the central pin and each master had a characteristic manner of decorating this pin. One attached a small painted flower to cover, another used an open-petaled daisy made of golden metal, while another looped the wire into a swirl shape. Another means of identification was the decoration of the blades of the pinwheels themselves; one master hand-glued small circles of silver metallic paper to each blade. He termed these "lucky stars" or "little silvers" and felt that they added an extra auspicious touch to his creations.

Another clue to different craftsmen is the fondness for certain raw materials, colors, or decorative elements. The Pinwheel master referred to above used only four metallic colors (red, green, gold, and rose), and often arranged them in the same order. Another master used only clear pinwheels printed in multicolored stripes, while a third preferred thicker, opaque varieties in a red-orange color. Masters also made use of particular elements; one workshop was the only one crafting handmade pleated paper lanterns as trim, while another workshop heavily favored chenille trimmings in the form of auspicious birds such as peacocks. Another Pinwheel master was known for metal frames in modern shapes like hearts and stars, and pressed metal trimmings in the form of lucky animals or other elements. Finally, the very largest Pinwheels (examples can be six feet in height and three feet in width) were handcrafted. The craftsman with the preference for red-orange pinwheels operated the only home workshop regularly producing the largest varieties, up to six feet in height; these could be recognized by size but also by his fondness for either round or gourd shapes. The most elaborate and eccentric Pinwheels, of which only a few were available at each Lunar New Year, if at all, were handmade by the odd craftsmen, not one of the five most active producers. These eccentric Pinwheels were elaborately and unpredictably trimmed and while expensive, were sought after by knowledgeable consumers whenever they appeared.

The above are the more subtle means of identifying individual craftsmen; the Flower Cannons, made for the birthdays of the most popular deities, provide more obvious examples. Since the workshops making these towering creations paint their name and address on the base, worshippers, admirers and deities alike are left in no doubt as to who made it (see Chapter 7). But, as for Pinwheel crafters, a Flower Cannon maker may also be identified by its decorative and auspicious elements.

The Shopkeepers

Shopkeepers need to take an active role in learning their trade just as the paper masters do. A number of shopkeepers have inherited the family business and been learning all their lives, helping their parents or relatives in the shop. These individuals are often quite knowledgeable, for they also inherit all the experiences of elderly family members well-versed in the meanings of paper offerings. Although, as one said, this active method of learning still requires effort.

When I starting working, when I was very young, I worked with my parents. But, I just observed how people did it; knowledge like this is not learnable, so I had to do it all by myself. For example, when a person came to buy something and I served her, I got the experience and knowledge. It was a matter of progress, and I learned it little by little. Sometimes, the old people would tell me how to do something or what items meant. Or, I just stood aside to listen if old people were explaining an item to someone else. My parents couldn't teach me item by item because paper items are too detailed, and no one could learn it all without active experience.

Some shopkeepers acquire an interest in paper offerings later in life or at retirement, having learned from friends. One woman master of funeral clothing explained how she had been purchasing from one shop for years, becoming more and more interested in the unusual items that the elderly shopkeeper had accumulated. When he became too old to continue, he begged her to take over the business and she did so. Some of the younger shopkeepers decide to take up the business because of their personal interest and curiosity. They embark on a crash course of study, making inquiries at established shops, asking elderly acquaintances, making extra visits to temples, and reading anything they can find on the topic. Even experienced shopkeepers must keep abreast of developments in the trade and familiarize themselves with paper items no longer readily available due to their age or rarity. Also, many shops sell items distinctive to one or another of Hong Kong's dialect groups, such as the Chaozhou and fishing communities. Mastering the ritual significance of these differing assemblages demands additional time and effort, even if one is a member of such communities by birth.

One respondent complained, "This business is too complicated, far too complicated. Even working in it for a long time, I find out new things, and my wife, who has been working with me for seven years, still encounters things she has never seen before, the things rarely asked for by customers." Repeated visits and interviews in retail shops made clear that even the most experienced shopkeepers were always acquiring more knowledge of their trade. As often as not, the shopkeeper would suddenly produce a special item, something we had never heard of in any of the one hundred or so previous interviews, so interviews were often begun in anticipation of "what might turn up this time."

7

Colors, Sounds, and Symbols:

The Making of an Auspicious Object

The widespread use of paper offerings in Hong Kong rituals underscores their identification as auspicious objects. While objects can acquire power in a number of ways,[1] one method is the extensive use of elements which are themselves auspicious. The decorative elements in a paper offering not only enhance its beauty but also convey ideas and associations to the worshipper. In a sense, the offerings can be read as texts, in which the combinations of auspicious elements are understood by the worshipper.

The Symbolism of Color

The first feature of paper offerings that attracts the eye is their brilliant, exuberant color — red, gold, rose, orange, plum, and green — which underscore the joyousness and auspiciousness of the worship. As Williams once observed, to be effective, "a colour must be brilliant" (1976: 77, see also Anderson 1970: 170), or in the words of a master, "bright and lively." Indeed, the dazzling colors of offerings, and their magnificent and complicated constructions, are part of the "sensory manipulation in the interests of religion" which is a critical theme in Chinese culture (Anderson 1977: 22). While it has been written that bright colors, especially the use of bright reds and greens in combination, are no longer favored by peasants in Mainland China (Laing 1989: 164), Hong Kong residents hold a different opinion. The brilliant color of paper offerings is echoed in other areas of Chinese traditional material culture, such as the decoration of temples and ancestral halls, study halls and homes, furniture, embroidery, painting, clothing, and children's toys. In these contexts, color, while a vital component of decoration, is never simply decorative. Colors convey messages both subtle and intense, messages which are understood independently, and which further emphasize meanings generated by the elements of decoration.

Not simply red

Red in various tints is the most commonly encountered color in a paper offering. Red "is the color of the summer, of the South and also of the ancient realm of Zhou (c. 1050–256 BC)" (Eberhard 1986: 248), and of blood, "life's sustaining substance" (Carter 1948: 8). On the stage a red-faced actor represents a holy person, as red is a symbol of virtue, truth, and sincerity (Williams 1976: 79). Red garments also identify one of the gods of good fortune who bestows high office and riches to the believer (Eberhard 1986: 248), and E. N. Anderson noted that images of deities in the temples were "all alike in that they feature brilliant colors, especially the magically fortunate red" (1970: 170).

The traditional distinction between the white affairs (白事), sad occasions such as funerals, and the red affairs (紅事), happy events such as weddings and childbirth, is followed in Hong Kong. Red protects against evil or bad luck, and is used as a prophylactic in funeral clothing and rituals (Wolf 1970), and as the color of choice for traditional Chinese wedding gowns and other items associated with marriage (Carter 1948: 8; Garrett 1994: 31). As the predominant color of any happy occasion, red is especially prominent during the Lunar New Year. During the New Year, the phrase, "To pin flowers [in the hair] and hang up the red" (參花掛紅) denotes the gaiety of the season, when people dress up in new clothes and celebrate. Red predominates in the traditional decorations, when market stalls display bolts of intense red ribbon, to be used at home for tying around ceramic pots of narcissus, peonies, oranges or kumquats, or any other item the household wants to make happy. Red paper envelopes (利是) are used for the gifts of lucky money given to family and friends at this time, as on other auspicious occasions. It was once considered highly improper to present gifts of money in any other manner (Burkhardt 1954: 5), and a red envelope is still the approved way to give such a gift. Red predominates in all the secular decorations and hangings for the home, including the pair of red papers painted with lucky couplets (揮春). Further, the red of firecrackers can be seen in the large heaps of spent paper; both sound and color are protection against evil. Red is the color evocative of all the wishes for good luck, good fortune, prosperity, happiness, and protection. It is the "emblem of joy and is employed for all festive occasions" (Williams 1976: 76).

Red is the favorite color for a variety of paper offerings, first as the paper or the printing ink for many of the non-pitched everyday offerings, including the Five Treasures Document, the Honorable People Paper, Longevity Gold and the Solving of 100 Problems. Red, and its partner green, is traditionally used for the Honorable People Papers, and many of the Chaozhou offerings (such as the Peaceful Money and the Money to Escape from Difficulty, 脫難錢) make use of fine red paper. Red is the traditional color for the paper gowns offered to the gods, especially female deities such as Tian Hou, and is a major component of many pitched offerings, including the Lucky Basins, Flower Cannons, Golden Flowers, and Pinwheels. On the Flower Cannons, red is the favorite color for the paper covering the base, for the round paper plaques at the top proclaiming the name of the association who commissioned the offering, and for the numerous items trimming the body of the cannon, including the clusters of red-dyed eggs, hung on the body of the cannon and sought by couples hoping to have children in the coming year.

The Golden Flowers make very good use of red, sometimes in an outer row of red pompom trimming, and pink, red's near relative, is favored for the silk or paper flowers set in the middle. The accompanying Spirit Red, centered with an elaborate rosette, is also red. This banner is purchased separately for trimming dragon boats during the Dragon Boat races of the fifth lunar month (Ward and Law 1993). Finally, Pinwheels are made cheery with red accents in the form of the cellophane or foil pinwheels themselves, the crepe paper wrapping the bamboo frame, and in the various elements such as paper lanterns and flowers.

Yellow, gold, and green

The color yellow, or gold as it more commonly appears, is the color of majesty. "Yellow, the national colour, was sacred to the Emperor and assumed only by his Majesty and his sons, or the lineal descendants of his family" (Williams 1976: 76–77). Yellow is deemed effective against evil, and is most commonly found on charms against evil spirits: "A small yellow paper, having four characters upon it, meaning that the charm protects the house and expels pernicious influences, is also often put upon the ridge pole and other high parts of the house" (Doolittle 1865b: 310). In addition, yellow may denote fame, progress and advancement, all desirable things (Eberhard 1986: 322), and, as yellow jade, represents the earth itself (Carter 1948: 55). Its general auspiciousness makes yellow (or gold) the color of choice for a number of paper offerings, including the Money to Live and the Solving of 100 Problems. The color gold also appears in various forms, the most significant being the "gold" rubbed onto the paper money, on the many offerings for the Chaozhou community, and for golden ingots and replicas of gold jewelry — any context in which the precious metal itself is represented. Gold is also the color of choice for the traditional crowns for Monkey, fanciful creations of gold paper loops.

Green is associated with precious jade, the Chinese stone of choice. Green as "indicating the awakening of nature in the spring" (Laufer 1989: 172), is associated with fertility and growing things. "Green is one of the colours that life takes on and it is the emblem of the spring . . . Several of the gods and goddesses, e.g. the god of literature, go about in green robes" (Eberhard 1986: 134). Green is the color associated with water, the first of the five elements (Williams 1976: 79, 186). Green appears, in a vivid hue paired with an equally vivid red, in the Honorable People Papers, and also defines the Prosperous/Green Horse Paper featured in rituals seeking protection from evil. Finally, the flower adornments on many pitched items are enhanced by green leaves and stems, while some masters add scepters in green paper to represent green jade.

The difficult colors

White, black and blue are traditionally associated with the points of the compass (west, north, and east, respectively), with the elements (Williams 1976: 79), and with heaven (Carter 1948: 55). Despite this, these colors are problematic when used on paper offerings because of their parallel association with death and unpleasant events. "When a parent dies, all projected affairs are automatically suspended and signs of happiness hidden away . . . all things colored red, pink, or purple are put away or covered over with white, blue, or black material" (Yang 1945: 86). This same inauspicious nature is underlined in the use of these unlucky colors for funeral goods such as the replicas of vehicles, which are usually made in blue. Shopkeepers and paper masters stressed that the difficult colors should be avoided in all other paper offerings, but despite this caution, the demands of manufacturing often modify this prohibition. For example, white is a difficult color to avoid, as it is used for the faces of the wax or plastic images of deities set into a number of the larger offerings and is the underlying color of the cloth painted over for the three-dimensional models of the auspicious animals needed for a proper Flower Cannon. Further, even difficult tints are traditionally appropriate for the paper clothing offered to the gods such as the blue color associated with Wong Tai Sin. As one master explained, "The colors of gods' clothing usually follow the traditional ways and it follows that the colors of the clothing of the gods' images must conform. For example, the images of Wong Tai Sin often wear blue clothing so I use blue for the paper clothing I make." Traditionally, white is the proper color for the clothing of Guan Yin, one of the most revered goddesses of the Chinese pantheon; in this context, white signifies purity.

Most worshippers make little of the symbolic contradiction of using these colors as long as there are not large expanses of pure white or black showing, which would elicit disapproving comments, certainly among elderly worshippers. In actual practice, craftsmen avoid excessive use of such problematic colors by substituting pastel colors. This is particularly obvious in the everyday offerings, whose base color is generally a variety of tan, cream or beige, the latter described in Hong Kong as "rice color" (米色).

Auspicious Elements

The use of vibrant color in paper offerings not only makes them attractive, but conveys auspicious meanings. The power of color is reinforced by the inclusion of auspicious elements, which are never merely decorative, but which signify the hopes of the worshipper. Their good meanings are reinforced due to their place in China's artistic heritage, in which such symbols, motifs, and legends appeared in all artistic productions (Stahlberg and Nesi 1980). Auspicious elements on offerings to the gods are believed to be effective in bringing both specific and general concerns to the attention of these deities, while simultaneously expressing the believers' gratitude and love. Similar sentiments are at work in the offerings for the ancestors, even though these offerings are more oriented towards the concrete conditions of life and signify the blessings and emotions that link ancestor and descendant together. Whether for god or ancestor, all offerings perform in the dual capacities of expressing wishes and gratitude, and auspicious elements enhance their ability to do this.

While the mere appearance of auspicious elements and colors on paper offerings is thought efficacious, the ability of the offering to produce a good result is enhanced by certain crafting practices. In pitched offerings, craftsmen may arrange and rearrange the elements of offerings to increase their good effects. A large number of elements may be grouped together, the sheer numbers resulting in a massing effect that increases benefits. Similarly, multiple appearances of selected elements multiply the effect and underscore the meanings associated with each. This conscious repetition of items allows the crafter to intensify the meaning. In this process, the crafter's action is similar to devices in literature, in which the "steady repetition of key phrases . . . created meanings larger than the words themselves" (Reynolds 1999: 37). Finally, when different items with similar meanings are combined, their individual strengths are amplified.

> Indicative of both Chinese eclecticism and a penchant for combining elements into numerical categories, many artistic symbols were grouped together . . . Plants and animals were often grouped together — the phoenix and the peony, for example, to indicate opulence; the chrysanthemum and the grouse to connote good fortune; the heron and the lotus to symbolize integrity. Larger groupings were common as well. As the Three Friends of Winter, the bamboo, plum, and pine signified enduring friendship as well as the harmony of the Three Teachings . . . The dragon, phoenix, unicorn, and tortoise were grouped together as the Four Spiritual Animals. (Smith 1994: 194)

Flower Cannons and Pinwheels as Auspicious Objects

The efficacy of combinations of auspicious elements can be seen in two quite spectacular items of pitched paper crafting, Pinwheels and Flower Cannons, items in which crafters' creativity is most expressed. Both appear in ceremonies to worship the gods. The Pinwheels are especially prevalent during the Lunar New Year, while the Flower Cannons are most often associated with the deities' birthdays. Both require time and considerable skill to craft, and both are evocative of good luck, through a complex pattern of interwoven representations symbolic of good fortune. In symbolic terms the Flower Cannons are quite complicated, expressing a variety of social and personal goals, including individual worshippers' desires for aid or gratitude for favors, and community expressions of both solidarity and rivalry (Scott 1997b). Despite the great variety of deities to whom they may be dedicated, Flower Cannons are most often associated with Tian Hou. During her festival days, Flower Cannons are carried into the temple grounds by successive lines of worshippers, and make a spectacular centerpiece to the celebrations.

Flower Cannons are adorned with a complicated variety of auspicious, decorative elements. As Osgood (1975: 890) once observed, "its gaudiness would have to be seen in full color for a meaningful reaction." However, the "meaningful reaction" stems not from worshippers' amazement at the Cannon's appearance (to them, it is not gaudy) but from their sincere belief in the Cannons being meaningful creations. In its various layers of construction, from the base to the very top, Flower Cannons bear a number of necessary elements: a pair of dragons, the figures of the Eight Immortals (八仙), the Three Star Gods (三星), a pair of Golden Flowers and their accompanying Spirit Red, and the representation of a bat.

Like the Flower Cannons, the body of the Pinwheel as a whole reinforces its overall good meaning, as the different sections complement one another. Individual details are not merely decorative, but are part of a whole, containing messages of hope, gratitude, and security. Pinwheels are made with a number of pinwheels and auspicious elements affixed to a frame. As the pinwheels revolve in the wind, the individual pinwheels secure and multiply the states of being or the spiritual benefits desired by the worshipper. Those who suffer from bad luck, are dissatisfied with their living conditions, or are concerned about family and personal issues, hope to effect a change in their fortunes, or at least, an easing of difficulty, from the good effects of the Pinwheel. Purchased as a necessary accompaniment to temple worship, the Pinwheel is enriched by its holy setting and proximity to the deity. While still a prominent feature of their original temples (Che Gong Temple in Sha Tin and Wong Tai Sin Temple in north Kowloon), Pinwheels have been available at most Hong Kong temples since the 1950s.

While never described as gaudy, Pinwheels are also brightly colored and greatly admired for their beauty. As they are crafted in a variety of shapes and combinations, it is difficult to assert that any element, other than the individual pinwheels themselves and the red plaques at the top bearing the auspicious meaning, are necessary for their construction. The larger examples commonly bear red flags with the name of the deity, and the very largest hold pairs of Golden Flowers and their Spirit Reds. Both Pinwheels and Flower Cannons are adorned with combinations of the following auspicious elements.

Animals and plants

Animals, both mythical and real, have long been part of the iconography of traditional crafts. A pair of carp often adorns the sides of Pinwheels, or perhaps two pair of carp will be set within its upper and lower sections.

> Owing to its reproductive powers, the fish is a symbol of regeneration, and as it is happy in its own element or sphere, so it has come to be the emblem of harmony and connubial bliss; . . . it is also one of the charms to avert evil, and is included among the auspicious signs on the FOOTPRINTS OF BUDDHA (q.v.) . . . The carp, with its scaly armour, which is regarded as a symbol of martial attributes, is admired because it struggles against the current, and it has therefore become the emblem of perseverance. (Williams 1976: 185; see also Eberhard 1986: 57–58)

In Hong Kong, these fish are also popular representations of abundance and, as expressed in the popular New Year phrase, "having both a head and a tail" (有頭有尾), they also signify that which is never-ending.

Bats, described by pinwheel craftsmen as heavenly rats, fairy rats, or flying rats (天鼠, 仙鼠, 飛鼠), are "emblematic of happiness and longevity" (Williams 1976: 35), and five bats together represent the five blessings of long life, riches, health, love of virtue, and natural death (Eberhard 1986: 32; Medley 1964: 95). Silver metallic paper bat cutouts hand-painted in red and pink are set at the tops or along the sides of the body of pinwheels. The images of bats on Flower Cannons are much more interesting, as these are highly individualistic (a feature also helping to identify their crafters) and many have semi-smiling or quizzical visages of considerable charm. As wide as the cannon itself, they are made of stiffened cloth affixed to a frame, and painted in red, pink, green, and orange, with wide curving wings, and fully molded expressive faces with large eyes and (sometimes furry) ears. Affixed to the top of the cannon, they look straight ahead, fixing the eye of the beholder as they look to the temple. As the bats represent generalized good fortune, they are much sought after during the auctions of Flower Cannons which end the celebrations for the birthday of Tian Hou (Johnson 1971; Watson 1996).

Mythical animals also appear on Pinwheels and Flower Cannons. The dragon is the most recognized of all Chinese symbolic elements, representing not only the land of China and the Chinese people, but divinity and beneficence. Items bearing the images of dragons are considered as auspicious as the dragon itself, and it is one of the necessary elements on any object. Small modern Pinwheels often carry two-dimensional golden images of horses and dragons machine-pressed from gold-toned metal, evoking the popular local phrase "Dragon and Horse Spirit" (龍馬精神). Dragons may also appear in conjunction with the phoenix, the paper cutouts set facing each other along the sides of the larger Pinwheels. The phoenix, which is "only supposed to appear in times of peace and prosperity" (Williams 1976: 325), appears as well on the Flower Cannon. Dragons and phoenix together represent male and female, and for this reason they are ubiquitous decorations at weddings and subjects of items representing the marital state. Unicorns, "a fabulous creature of good omen, and the symbol of longevity, grandeur, felicity, illustrious offspring, and wise administration" (Williams 1976: 414) are put to good use. Lion dogs, representing the lions who guard official buildings and temples (Eberhard 1986: 164) are very finely modeled of cloth on a frame and elegantly painted and trimmed with sequins and other adornments. One fine cannon recorded by the author in 1985 was adorned with a pair of large lion dogs complete with yellow furry bodies, red yarn manes, and large white furry feet with red soles.

Occasionally, elements from living animals are placed on paper offerings. Flower Cannon association members who have had children within the year may attach red-dyed eggs to the cannons to thank the deity for their children; these eggs are eagerly sought by couples who are themselves hoping for children. The Golden Flowers contain, in their medium and large sizes, varying numbers of paired peacock feathers. The peacock is another auspicious bird which symbolizes dignity and beauty, and "drives evil away" (Eberhard 1986: 229; Williams 1976: 317). In the same manner as for the carp, the peacock feathers adorning the Golden Flowers also symbolized "[having both] the beginning and the ending," or completeness, a reassuring theme for the Lunar New Year when the new pairs are purchased.

Both Pinwheels and Flower Cannons hold plant symbolism. The largest Pinwheels may hold trios of plastic tangerines, which are given at the New Year and are wishes for happiness and prosperity (Morgan 1942: 113). A variety of generic flower shapes are employed on both Pinwheels and Flower Cannons, among which are chrysanthemums, flowers denoting a life of ease in retirement (Williams 1976: 70) and joviality (Morgan 1942: 121). If the Flower Cannon is dedicated to Tian Hou, masters suggest using paper peonies because of their association with majesty, although the cannons also bear silk roses (representing the fourth month, Yetts 1941: 4), morning glories, and cloves (which have no special meaning but are popular for their fragrant flowers). Paper masters select most flowers because they are convinced of the flower's good meaning, not because of its adherence to classical distinctions based on season (Williams 1976; Yetts 1941). For example, the rose, while representing the fourth month, has become such a loved flower that it appears on many pitched items, including the Golden Flowers.

Other auspicious elements

In addition to these more commonly appearing elements, both Flower Cannons and Pinwheels may be adorned with other meaningful items allowing some freedom of expression on the part of the master. Such elements on Flower Cannons include models of ships, lanterns, replicas of strings of gold coins, clocks and lanterns; and for the Pinwheels include coins, small swords, or bells. Ship models are understandable since Tian Hou and Tan Gong, the most notable recipients of Flower Cannons, are revered by fishermen, whose lives depend on the kindness of the sea. These models also refer to Buddhist thinking in that they can transport one to a better life after death. Golden coins express a desire for general prosperity. The clocks and candles are desired by Flower Cannon craftsmen, who choose them for their decorative effect, but the lanterns represent fertility (Eberhard 1986: 159), and echo the desires of members of Flower Cannon associations for children in the next year. The Pinwheels' use of gold or silver toned metal bells evokes the dispelling of evil spirits (Williams 1976: 39), while the swords symbolize the "cutting away of all doubts and perplexities" (Williams 1976: 384).

The body of the Golden Flower further reflects this heavenly association — the bodies of the larger examples contain small images of the deities for good fortune. Most often the figures are supposed to be the God of Wealth, an identification supported by the presence of red and white painted foil plaques below the images, on which the characters are brushed. It is no matter that there are always two figures, as the god of riches is "represented sometimes as a single being, sometimes as a dual being, sometimes as a group of deities" (Eberhard 1986: 251). A typical depiction of the God of Wealth has him dressed in bright clothing (red or pink) cut from metallic or fine paper and perhaps trimmed with tiny pompoms, and wearing a hat of crepe paper.

More deities can be represented on larger Golden Flowers. One master crafter explained that forty years earlier, when he began his apprenticeship, large Golden Flowers contained fine images of the Eight Immortals; such elaborate examples are no longer made in Hong Kong. The Eight Immortals represent the different conditions of life (poverty, wealth, aristocracy, plebeianism, age, youth, masculinity, and femininity) (Williams 1976: 151–2). The Eight Immortals are particularly popular, but the Three Stars are also greatly admired. The Three Star Gods are known as the Happiness, Official Rank (or Affluence) and Longevity stars (Burkhardt 1953: 126; Eberhard 1986: 167).

> The San Hsing are often represented by three porcelain statues: the statue carrying one or two infants represents Happiness; the central statue holding an emblem of authority represents Success; and the smiling statue carrying a long staff in his left hand and a peach in his right hand represents Longevity. (Wong 1967: 69)

Also, locally crafted examples once carried images of the Number One Scholar (or *zhuang yuan*, 壯元). While the Number One Scholar could only be one person in real life, craftsmen were nevertheless free to include more than one of these images on their flowers.

One craftsman gave a more poetic explanation for the figures on the Golden Flowers. "There are different numbers of people in the central part of the spirit flower. Two persons together is a symbol which represents the good relations of a married couple. Three persons together represent the three stars in the sky." He meant that two figures represented the gods of He He (和合), and three figures represented the Three Star Gods. Another interpretation of these two figures is that they represent the Immortal Twins of Harmony and Union (He He Er Xian, 和合二仙), both of whom represent wealth and the removal of bureaucratic obstacles; anything bearing their likeness is considered auspicious (Stevens 1997: 125).

The images of the deities are also special features of the Flower Cannon.[2] Respondents were not always clear on why such images are put on the cannon, but all agreed that they were for good luck. Such images do increase the efficacy of the cannon in securing benefits for worshippers, and there is plenty of space on the cannon for such groups of modeled figures. The most important is the wooden image of Tian Hou herself, enshrined in a wooden and glass case set into the cannon in a secure niche built into the body. These images are normally found in the temple, but are taken out on a "tour" during the festival in the body of the cannon, which then acts as a form of temple (Scott 1997b). Sometimes this image is accompanied by the Golden Boy (金童) and the Jade Girl (玉女). The Jade Girl and the Golden Boy are aides to Guan Yin; she carries messages and he guards the incense (Stevens 1997: 53). Cannons may also hold the images of the Eight Immortals and the Three Stars, as well as the spirit guardians of the doors (門神) (Stevens 1997: 177; Burkhardt 1953: 71).

Of all the pitched paper offerings, the Flower Cannons and the Pinwheels permit, and even encourage, the creativity of the imaginative craftsperson. While most Flower Cannon masters include the elements listed above, the most skilled are famed for their interpretations of these elements: for how well they crafted each element, and their ability to combine the various elements into an eye-catching and elegant design. The creative potential for Pinwheels is most obvious in the fully handcrafted examples from the few remaining home workshops, which often contain unusual or specially created design elements. For example, an acclaimed Pinwheel master once created a few large examples containing the figures of the Eight Immortals, each one individually painted with great care on foil paper. He had already designed four other special models, including one trimmed with golden circles representing golden coins, that he termed a Gold Money Pinwheel (金錢車). The same master created a special cut paper "grass tail," representing the scepter, which to him signified the phrase, "All things come to pass in accordance with the heart's desire" (心想事成). Avoiding the original (and to his mind, inauspicious) color of white jade, he painted it a fresh green, a color which to him represented both life and luck. While remaining conservative in his adherence to traditional crafting and treatment, this master was quite innovative and thus typical of the Pinwheel masters, who spent considerable time reflecting on the form, content, and meaning of their creations.

No matter which auspicious elements are included on any pitched paper offering, all are carefully considered and skillfully crafted. Their combinations emphasize both individual and group desires for good luck, long life, protection, prosperity, family security, and the reverence for the deities; all the good things that worshippers seek. The resulting objects are particularly meaningful structures whose imagery can be understood, considered, and appreciated by all — those who make them, those who use them in worship, and those who simply observe them.

Playing with Words, Numbers, and Shapes

Another source of good luck stems from a conscious play on words, which is due to the homologous character of spoken Cantonese, in which one item of similar sound takes on the meaning of another. As Burkhardt observed, "This similarity of sound forms the basis of much of their symbolism in art, and they are quite willing to sacrifice a tone to drag in a decorative object to convey their good wishes for happiness or prosperity" (1953: 111). For example, the pair of carp described above on the Pinwheels are considered good "as the emblems of wealth or abundance, on account of the similarity in the pronunciation of the words yu, fish, and yu, superfluity" (Williams 1976: 185). The character for the bat is a homonym for prosperity, and so the bat has come to symbolize good fortune (Eberhard 1986: 32), a belief underscored by the painting of the character for prosperity on the bat's head (with the meaning of "Vast prosperity all the Days," 鴻福齊天). Further, the red bat is very auspicious, as it is "a harbinger of especially good fortune, not only because red is the colour which wards off demons, but also because the Chinese word for red (hong) sounds the same as the word for 'enormous' " (Eberhard 1986: 32). The value of gold as a color and a material is given expression in the use of items suggesting it; for example, the word for tangerine (found on the Pinwheels) sounds the same as the word for gold. Similarly, the word green is a homonym with the word for good fortune, making green a good color to use.[3]

Pinwheel makers provided numerous explanations of how the numbers of pinwheels on the frame could provide yet other auspicious meanings. For example, a pinwheel frame of eleven pinwheels has three pinwheels at the top, with the meaning of growth or life (生), as the sound of the character for three echoes that of the character for life. The remaining eight pinwheels are set below, as the character for eight sounds like the term "to make a profit" (一本萬利). Other sound or number combinations are equally suggestive. Six pinwheels represent never-ending luck (好運不停), while nine pinwheels evoke the sound of the word that means "a long time" (久), evoking longevity. In fuller form this also refers to the phrase "never-ending luck," or "good fortune" (好運). The number nine, when equally divided into three parts, sounds like the character for life repeated three times.

The shape of an offering also enhances its auspicious nature. Pinwheels may be made in a variety of forms, including star and heart shapes, but most are either circular or in the shape of a bottle gourd. As far as can be determined, the medium and large Pinwheels made in the decade or so after the Second World War were nearly all made in these two basic shapes. The largest varieties currently available are still gourd-shaped, created by binding together a series of two to three circles of increasing size, the smallest at the top, to form the characteristic gourd shape. The bottle gourd has been described by scholars as a miniature replica of heaven and earth (Eberhard 1986: 46), and "the symbol of mystery and necromancy and the emblem of Li Tieh-Kuai, one of the EIGHT IMMORTALS (q.v.) of Taoism, who holds it in his hand while spirals of smoke ascend from it, denoting his power of setting his spirit free from his body" (Williams 1976: 217). Pinwheel masters agree, describing gourds as the fruits carried by the deities and which represent long life as well as protection from evil. As one master explained:

> The shape of the Pinwheel is a gourd. In Chinese tradition, the gourd is very useful as we can eat its flesh and we can use its skin as a vessel for tea. The fishermen even use it as a buoy. It is thus a valuable fruit and is also regarded as auspicious. It is also believed that it can drive away evil influences.

Its ability to dispel evil was noted by earlier observers. "The gourd shell, or a painting of the gourd on wood or paper, or a small wooden gourd, or a paper cut in shape like a perpendicular section of the gourd, or a paper lantern in shape of a gourd, is in frequent use as a charm to dissipate or ward off pernicious influences" (Doolittle 1865b: 315).

While many assert that the gourd is effective against evil, this does not imply that the Pinwheels have any relationship with ghosts, or with protection from them; no respondents mentioned this as a possibility.

Pitched and non-pitched offerings differ in the degree to which their content may be manipulated. Non-pitched printed offerings allow fewer possibilities, for their designs are more traditional and set within a specific context. The texts which they bear are of some antiquity and are perceived as efficacious as written; they cannot, then, be meaningfully altered or edited by subsequent users for fear of destroying their beneficence. The enhancement of these objects depends more on variations in the amount of items used and manner of usage rather than alterations to their surface content. Pitched offerings do not only afford greater possibilities for individual crafting skills and imagination, but also more opportunities for creatively enhancing the meaning and significance of the finished item (albeit set within the trade's and the customers' conceptions of a proper object). Craftsmen can draw upon an extensive traditional repertoire of symbolic elements, manipulations of sounds and characters, and colors, as well as take advantage of emerging popular associations and new ways to combine and recombine aspects of this repertoire.

All this allows for the creation of truly wonderful examples of the art of paper offerings, examples which combine ritual significance with artistic achievement. Further, professional crafting practices of combining, recombining, repetition and massing of elements serve to emphasize and amplify messages. The result is often a magnificent item that is replete with meaning and readable in much the same manner as a text. Scholarly opinion is divided on the readability of artifacts of material culture, with some explaining the risks inherent in too facile assumptions of direct correlations between objects and texts; material culture can be limited in what it can communicate (McCracken 1988). On the other hand, scholars such as Lubar and Kingery have noted, "Too seldom do we read objects as we read books" (1993: viii). It is fair to say that Hong Kong worshippers do indeed read the paper items they use. They can, of course, read the lines of texts that appear on many of the non-pitched items, and perceive their underlying efficacy even if they no longer use such specialized vocabulary or phrasing in everyday life. But in addition, they understand the iconography of the materials and are attuned to the long historical, social, and cultural contexts of color and design element. This sensitivity enables them to go beyond the surfaces of the items, beautiful as these are, to appreciate the meanings therein. Worshippers are able to focus on the messages, the purposes, of worship and can construct, deconstruct, and reconstruct individual items of paper offering. What this suggests is that, as items of material culture, Hong Kong's paper offerings allow considerable scope for expression and convey very complex meanings to the worshipper, while simultaneously allowing the worshipper to construct personal interpretations.

8

Customers and Customs

The actual number of Hong Kong worshippers using paper offerings is difficult to estimate. Results of the June 2003 survey revealed that 26 percent of respondents described their religious belief as, "ancestor worship/Chinese folk belief." Within the sample as a whole (776), 85 percent disagreed with the statement, "I do not believe in burning paper offerings," and respondents burned paper offerings for the following occasions: Qing Ming (56.7 percent), Chong Yang (43.7 percent), Festival of the Hungry Ghosts (39.9 percent), and the Lunar New Year (37.5 percent). Interviews with the owners of retail paper shops, wholesalers and workshops have already underscored the continuance of traditional practices, and observation of actual behaviors provides still more data on the use of paper offerings. On any day, visitors can observe worshippers going about their rituals in any of Hong Kong's temples, well supplied with the papers they wish to offer to the deities. During the Lunar New Year, tens of thousands of worshippers throng the major temples. The combination of survey, interview, and observational data indicates that considerable numbers of people still buy paper offerings and consider them an important part of their daily worship.

The question of who uses paper offerings is complex, because there are no absolutes; the best that can be said is that use is not confined to the elderly, the minimally educated, and the poor. Hong Kong's paper shops serve a regular clientele, providing for both daily worship and the special celebrations highlighting the yearly ritual cycle, with customers drawn mostly from the immediate neighborhood. If the shop is near a temple it will attract a larger number of customers, especially during festivals, and shops near the tourist areas have even reported increasing numbers of foreign visitors. Due to the continuous redevelopment of Hong Kong's pre-Second World War urban districts, there is always some client turnover as residents move in and out of old neighborhoods. Despite this, loyalty to a shop is quite common and old customers who have moved to other districts, even those quite far away, frequently return to the old neighborhood to make their purchases.

Young and Old

Who takes responsibility for domestic worship is still debatable. Do young people understand the offerings and how to use them? When I asked my own students here in Hong Kong to tell me about paper items, many of them said that they did not understand these things, they could not even name them; I was the one who did the explaining. Some colleagues declare that young people just do not care about paper offerings (or any tradition) any more. This evaluation seems to be a perennial theme in writings about Chinese traditional practices. Dard Hunter, the author of the noted study of paper offerings made in China in the 1930s, wrote that: "The youth of China does not accept whole-heartedly the ancient practices of their forefathers and they are not slow in casting aside many of the symbolic ceremonies to which their progenitors were so devoted" (1937: 79). Yet, in the next breath, these same students who professed ignorance of the offerings will assert with pride that paper offerings are part of a unique Chinese tradition. Other surveys conducted in classes indicated that students did recognize many of the most common items and knew in broadest outline how they were used, even if they did not always join their parents in worship. Certainly, during examination periods, Hong Kong's temples, especially the Wong Tai Sin Temple, see many students giving offerings and praying for good results. And, while shopkeepers and customers alike assert that few spend time formally instructing children in the practices of worship, it appears that many parents do explain the basics of worship to their children, while taking them along on visits to paper shops, asking them to assist in domestic worship, taking them to worship in the temples, and to the graves of relatives during Chong Yang and Qing Ming. Participation in these activities, a form of religious socialization which extends over many years, is a form of learning by doing, listening, and observing and is a critical means of recruitment into this world of customary traditional belief and practice.

Such socialization stills exists, despite literature which has suggested a decline in overall belief and a lessening of interest in tradition by Hong Kong's young people. Potter's early study of traditional religion in the New Territories indicated that belief was still strong among elderly women, and "by no means absent among the younger generation" (1969: 21), a situation he attributed to the persistence of the villagers' traditional world view (1969: 22). Myers' later analyses of surveys in the Kwun Tong District in 1975 (Ng 1975; Myers 1981) suggested that participants in domestic worship were primarily older members of the family; for ancestral ceremonies, "only 50% of the children in households where the ancestral rites are practiced join in the ceremonies" (1981: 280), and for the overall adoption of traditional practices, only 24.2 percent of children participated (1981: 282). He concluded:

> As we have seen with respect to ancestral worship and the cult of the deities, family loyalty, regional customs and cultural identity are no longer viewed, especially by the younger generation of Kwun Tong residents, as sufficient cause for pursuing traditional rites. (1981: 287)

This picture is by no means complete or unambiguous. Similar results were obtained in surveys from 1988 and 1995, although the 1988 results recorded a greater percentage of believers in folk religion after age thirty-five (Hui 1991: 105). Such findings imply that young people's belief in folk religion declined between 1988 and 1995, but more recent surveys indicate that percentages of believers in folk religion increase with age, while percentages of respondents declaring no religious belief also declined as the ages of respondents increased (Cheng and Wong 1997: 302). In their studies at the Wong Tai Sin Temple, Lang and Ragvald discovered that the temple always attracted new worshippers, and that young people, who visited the temple for various reasons as teenagers return to worship as they become older, "in the pattern more typical of adult worshippers" (1993: 90). These findings would suggest the more active practice of faith later in life.

The clientele of most paper shops is made up of a wide range of individuals, from teenagers to the elderly. Observations at temples and at retail shops and the responses of most shopkeepers suggest that their regular customers are mainly middle-aged or older, but it cannot be inferred from this that the world of paper offerings is inhabited exclusively by the mature and the elderly, for shopkeepers were adamant that they served a wide range of ages. Shopkeepers and paper offering masters alike rejected any direct correlation between age and the capacity for religious belief in any context, whether in ceremonies for deities or ancestors, or to placate ghosts, explaining that sometimes even young children were very pious. What is more significant is their reasoning that the younger generation would eventually feel the need to believe (for example, in the gods) and seek out the offerings needed. As one master explained:

> The elderly said that the young generation would not worship. Young people, such as those on this estate, are mostly just married with few children. Most of them do not believe, but later on, they nevertheless believe and worship. Why? Once their children have something wrong, or get sick, or they have trouble after moving in, they wonder what to do, why this has happened, and so set an altar to worship the gods and get help.

As well, newlyweds begin domestic offerings, if they have not already acquired the practice, because one of the responsibilities of marriage is the protection of the family through worship. Many young women, now under the watchful eye of a mother-in-law or family elders, become responsible for this daily practice. In the words of a young shop owner:

> Once when there is something happening that she [the young customer] is unable to solve, in her soul she feels very empty and needs some comfort, so she turns to worship for comfort. It [worshipping] is also a matter of home duties, because women get married and are in charge of home worship . . . Personal interest is also a reason, for once women get married they have their children and they hope that their children would be blessed and healthy. If you observe those paper shops in public housing estates, you can find a lot of young married women going to buy paper offerings during festivals. They were young girls just one

year before and at that time they had never touched those paper items; however, when they got married and had children, they would find that only worshipping would help when they had troubles. This is very common.

In these examples, the main factor was not chronological age alone, but the assumption of responsibility, particularly that associated with marriage (Lang and Ragvald 1993). Similar positive correlations between marriage and religious belief were observed in the already mentioned surveys of 1988 (Hui 1991) and 1995, in which more single people (70 percent) than married (59.7 percent) did not believe in any religion (Cheng and Wong 1997: 304). Yet, many shopkeepers insisted that the unmarried could not be discounted. "Many of these also are strong believers, for they follow their parents." A minority of shopkeepers even report pre-teens as serious and sincere worshippers.

Recent observations made at Chong Yang observances for the dead suggested that learning about religious practice is alive and well among the young, with a very large percentage of young families participating, most with children actively assisting, for example, packing Fu Jian Bags for the deceased. Girls and boys as young as six or seven were observed carefully folding the Gold and Silver Paper into the requisite ingot shapes and sorting out the other paper items before packing them in the bags. Young unmarried people become believers in the powers of gods and the efficacy of paper offerings through years of observing their parents' (and neighbors') practices or through experiencing personal misfortune, yet have not assumed formal responsibility for domestic worship. They are not yet customers and do not yet purchase offerings, yet shopkeepers know of their existence through interaction with them when they accompany their parents to the shop, and from their own years of experience in the trade.

Class and Education

It has been asserted that a characteristic of popular religion is its referent to the religion of the lower classes, a perspective which allows for scholarly recognition of social status, the questioning of egalitarian presuppositions, and the understanding that participants in religious activities view these activities differently according to their social position (Teiser 1976: 24–25). While the last aspect (position affecting point of view) is reasonable, in Hong Kong social position is difficult to factor in. Lang and Ragvald's study of worshippers at the Wong Tai Sin Temple concluded that worshippers accounted for the same percentage of lower-income families as found in Hong Kong's population as a whole, and that "lower-income families constitute the majority of the temples' clients." However, during the New Year worship, many businessmen came to the temple to thank Wong Tai Sin for the year's prosperity (1993: 79). The multiplicity of worshipping practices result from many factors including, but not emphasizing, class. The understanding and use of paper offerings and the beliefs surrounding this use are not restricted solely to the uneducated or to the working class any more than to the elderly. Paper offerings and educational level/occupational status do not correlate, and use of such items is not a sign of backwardness. If a number of the educated young (and old) do not themselves use paper offerings on a regular basis, many still come from backgrounds where someone in their family still uses (or did use) paper, and many understand the practice. At the least, explaining the persistence of paper offerings as a form of ignorance ignores the obvious sincerity with which worshippers conduct their beliefs, and implies that the entire complex is a mere superstition that educated people will — or should — discard. The latter idea is an established theme in many of the twentieth-century movements to modernize China, yet paper offerings have survived the innumerable campaigns in Mainland China for their eradication.

Male and Female

In 1890, William Townsend noted Robert Morrison's observation on Chinese women and religion.

> Their nature is much more religious than that of the men. The men trifle with their beliefs; the women are in earnest. They are capable of a practical faith, the men much less so . . . It is they who visit the temples. The incense pots which smoulder before the placid countenance of Buddha are filled and kindled by them. It is they who may be seen prostrating and K'o T'owing before the monstrous images alike of general and local deities. They burn ten sheets of paper to the men's one . . . The men can do without worship, the women cannot. (1890: 266–7)

While a common perception, my respondents consistently rejected suggestions that worship and the use of paper offerings was, in any context public or private, strictly engendered — more precisely, they denied that it was the sole responsibility of women. This does not mean that women do not play a leading role (see, for example, Berkowitz 1975) nor that worship is not colored by gender, but that the nature of masculine and feminine participation is rather more complex. In the *People of Kwun Tong Survey* in 1975 (Ng 1975), of the sample of 818 households, half contained husbands and wives both professing to be active participants in ancestral rites (Myers 1981: 279). However, results of other surveys in 1988 indicated that a larger proportion of males (66.4 percent) than females (49.9 percent) claimed no belief in any religion, with male believers in Chinese traditional religion nearly half the number of female believers (Hui 1991: 104). A similar survey in 1995 produced similar results (Cheng and Wong 1997: 302).

Despite these results, paper professionals interviewed in this study are quite emphatic in their views, which matched more closely the results of the 1975 survey. Not one retail shopkeeper, executive of a paper wholesaling company, or workshop master described the purchase and use of paper offerings in engendered terms. The proportion of male and female customers does vary from shop to shop, but while there are fewer male customers overall, shopkeepers assert that men are as sincere and observant in their worshipping habits as their female counterparts. Furthermore, male customers are equally knowledgeable about paper offerings, but because of their jobs, they are simply too busy to see to the purchases (or the worship, even of ancestors) on a daily basis, a justification earlier recorded in Taiwan for the greater purchasing done by women (Gallin 1966: 148).[1] Many men ask or expect their wives or daughters-in-law to do the purchasing for them. These assessments of their customers also appear to discount a fact that most shopkeepers understand very well — that Hong Kong women have long been part of the workforce and hold regular jobs which would also limit their time to attend to the necessities of worship, including paper purchasing. That leaves the responsibility for this task to older women who are not in the job market.

Observations at retail shops during daytime visits and interviews suggest that the majority of customers are indeed women, middle-aged and older housewives who are unemployed, employed part-time, or working at home on a piecework basis. These women are freer to see to both domestic worship and temple worship during major religious holidays, and to purchase the paper offerings. As well, younger women still come into the shops, despite being heavily occupied with work or school-related responsibilities. Assuming the responsibility for domestic worship and having more free time have also been cited by other local scholars to explain the greater proportion of women worshippers at the temple. Lang and Ragvald listed the greater potential for health problems and women's lack of social power as additional reasons for female worship; worship at the temple offers access to heavenly aid to deal with these issues (1993: 80).

What is most important within my respondents' sometimes contradictory comments is not the precise proportion of male to female customers, nor the rationale of employment or any other factor as determining gender involvement, nor even the "appropriate" contexts (domestic or public) for worship by men and women, but the trade's reluctance to accept any innate, automatic, or gender-based assignment of, or limitations on, the responsibilities for worship and the purchase of offerings. Following this perspective, masculine employment was a secondary rationalization to explain the larger number of women customers. Some support for the shopkeepers' assessment may be obtained during any of the special religious celebrations. A visit to any temple during these times will demonstrate both a good proportion of men to women, and of youngsters and teenagers to the aged, all involved in temple activities, worshipping and making offerings to the deities.

The Knowledgeable Customer

How knowledgeable are customers about the offerings they purchase? Do they fully understand the significance of the items, or are they simply doing what others do without considering symbolic or religious content? The survey of June 2003 indicated that 98.6 percent of respondents asserted that they understood paper offerings, and that further, all the members of their families also understood the objects; such results echo smaller indicative surveys conducted in the early 1990s. Shopkeepers and paper masters' assessments of their customers' understanding reflect a range of customer expertise. Shopkeepers' evaluations indicate that most customers possess a reasonable — and some an excellent — working knowledge of the meaning and use of the everyday offerings they buy. This means that customers were familiar with the offerings for both everyday worship and for particular occasions, and why certain items should be used. Customers also understood what effects, if any, the offerings could be expected to produce, and why they were efficacious.

A similar situation holds for the iconography of paper offerings, the auspicious symbols depicted on them. While not always fully conversant with the fine points of their significance, most customers could identify many of the individual symbols and design elements depicted on the everyday offerings, and could explain the meaning of these symbols. Worshipper recognition and understanding is strengthened because the same symbols and designs appear in many other contexts of everyday life, as decorative elements of architecture, embroidery, painting, wood carving, and painted temple decorations. While their beauty is appreciated in these forms, it has been suggested that their appearance in such contexts began as a way of instructing illiterates in the proper elite values of society such as patriotism, loyalty to the emperor, loyalty to the state, and filial piety (Eberhard 1967b: 31–32).[2] Whatever the original purpose, the understanding of the symbols and designs on paper offerings is enhanced by their persistence in other areas of everyday life.

Due to what Cave referred to as the "very considerable conservatism" in Chinese arts and other manufactures, meanings, especially those represented in religious materials, have tended to remain stable (1998: 20). Also, production was bound by strict conventions. As he explained:

> . . . there was a considerable degree of uniformity in the artistic and iconographic conventions. Many worshippers might be illiterate, and the inclusion of familiar symbols of good fortune was important, as was making the particular demon, saint, or god instantly recognizable. (Cave 1998: 37)

Some shopkeepers agree, explaining that items like the Longevity Gold, White Money, and Gold and Silver Paper look the same as they did in the past,[3] since they have been used "since the beginning of the world."

As numerous Hong Kong-based researchers will attest, a common response to inquiries about the meaning of an activity or an object includes a variation of, "Everyone knows that already."[4] What is being investigated is so much a part of general experience that further reflection is deemed unnecessary. For example, when queried as to why offerings were made to the gods, many worshippers responded with one word, "tradition," or when pressed, "Chinese tradition" or "Chinese culture" or "That is what is right to do." Giving offerings is a deeply held custom of some antiquity, an obvious fact that customers and worshippers understand. In that sense, purchasing and using paper offerings does not require long, complicated explanations; everyone knows that if one is a worshipper, this is what one does. Even customers who are Buddhists, Catholics, or Christians (Protestants) accept this perspective.[5] What is most important is not whether customers' opinions can be proven as true, but that they firmly believe them to be.

Shopkeepers agreed that even knowledgeable customers needed to ask advice from time to time. As special religious festivals occur only once a year, some customers may not remember from year to year just what is needed. As already demonstrated, paper offerings for these festivals can be quite complex. For example, a packed assemblage such as those for the Festival of the Hungry Ghosts may contain up to twenty items, each with its own iconography and symbolic content. Customers may not understand the meanings, often complicated, of each of these items, or the significance of the printed symbols or designs, or the names of the individual components, or why each item is necessary for that assemblage. Further, they may not know which paper combinations are suitable for more rarely occurring rituals and events which require more specialized paper, such as moving to new homes. While sickness was not uncommon, it appeared to be another problem for which the specific paper combinations were difficult to remember, especially if one's own elderly relatives were not nearby to assist. There are solutions for all these uncertainties: customers could have the shopkeeper pack the materials, buy a pre-packed assemblage, or consult the *Tung Sing* when they did not know.

Despite all these alternatives, some customers simply cannot remember the finer points of paper offerings, no matter how often the shopkeeper provides suggestions or solutions. One respondent declared, with some exasperation:

> They ask about many occasions. Even if they ask this time they will ask next time. They don't remember because it is too complicated. It is not strange that tomorrow they would ask you again even if they have asked you today. Tomorrow, they'll forget about what they have asked you today!

The Flexibility of Belief

Belief is flexible and changeable. As Cammann observed, "in any study of Chinese symbols, the context is all-important" and "symbols, like words, can become obsolete or change their meaning with time" (1968: 787). The question of customer knowledge ability becomes more complex when it is set against the considerable variations in belief and practice. Worshippers need not agree on all the most common uses of an item, on the details of its individual history, or on the meaning of each and every detail of its iconography. Differences arise from the intricacies of the paper itself, the worshipper's ethnic background, and his or her personal belief and family practices. This uncertainty allows for alternate explanations, as people fill in the gaps with what they think is correct.[6]

More significant complicating factors are regionalism and ethnic differences within China. The way worshippers use different items of paper does not necessarily reflect confusion or ignorance, but may be the result of "different regions and language groups . . . so there were gods [and varieties of ceremonial papers] which were common with one language group and rare with another" (Cave 1998: 37). What Cave meant was that there were variations, even in the printed text, according to the worshipper's home place. Such was the experience of many shopkeepers.

> The worship of gods and ancestors is so widespread that everywhere [in China] has its own way of worship. People cling to the way of their origins. You cannot argue with these customers, but just give them what they ask for, for they have been worshipping in their own way for years and will not believe what you say. For example, people from Dongguan (東莞) use white paper money to worship gods, but in Hong Kong, this is not generally done.

Shopkeepers and paper masters said they were expected to recognize the numerous variations based on regional or ethnic differences, in order to serve their customers and stock the shop. For example, the Chaozhou craft particularly large, elaborate and elegant items for their worship, especially during the New Year.[7] As they are a notable section of Hong Kong's population (see, for example, Sparks 1976a; Myers 1981), some shops sell only Chaozhou items. Similarly, Hong Kong's fishermen (水上人) make use of a complicated repertoire of paper offerings specific to them alone (a sample of these will be taken up in Chapter 9); these, too, are usually sold in shops, mostly on Hong Kong Island, which cater heavily to their needs. The specific paper offerings characterizing other Hong Kong residents such as those of Shanghai (上海), Hakka (客家), and Dongguan (東莞) origin are much more difficult to understand and to find, although a fair number of shops carry a few items of Shanghai origin, notably the Shanghai silver money for the gods. No exclusively Dongguan or Hakka paper shops exist, and the items distinctive of these groups are rare and little understood by most shopkeepers. Despite customer and professional assertions that the complex of paper offerings is something that everyone knows about, a more accurate depiction would be that everyone knows about the practices in their place of origin. While the concept of giving offerings is widespread if one is a believer, both content and behavior are heavily influenced by where the worshipper learned to worship.

Ethnicity or place of origin is not the final consideration; there is a wide range of what can only be described as purely familial or individual variations in both knowledge and practice. Individual worshippers, shopkeepers, and paper masters all present their own versions of how to worship, explaining their personal idiosyncrasies by saying, "Ten fingers are not the same length" (十隻手指沒有一樣長), a Chinese idiom meaning that people are not all the same. Differences in worship come about from variations introduced within the family, from parents to children to grandchildren. Over time, even individual families can develop distinctive patterns of worship.

The most commonly used items for gods and ancestors provide good examples of variations at the individual level. Most customers know the variety and amount of paper offerings needed for the gods, whether to request their assistance, express gratitude for favors received, or celebrate the deities' birthdays. Nearly all will offer Longevity Gold and the elaborate paper clothing. Likewise, most customers automatically purchase the Gold and Silver Paper and the clothing packages for the ancestors. Yet even in examples such as these, about which there is considerable agreement, individual worshippers vary their practices. Some devout customers increase their offerings, perhaps giving a larger-than-usual amount of Longevity Gold to the deity, or of Gold and Silver Paper and Money to Live to the ancestors. Those convinced of suffering from ghostly-generated illnesses will also burn much more than is strictly necessary, for psychological comfort. What is strictly necessary is defined in a very personal way.

Substituting one item for another is also a recognized practice.

The believer decides what kind of clothing will be given; some offer to the gods various kinds of clothing and personal items, such as gold paper jewelry and watches, that others feel are only suitable for the ancestors (Scott 1997b). Some offer Longevity Gold to the ancestors when shopkeepers generally agree that it is for the gods. Still other purchasers vary the appropriate colors of clothing (giving blue or green clothing instead of red) or offer to one deity the items usually associated with another, while others create a one-of-a-kind object which they feel is important to offer, perhaps because they envisioned it in a dream. Similarly, there is nothing to stop the devout worshipper who pities the ghosts from offering them large amounts of what would usually be ancestors' clothing. Recently available packages of offerings for the Festival of the Hungry Ghosts, the Clothing Burned at the Street (燒街衣), suggest that certain shops are now following the worshippers' leads in rethinking their complexity and content. Such personal practices should not be interpreted as carelessness, the results of the fast-paced lifestyles of a modern metropolis, or by a lessening of devotion. On the contrary, they imply great care and concern for the recipients of the offerings. Shopkeepers will point out the idiosyncrasies of their customers, but while a few may disapprove of these personal variations, the trade neither demands nor expects total agreement on any one pattern of worship. Tolerance and flexibility are fundamental features of the trade itself, stemming from its development and working philosophy as well as from the ideology of worship.

9

Life in Paper

Everything has changed and yet nothing has changed. Even new houses have ancestral altars and a Stove God as well as a television set, and I have seen fire-walking performed on a baseball diamond. The reader will have to exercise some historical imagination to understand the conditions that gave rise to the beliefs I discuss, but he must not forget that these beliefs endure and will influence the future. (Wolf 1974: 133)

While Arthur Wolf's comments described the modernizing Taiwan of the 1970s, they are appropriate for Hong Kong, especially his recognition that beliefs endure. How has this customary practice, the crafting and use of paper offerings, proven so enduring and successful? The settings and context for the items and the meanings they have for worshippers and professionals are part of the answer. First among these are the political attitudes towards religious belief and practice and the flexibility of the trade.

Political Attitudes

An important factor is the attitudes of national and local government, as such attitudes may constitute serious impediments to the continuance of customary practices. Since the Chinese Revolution of 1911, both reformers and officials of successive governments have taken a dim view of what they termed superstition and backwardness among the population. Accordingly, official actions towards behaviors and practices so characterized have ranged from ridicule to determined persecution. Clarence Day reported with some concern in the Shanghai Times on November 1, 1928, that:

> The selling and burning of incense, candles, and paper money for idol worship and for the dead will be strictly prohibited in Kwangsi province beginning from January 1, 1929, according to a decision reached at a recent meeting of the Kwangsi provincial government. (cited in Day 1929: 11)

While not fully convinced that "ancient religious practices of the people" would easily disappear, Day was nevertheless moved to note this disturbing report (1929: 11). A similar conclusion was drawn in a more recent study concerning the contest between worshippers and the Republican government over the conduct of the Festival of the Hungry Ghosts and the Double Seven Festival in Guangzhou in the late 1920s (Poon 2004).

The government of the People's Republic of China was no more supportive of traditional belief and its associated practices than was its predecessor. The tensions between the old and new belief systems were rooted in many contradictions, among them the emphasis in the old system on otherworldly beings and their effects on everyday life and the rationalistic alternative advanced by the socialist government. Traditional religious rituals were also wasteful of the financial and human resources needed for national reconstruction (Whyte and Parish 1984: 302–4). The state remained at best ambivalent, and often ruthless, about traditional festivals, traditional practices, institutions, temples and churches, all of which suffered severely under such successive campaigns, culminating in the Great Proletarian Cultural Revolution of 1966–7 and its intent to destroy the "four olds" — old thought, old customs, old culture, and old morals (see, for example, Chan, Madsen and Unger 1984; Liu 2003; Spence 1990).

The situation began to change under the Reform Period initiated by Deng Xiaoping in 1978, and under the new constitution of 1982, which affirmed the official policy of respect for and protection of the freedom of religious belief. But while it recognized the five protected religions — Buddhism, Daoism, Islam, and Protestant and Catholic Christianity — the same constitution also affirmed that sects were to be suppressed (MacInnis 1989). Superstition (popular religion) was to be kept distinct from real religion and discouraged, although domestic worship was tolerated (Feuchtwang and Wang 1991: 262–3), despite its inclusion of "the popular gods of heaven, earth, the underworld, the ancestral cult, the gods of the house doorpost, the kitchen stove, and so forth. In other words, what is well known to be the basic traditional religious system of the Chinese people . . ." (Cohen 1991: 129). Scholarly opinions on the survival of popular religious rituals and beliefs vary, with some believing that religious practices have seriously altered or have been destroyed after nearly fifty years of socialist pressure (Siu 1989), while others feel that the opportunities presented by economic liberalization have assisted religious revival (Feuchtwang 1986). Urban populations appear to have been most affected, with traditional funeral ceremonies, including the burning of paper offerings, severely curtailed (Watson 1991; Whyte 1988). As late as 1996, well into the second decade of the Reform Period, articles in Hong Kong newspapers were reporting bans on "superstitious" practices such as "the manufacture, sale and burning of funeral objects" (*South China Morning Post*, December 10, 1996). Yet, controls have been progressively eased on selected public manifestations of traditional belief and religious materials such as paper offerings are again available (Ikels 1996: 250, Liu 2003). Answers to the questions of what to do about traditional religion and its practices, and of how to handle an assumed antagonism between tradition and modernity, are still being formed, despite the greater flexibility of the Reform Period.

In Hong Kong, the situation has been different. In 1983, Barbara Ward explained the persistence of tradition and traditional practices in Hong Kong's New Territories by noting:

> An interesting paper could be written about the paradox that the preservation of the traditional has been a direct result of colonialism . . . Suffice it to say here that, contrary to popular opinion to-day, it was not usually the intention of the British colonial administrators (District Officers and the like) to impose alien ways and force change but to leave well alone (as long as in their eyes it was well) and interfere as little as possible. (Ward 1983: 121)

The origin of this long-standing policy was the February 2, 1841, proclamation by Captain Charles Elliot, the Superintendent of Trade, to the effect that "the natives of the Island of Hong Kong and all natives of China thereto resorting, shall be governed according to the laws and customs of China, every description of torture excepted" (Endacott 1964: 28). A second proclamation issued shortly thereafter reconfirmed the Chinese rights of "free exercise of their religious rites, ceremonies, and social customs" (Endacott and Hinton 1962: 54). There was little pressure to force the Chinese inhabitants to follow British custom as "there was general agreement that they should be allowed to enjoy their own customs, laws and general way of life undisturbed", an agreement which was further supported in instructions given to Sir Henry Pottinger in June of 1843, stating that the Chinese were to be subject to their own law (Endacott 1964: 29, 32).

Such proclamations set the stage for a governmental policy of religious tolerance, although as the performance of religious festivals also united and strengthened local communities, the Hong Kong government began to take greater interest in supervising such activities, resulting in the Chinese Temple Ordinance of 1928. While the aim of the Ordinance was to limit abuse of worshippers and the misuse of religious functions and funds, another suggested aim was the government's desire to intervene in religious faith and practice (Kani 1982: 160). Except for the requirement for permits for temporary structures, the 1960s proscription of the "bomb snatching" (scrambling for lucky coins fired from the Flower Cannons) at the Tian Hou festivals, and the recent restrictions on the burning of paper offerings due to fire or environmental concerns, Hong Kong residents have been free to worship, at home and in public, as they wish, and the production, sale, and use of supporting items of material culture such as paper offerings have not been affected, although original forms of religious activities have modified in a colonial context (Liu 2003: 376). There is little concern that "participating in something Chinese" (Cohen 1991: 125) through the practices of traditional worship has been seriously damaged by the Hong Kong government, which has not imposed restrictions or assumed a lack of compatibility between customary practices and modern life.

Flexibility in Trade and Practice

Another possible impediment to survival would be the practices and attitudes of the trade in question: Can it adapt to changing circumstances? The paper offering trade exhibits a high level of flexibility that has contributed to its survival as an industry; its apprenticeship practices are quite unlike those of other Chinese trades, and indeed unlike those apprenticeship systems described for traditional trades elsewhere (Coy 1989). Much of this flexibility stems from the training of young professionals, which is not as rigid nor as formalized as has been reported for other classical trades (a characteristic of which the trade is conscious). Masters emphasize a hands-on approach which allows the learner to learn by watching and then doing, both for the pitched (modeled) and non-pitched (soft) offerings. Masters do not hover over the young workers, as independence and self-reliance are crucial skills for a professional paper crafter. Elderly paper masters explained how, when they were young workers, their relationships with their masters, while hierarchical and not totally free of hardship, were not marked by the extreme misery one so often encounters when examining forms of traditional apprenticeship in China or elsewhere in the world. Young workers were not treated as equals, but neither were they treated like slaves, constantly beaten or otherwise mistreated. They could obtain help from masters who were not as obsessed with the protection of trade secrets as were the masters of other traditional industries. It was even possible for them to study under many paper masters as they were not bound forever to one.

Young learners are expected to actively learn new techniques and to examine new things, to gain inspiration for their own crafting. Within the funeral offering section they are not trained to merely reproduce classical elements of the basic set (although this is deemed a vital component of their training) but to be aware of new technology and changes in the society at large. Constant learning and self-improvement are necessary because even the most learned of paper masters cannot provide training for all aspects of the trade. If the young workers cannot develop the capacity for creativity, for paying attention to technological changes, or for going out and learning on their own, they will never be successful or become true masters. The paper offering industry, while one of the most traditional, has in fact proven itself highly capable of responding to changing times, while simultaneously providing items of classical significance and meaning to its customers.

A second area of flexibility concerns shop practices. Hong Kong's retail offering trade, if never subjected to official pressures as agents of superstition, does face the problem of finding enough space to work in land-deficient Hong Kong. The situation for wholesalers and for the workshops is often difficult, for the larger spaces these businesses require to craft and then to store the bulky pitched items are increasingly difficult to acquire. The lucky few owning their own premises have solved the problem, even if they may be squeezed for space during busy seasons, but renters face serious difficulties. Some craftspeople move further away from urban areas, but moving does not automatically guarantee relief from high rent, and also adds to transport and commuting time. Retail shops are not immune to real estate pressures either. Many of those located in the older, pre-Second World War neighborhoods of Kowloon and Hong Kong Island have had to move out due to redevelopment; increased rents in the newly rebuilt high-rises and modernized shopping centers built on the sites of their old shops are too much to pay. Even if they do not need to move, shopkeepers may discover that their old clientele have been scattered into new housing elsewhere. While many of these old customers will return to the shop to make their purchases, adjusting to a new set of customers adds more work for elderly proprietors.

Despite such property-based difficulties, the state of the industry today is basically healthy. The funeral offerings component is expanding rather than contracting, while the everyday offerings are stable. Retailers have adopted various strategies to retain and attract customers. One strategy already mentioned is the pre-assembled packages of paper offerings, the most common examples being the offerings for the gods. Such offering packages, which have been available for over twenty years, are now a staple of the paper offering business. Nearly all the Hong Kong retail or wholesale paper shops offer these packages, and they may even be purchased at a local supermarket chain as part of other necessary supplies of everyday life. Their simplicity makes easier the choosing of offerings, making them more accessible and convenient for all customers; this is especially true for the novice worshipper, but convenience is important to all Hong Kong consumers. The point is that the trade is well able to devise practical adaptations to changes in worship styles.

Retail shops have developed still other strategies for coping with possible fluctuations in the business. A number are still family-owned and operated, which means that expenses can be reduced through the unpaid labor of family members. Another strategy is the diversification of stock, in order to provide a more complete service. The traditional pattern of retailing in Hong Kong used to be considerable specialization among shops, even among those selling religious items. There are still old shops specializing in the manufacture and/or selling of incense sticks and items carved from sandalwood, or selling brass worshipping accoutrements such as temple hangings, incense burners and lotus lamps. The painted porcelain or wooden images of deities, or their likenesses painted on wooden or glass boards, are sold in special shops along with the red and gold painted wooden domestic altars. Within the last thirty years or so, however, retail paper shops have begun to sell more of these items, especially the vessels for the altars. Diversification of stock may also include stocking ordinary stationery, writing paper, school notebooks and the like, selections of toys and games, napkins, wrapping paper, and Hong Kong's beloved red, white and blue striped plastic carry-alls. During the Mid-Autumn Festival, even very traditional paper shops sell a wide variety of lanterns, from the classical rabbits, melons and lotus roots pitched on bamboo frames covered with crepe paper, to animals in cellophane, to the latest plastic versions of Japanese cartoon characters.

The trade is further enhanced by its acceptance of the different offering practices of its customers. Hong Kong respondents' explanations and behaviors emphasize both the general understandings and the great variability of beliefs and practices. There is general agreement on the need to give paper offerings and on the occasions on which these offerings are used, and worshippers understand the most common everyday items. In short, they agree on the basic whats, wheres, and whens. Respondents also participate in the religious events of the lunar calendar, and accept the three great categories of supernaturals — gods, ghosts, and ancestors — although the content of these categories may vary. Yet, there is great variation in idea and practice as well, arising from regional or ethnic differences, as well as family practices and individual taste.[1] As shopkeepers explained, each province and region, and sometimes each county and village, had its own version of what to use and how to use it. In its recognition of individual variation, the paper offerings trade has proven flexible and adaptable to modern conditions, a circumstance which has at least lessened many economic impediments to conducting a successful and enduring business.

Traditions and Identities

A key to the question of why such practices continue is to be found in the meanings that worshippers find in the items and in the practices of worship. One area to consider is the possible contribution of traditional practice to the discourse on modern Hong Kong Chinese identity, including such ethnic variations as remain. Two facets of this discourse are of concern here. First are the debates over Westernization and Chinese tradition. Discussions of Hong Kong's modern identity feature the recurring themes of "westernization" and the "interplay of east and west" (Baker 1983; Evans and Tam 1997), and of "internationalization" and the world system (Johnson 1997: 135). In these discussions, the role of traditional culture is at best ambiguous. Part of the difficulty is defining the content of "traditional Chinese culture," a difficulty scholars have recognized: "there might always be a risk that what is considered traditional in this discourse might turn out largely to be a straw-man" lacking "systematic empirical data of the traditional values of the common Chinese people in the past" (Lau and Kuan 1988: 3). Evans and Tam have asked, ". . . is the substitution of an ideal, fantasy past [for the real values of the Chinese past] an adequate substitute? And why is it needed for an analysis of contemporary Hong Kong culture?" (1997: 9).

Other scholars have taken the position that in the late Imperial period, literati and peasants shared a "vision of the acceptable way of life . . . based on shared oral tradition and the central role of ritual" (Watson 1991: 369). They lived in a society in which classical opera, elementary education, and the correct performance of the public rituals of the life cycle were critical to understanding this question of the Chinese traditional cultural identity (Watson 1991: 369–71; see also Johnson 1987; Rawski 1979; Ward 1985a). The result was a unified, shared culture and, further, that "the vast majority of Chinese, irrespective of class background, life experience, or education, shared this vision of the acceptable way of life during the late imperial era" (Watson 1991: 368). Cohen has addressed this issue in a similar fashion, arguing that in late traditional China, there was "a common culture in the sense of shared behavior, institutions, and beliefs . . . it was also a unified culture in that it provided standards according to which people identified themselves as Chinese" (Cohen 1991: 114). Traditional culture was critical to this process of identification, in that "it linked being Chinese to a firm consciousness of participating in a nationwide system of political, social, religious, and symbolic relationships" (Cohen 1991: 123), which conferred a sense of "what being Chinese was all about" (Cohen 1991: 125).

Giving offerings to the ancestors, the gods, and the ghosts as part of ritual has continued to be one means of participating in something Chinese, because certain traditional values remain a vital part of Hong Kong life. As Wong Siu-lun observed in 1986, "The Hong Kong Chinese may be described as Westernized only in a superficial sense . . . a substantial number of them still adhere to traditional Chinese mores on various aspects of social living" (1986: 307). If people construct their own cultures and cultural identities, they do so with what Evans and Tam have termed "culturally identifiable parameters" whose importance and interpretation they need not fully agree upon but which function as cultural symbols or reference points that are accepted as important (1997: 12). Two of these reference points are the Confucian concept of filial piety and the practice of giving offerings.

Social surveys conducted in Hong Kong in 1985 and 1986 by Lau Siu-kai and Kuan Hsin-chi found that a high percentage (87.6 percent in 1985) of the population either strongly agreed or agreed that a good society required the practice of filial piety; care of parents being particularly important (Lau and Kuan 1988: 59). Further surveys conducted in 1990 found that a majority of respondents (56.1 percent) agreed that children must support their parents (Lee 1992: 22). As care of ancestors is quite a visible extension of the care of parents (albeit in the next world), the incidence of burning offerings would be further support of filial piety. Data from the survey of June 2003 indicated that 56.7 percent of all respondents burned offerings to their ancestors at Qing Ming, and a further 43.7 percent did so at Chong Yang. The importance of filial piety in modern Hong Kong's social life is underscored by paper. The second point of reference, the need to give offerings in worship, has been amply discussed in previous chapters. Shopkeepers will explain that they have customers who are Buddhists or Christians, but who still purchase paper offerings for ancestors. Worshippers are convinced that burning paper offerings is a practice of great antiquity which needs no explanation, for it is so much a part of everyday life.

Ethnic variations

The ethnic identification of Han Chinese, and how to conceptualize it, is a second facet in which to explore how tradition intersects with identity. Here, paper offerings, when set within ritual practices, provide a little explored but fascinating glimpse into such patterns of ethnic distinctiveness as still exist. Studies of general ethnicity in Hong Kong (Anderson 1967, 1970; Guldin 1977, 1982, 1997; Sparks 1976a, 1976b; Ward 1965) have explored different Chinese ethnic identities as they exist now and in the recent past; a smaller group of these (Anderson 1967, 1970; Choi 1995; Ward 1965) consider the function of ritual in ethnic identification. While classic means of ethnic identification such as language/dialect or occupation/economic factors (Baker 1983) have altered or faded over time, particular rituals and worshipping practices remain, as evidenced in the Festival of the Hungry Ghosts sponsored by the Chaozhou community, the Jiao Festival in Cheung Chau Island (Choi 1995), or the unique rituals and deities of the fishermen (Anderson 1970). Paper offerings are one remaining material embodiment of ethnic identification, for Hong Kong Chinese worshippers of different ethnic backgrounds burn different kinds of paper offerings, or add or substitute their own distinctive materials to the everyday items (Gold and Silver Paper, Longevity Gold, Honorable People Papers, White Money, and so on) used by other Cantonese. Of all the variations within the complement of paper offerings used in Hong Kong, the most notably distinctive papers are those of the Chaozhou, for which the manufacture of selected items has already been described in Chapter 6 (and listed in note 7 of Chapter 8), and which will not be repeated here. A second very distinctive complement of offerings is still used by the Hong Kong fishermen.

The paper offerings of the Hong Kong fishermen,[2] a group of Han Chinese once set apart from other Chinese (Anderson 1967, 1988; Ch'u 1961; Ward 1965), are related to making good catches and being protected while at sea. Fishermen's religious beliefs and practices have been set out by Anderson (1970), but it remains to fully connect these beliefs and rituals to the offerings that accompany them. Fishermen employ numerous paper items to beseech the deities for protection. Shops specializing in these offerings sell small models of different boats (to be offered to the deities) complete with sails and in auspicious colors such red and green. Two of these are the Flower Boat (花艇), decorated with flowers, and the Big Boat (大船), which is actually a small replica of a fishing boat. Whenever the fishing boats set sail, one Big Boat is sent out to sea to bless the fleet and ensure safety. These boats are either burned or set afloat on the waters, depending on the ceremony. Big Boats are also burned each time a fishing boat is repaired. Fishermen also use a special form of gate passing paper, called the Boat Tablet (船牌) or the

Boat Close (船關), to protect the boat from harm. A variety of symbolic fish traps, such as the Water Gate (水閘) and the Fish Gate (魚門) are burned to ensure good catches. The Fish Gate is burned to ask the gods to open the door of the sea so that the fish can be caught as they leave. At the Lunar New Year, a special set of papers including a Water Duck (水鴨) and a Water Ladder (水梯) is burned to ensure that children who fall into the sea will not drown but only float (like a duck).

Still other items ensure the protection of the gods. Clothing for the Boat Head (船頭衣, the Boat Head being a popular deity), and Small Water Clothing (水衣仔) are burned before sailing, and the deities most revered by the fishermen, Tian Hou and Hung Shing Kung, receive special gifts neatly packed in paper chests before burning. The deities also receive the Flower to Thank God (還神花), taken to the temple or affixed to the head of the boat at the Lunar New Year to thank the deities for their assistance during the year. Items for the ancestors include the Flower Boat (花艇) decorated with paper flowers and containing a paper servant (some shopkeepers say this boat is also for the gods) and small chests for paper clothing, painted in black rather than red. Fishermen also use the Longevity Gold, Gold and Silver Paper, Honorable People Papers and the Five Treasures Documents burned by land-dwelling Cantonese. While there is some mixture of items from both repertoires, fishermen's paper offerings remain perhaps the last true marker of distinctiveness for this group of Hong Kong citizens.

The Practices of Chinese Religion

The question of the endurance of paper offerings has led to a consideration of political realities, trade flexibility, and modern identity, the areas in the background of this customary practice. Returning to the key question of how the crafting and use of paper offering have endured involves reviewing the everyday practices of ordinary people and their attitudes towards religious practice. Taken another way, it could also be approached by investigating how ordinary Hong Kong worshippers imagine the spiritual world they are encountering. If religious practices allow a glimpse into how worshippers understand their world, then it can also allow glimpses into how they view worlds other than this one. What is the form and substance of these other worlds? A classic depiction of the heavenly pantheon and the world of Chinese deities may be found in Arthur Wolf's classical study of 1974. Wolf's insight was that of a supernatural bureaucracy, one in which each deity had a place in the hierarchy comparable to its imperial counterpart on earth. "In sum, what we see in looking at the Chinese supernatural through the eyes of the peasant is a detailed image of Chinese officialdom," one so potent that it was able to create "a religion in its own image" (Wolf 1978: 145). This depiction of the supernatural world was made more concrete by popular images of the deities, which portrayed many of them in the clothing of officials and bureaucrats (see, for example, the carved images of the gods reproduced in Stevens 1997).

The bureaucratic metaphor received further support from vivid artistic depictions of the underworld and its courts of Hell, at which souls are judged and punished (Clarke 1898; Eberhard 1967a; Pas 1989). These depictions of Hell, whether in the form of eighteen (or sixteen) or eight (or ten) courts, were closely associated with their counterparts on earth, the yamens in which those accused of crimes were brought before the magistrate for assessment of their guilt or innocence. Each yamen was presided over by its own judge and was empowered to carry out its own forms of punishment. Popular prints and paintings were quite detailed in depicting the physical layout of each of these courts, including the dress and accoutrements of the judge and his assistants, and of course, the gruesome nature of the punishments and tortures to be meted out to the guilty. Such striking depictions were for the instruction of the living worshipper and their concreteness enabled the viewer to imagine what this component of the next world was like.

The vivid detail characterizing the depictions of the courts of Hell and the punishments therein, leads to considerations of another aspect of Hell, namely the actual living conditions of the deceased ancestors. Herein is seen another reason why paper offerings have endured. The careful and detailed depictions of ancestral worship recorded for other Chinese societies (see, for example, Ahern 1973; Gallin 1966; Watson 1988a) demonstrate the care that relatives of the deceased take to ensure their comfort, reflecting their belief that "ancestral spirits live in the other world much as they did in this one, they must be fed, cared for" (Gallin 1966: 233–4). Popular belief in Hong Kong also accepts this perception of the next world — a place that the living can imagine — further emphasizing the continuity worshippers feel exists between this world and the next. But how is this actually accomplished? How can a world just like this one be made real? If life in Hell is a reflection of life on earth, then these paper offerings endure to serve another purpose, which is to create in a very vivid and concrete manner the other world in which the ancestors now reside. The offerings, concrete replicas of everyday familiar objects, ensure that the next world is both comfortable and familiar to the dead; these items of material culture serve to recreate in a very concrete fashion the context of an ordinary, everyday life. As was explained by respondents, the ancestors really will wear the clothes, drive the cars, use the appliances, and spend the money provided for them, and will contact their descendants to tell them about their new lives. Respondents truly believe that this will happen, and that this other world exists. Further, in arranging for the purchase and burning of the objects, families can themselves visualize the world of the ancestors. Paper offerings are a means for both parties to craft this other world, and even further, to help manipulate it; the yellow Money to Live, it should be remembered, is burned to help the ancestor shorten the time until rebirth.

In such exchanges, the ideology of filial piety assumes a genuine concrete form, as ancestors are provided for, and Hell is made less of a terrible place, through offerings. This other world is actively created, as Hong Kong worshippers are anything but passive in their worship and in their determination to mold the world beyond this one. Worshippers are eager to provide not only sufficient amounts and varieties of materials, but the latest in technology, so that the world as it was known by the deceased is faithfully reproduced, maintained and kept up to date. It is in this context in which the great power of material objects to objectify, to create, entire worlds is best understood.

Parallel Lines

The many themes explored in the previous chapters about the world of paper offerings include the great variability of both opinion and practice among worshippers, the flexibility of thought and practice within the trade, and the adaptability (especially seen in the funeral offerings section) of the industry. In addition, it is clear that worshippers are not passive onlookers but active participants in all the rituals they perform, whether creating and recreating a world for the ancestors, attempting to enhance their own life chances, or thanking the deities. Other themes, appearing in various chapters, include the power of filial piety and the rightness and importance of giving paper offerings in worship. Burning paper offerings to thank or to beseech the deities, to appease or aid the lonely ghosts, and to care for the ancestors is something that the majority of worshippers feel is the right and necessary thing to do (Scott 1997a). One last issue is linked to the initial question on the endurance of the practice, and concerns what motivations lie behind all this activity, this rightness and appropriateness. Why give gifts to the gods, why assist the wandering spirits, and why, other than the demands of filial piety, work so hard to create a real life for one's deceased family members? Is there anything else that people are hoping to achieve and how do paper offerings help them achieve it?

Offerings for the ancestors

Burning paper offerings to the ancestors satisfies the requirements for the sacrifices which are, and were, a significant way to maintain the ongoing relationships between ancestors and descendants (Ebrey 1991). In his edited volume on death ritual, Watson has observed, "A central feature of Chinese funerals and postburial mortuary practices is the transfer of food, money, and goods to the deceased . . . In return the living expect to receive certain material benefits, including luck, wealth, and progeny" (1988a: 9). Both classical (De Groot 1892–1910; Doolittle 1865a; Williams 1976) and contemporary writings on Chinese funeral custom (for Hong Kong, see Hase 1984; Waters 1991) describe how ancestors are provided for in death. Individuals who were loved and provided for in life are also provided for when they leave this world, and reciprocal relationships maintained. A common perspective is that the condition of ancestors directly affects the fortunes of their living descendents, for burning funeral goods allows the givers to claim the deceased's property (Johnson 1910; Ahern 1973), or allows the deceased to become a "property-owning spirit, as a person without property cannot conceivably become an ancestor" (Tong 1993: 145). Descendants also benefit materially, a theme appearing in studies of Singaporean funerals, where mourners, at least privately, understand the benefits:

> I suggest that what is important is not simply the inheritance of the property of the deceased, but also the potential for greater benefits that motivate the descendants to spend so much money. It is believed that by converting the deceased into a rich ancestor, the now well-off ancestor will see fit, and is in fact expected, to return the favour and reward descendants with even more wealth. (Tong 1993: 153)

If this most persuasive and instrumental line of reasoning be true for Hong Kong, then it would add an explanation for the great variety of paper items available, the seemingly endless array of goods that can be offered to the ancestors (and also to the gods and even to the ghosts). In simple terms, it would be an echo of what has been termed the "hardnosed view of the Chinese ancestral cult" (Watson and Watson 2004: 444), a form of reciprocity in which one gives to receive something in return. Such reasoning would also harmonize with the often-quoted characterization of Hong Kong people as extremely materialistic and driven by consumerism (Chan 1994; Chaney 1971; Hayes 1975; Mitchell 1969). Lau Siu-kai devised the term "the fetishism of material wealth" (1982: 69) to explain this phenomenon (see also Lee, Cheung and Cheung 1979), born of the social conditions — the lack of moral constraints and absence of other channels for self-advancement — facing the original immigrants to Hong Kong. This combination of spiritual conspicuous consumption and an emphasis on egocentric gain should be sufficient to explain all this burning and point to the real meaning behind offerings.

Yet, the living cannot make any use of the offerings, cannot obtain concrete benefits in this world. For example, no one would wear an item of paper clothing for the dead even if it fit, and no one can use Hell Money at the grocery store. Recently, paper offerings have been used as decorations, suggesting a form of artistic recycling of the material, but this behavior is rare and nearly all examples concern foreigners, who enjoy paper items strictly for their artistic qualities and know little of, or choose to ignore, their original purpose.[3] It is possible that some public face might be gained from the display of paper funeral replicas before they are burned. This explanation has been advanced for modern Singapore: "These items are put on display and burned in open spaces, in full view of the public, demonstrating the virtue of the family in offering elaborate sacrifices, and thereby enhancing their own social status" (Tong 1993: 149). In Hong Kong's rural areas, offerings may be moved in the funeral procession to the burning site (Hase 1984: 158), and can be seen and evaluated by village eyes. But in the urban areas, funeral processions are no longer held; if burning offerings are chanced upon, observers can certainly make evaluations, but their reactions have no effect on the social standing or status of the strangers (to them) who are doing the burning.[4] Further, during the Qing Ming and Chong Yang Festivals, individuals and families are absorbed with the care of their own dead through cleaning the grave and giving offerings; observations during both festivals reveal participants' lack of attention to the offerings other families are assembling. Public displays of wealth or praise for public displays of piety are weak motivations, so what other explanation can be advanced?

"When I looked at the results, I was so moved that I wanted to cry. I found the Hong Kong people, often dubbed as obsessed with material satisfaction, do have a very rich spiritual life." This remark was not made by a worshipper, but by the president of the Hong Kong Bird Watching Society, referring to the results of a survey declaring the humble Eurasian tree sparrow as Hong Kong's favorite bird (Cheung 2004). Yet, it seems appropriate in this discussion of burning offerings, if there is a parallel explanation that extends beyond both materialism and egocentric motivation. Respondents from the June 2003 survey were asked if ancestors would give more benefits to their living relatives if a large quantity of paper offerings were burned to them; 77.8 percent disagreed. A resounding 84.4 percent of the sample also rejected the belief that ancestors would punish the descendants if paper offerings were not burned to them. These results contribute to the old debate on the nature of ancestors, suggesting that urbanites do not look on the departed as inquisitors or wrathful agents (Gallin 1966; Watson and Watson 2004). Providing for the deceased does give benefits, but these are all for the departed and the living cannot gain in strictly material terms. For example, the very popular yellow Money to Live, which appears many times in the preceding chapters, may be burned in the thousands. Its purpose is to secure a faster rebirth into a new life for the soul of the deceased; the giver obtains no material benefits, but rather, the satisfaction that he or she has taken concrete action to facilitate the process for the deceased. In the interviews conducted, the majority of respondents held the same opinions about burning greater quantities of more costly or elaborate offerings such as the special order, handcrafted varieties.

Worshippers interviewed saw no automatic link between the quantity or quality of offerings and ancestral blessings. At least, they did not have the conscious intention to benefit materially. Some respondents said that, while they vaguely remembered hearing of the idea that benefits could be gained in this way (although they could not recall just when or where they had heard about it) they did not believe it to be true, while others said that they saw no direct relationship between burning to the ancestors and obtaining any benefits whatsoever; they had separated the two concepts (Scott 1997a: 237). The reasons respondents provided for giving paper offerings included providing for the ancestors expressed one's devotion and respect, giving offerings reflected one's sincerity, gave psychological comfort, and eased one's heart. What is significant, as one lady expressed it, is that, "Offerings are necessary to show our sincerity and devoutness and the ancestors need them. We must respect them and help them to have a better life" (Scott 1997a: 236). In short, worshippers did benefit from giving offerings, but in a spiritual way far removed from the concrete rewards of this world.

Offerings for the gods

The giving of offerings based on egocentric or materialist motivations should also not be assumed in the worship of the gods, although here the situation is somewhat more complex. Temple worship is often accompanied by divination techniques, so that worshippers may receive answers to the questions most troubling them. It is significant that most inquiries now, as in the past, are not directed solely to financial affairs or personal advancement, but to illness, family problems, and family security — varieties on the theme, "keep my family safe and well." In his 1924 survey of prayer slips collected in north China, L. Newton Hayes found that illness topped the list of worshippers' concerns, followed by marriage problems and protection during travel. Wealth came last (Hayes 1924: 97).

Reporting on a 1989 survey conducted at Kowloon's Wong Tai Sin Temple, Lang and Ragvald found that most worshippers reported going to the temple to ask for help, advice or predictions from the god. Nearly one-fourth asked for aid for health and careers, while others asked about such things as family matters or about fate (1993: 83). A further 14 percent made general petitions for a peaceful life: "These people are basically asking for freedom from anxiety" (1993: 84). Worshippers were keen to show their gratitude for such help: "Around the end of the year (just before Chinese New Year) and during the New Year period, many people go to the temple to show their gratitude for the peace and good fortune of the previous year" (1993: 84). At one level, it is true that worshippers are seeking benefits from the gods, and are earnestly beseeching the gods' assistance. It is also true that a percentage of worshippers are worried about their businesses and their livelihoods. However, many entreaties are for benefits for others; mothers wishing for family security, grandmothers appealing for assistance for sick children or recovery from accidents, fathers hoping that their children will do well in school.

The most popular special pitched items offered to the gods suggest similar motivations. The Pinwheels, which are instruments for fate changing and the securing of blessings, contain a variety of wishes that the worshipper hopes the deity will fulfill. Each time the Pinwheel's blades revolve in the wind, the wish that is written as a couplet (the meaning/wish head 意頭) at the top of the Pinwheel is sent on to the god in a gentle reminder. The Pinwheel can send this wish to the deity throughout the year. Again, these wishes that are not materialistic and although a number are directed to general prosperity in business or any enterprise, an equal number of phrases concern family security or to a peaceful life. I once jokingly asked a well-regarded Pinwheel master whether he had ever crafted any Pinwheels for success in horse-racing or to winning Hong Kong's Mark Six Lottery. He was visibly offended at the suggestion, for he strongly believed that the Pinwheel was an item to treat with respect, something that should never be used for that kind of material gain. He further believed that employing the Pinwheel in this fashion would be offensive to the gods. A second manufacturer queried decided against the popular phrase, "Good luck in dog and horse-racing" (狗馬亨通), deeming it too vulgar and materialistic for his creations.

The Flower Cannons offered to Tian Hou are adorned with many decorative and auspicious items related to having children or safety on the sea, always paramount in the minds of sailors and fishermen. The most notable prosperity-related item is the bat placed at the top, for bats symbolize general prosperity and good fortune, but other decorative elements on the body refer to other wishes. The final pitched offering, the Golden Flowers of the Lunar New Year, are affixed to the images in the temples so that the gods may be adorned and receive new clothing for the year. Their purpose is to make the whole more beautiful and joyous, and to express worshippers' devotion; the accompanying ritual does not include asking for benefits. Survey results from June 2003 again support this general contention, for 78 percent of respondents disagreed with the statement that gods would give more blessings if a large quantity of paper offerings was burned to them, results echoing those for interviews at shops and with worshippers. As for the ancestors, the quantity and quality of offerings to the deities and anticipated material benefits had been delinked.

Offerings for the ghosts

Not to be ignored are the offerings for the ghosts. Even today, a majority of Hong Kong people fear, or at least are wary of, ghosts as entities that cause illness, accidents or bad fortune. Thus, one might expect to see little pity for them. Accounts from other Chinese societies explain that only meager or unprocessed offerings are given to ghosts to placate or bribe them to cease bothering the victim any more or to just go away (Harrell 1986: 105), an instrumental purpose. However, while during the Festival of the Hungry Ghosts, many people burn large quantities of paper offerings with these motivations in mind, they also burn offerings to be sure that these neglected souls receive some comfort. Survey results from the June 2003 survey indicated that 39.9 percent of respondents burned offerings at this period; a further 36.1 percent agreed that ghosts were not dirty things but poor creatures deserving assistance. These worshippers are well aware of classic Confucian thinking on the matter: "The Master said, 'For a man to sacrifice to a spirit which does not belong to him is flattery' " (Legge 1960: 154; see also Ebrey 1991). A man may sacrifice only to his own ancestors, and sacrifices to others are not only inappropriate but inefficacious. Yet, these worshippers have willingly extended the boundaries in the name of compassion. Outside of this festival period, some worshippers burning Longevity Gold to the gods say that the deity will use this money for the neglected souls in the underworld — an act of mercy by the gods made possible by the generosity of the living. And, while the majority of customers buy simple paper materials for the ghosts, an increasing number make a much greater investment, purchasing quite elaborate assemblages of gifts for them, and burning them throughout the year. One can only assume that, despite Ruist traditions, pity outweighs any other motivation for these worshippers, and certainly outweighs personal gain.[5] While worshippers well understand the Confucian strictures that sacrificing to the ancestors of others is not acceptable (Legge 1960), some also believe that the wandering spirits deserve pity and a share of offerings. The use of paper offerings in these contexts are material manifestations of an expanding appreciation of care and concern and a willingness to extend the boundaries of compassion.

Beyond Offerings

As early as 1970, E. N. Anderson, describing a segment of the marriage rituals among Hong Kong fishermen, noted, "The act, not the intent, is important" (1970: 177). His remark referred to the questions of orthodoxy and orthopraxy in Chinese ritual behavior, an issue well discussed by James Watson (1988a, 1991, 1993). Put simply, the "genius of the (presocialist) Chinese approach to cultural standardization . . . allowed for a high degree of variation within an overarching structure of unity" (1991: 372), and contradictions between a unified Chinese culture and a tolerance for regional distinctiveness were resolved by emphasizing correct practice and not correct belief in ritual (1991: 371). The experiences of paper offerings add to this insight, in that there is a structure of giving offerings, within which there are considerable variations in actual practice, worshipping styles being highly individualistic.

Yet, for most respondents, intent is still significant, for worship and offerings must be approached with the right frame of mind. But what is the "right frame of mind"? A minority of worshippers have extended this frame to its limit, believing that it is not necessary to give paper offerings at all. Their views were that the worshipper's state of mind was the most important element and that giving only small, simple items like flowers or incense were sufficient to reflect this. What such worshippers meant by "state of mind" was best expressed in their own words as the "state of one's heart" or, what is most important belongs to the heart (最緊要喺個心) a state in which the worshippers' love for the object of worship, their sincerity, and their unselfishness would be known, whether the object be gods, ghosts, or ancestors. If a worshipper had a good heart and was truly devoted to the god or goddess, truly loved and respected the ancestor, or sincerely pitied the spirits, then he or she needed only pray sincerely and offer small items. Deities, ghosts and ancestors would know.

Studies of social life in Imperial China provide some support for the significance of sincerity in thought and deed. Song scholarly support for a focus on inner cultivation was found in both the Great Learning and the Doctrine of the Mean — the desire to rectify hearts leading to the need to be sincere in thoughts (Schwartz 1985: 405). Speaking of classical attitudes towards the adoption of heirs of different surnames, the Neo-Confucian scholar Chu Hsi (Zhu Xi 朱熹, 1130–1200) observed, "However, it is all right if, when participating in the sacrifices, the adopted man has a totally sincere attitude of respect and filial piety" (Waltner 1990: 74). Waltner goes on to say, "But for Chu Hsi, sincerity (ch'eng, 誠) mediates between the prescriptions of the sacred text and the exigencies of the actual situation. Sincerity matters more than does the letter of the ritual . . . Sincerity of attitude must supplement and might supplant kinship" (Waltner 1990: 74). If sincerity and the right attitude is vital in so critical an area as the proper continuance of the family line, in a matter as serious as obtaining a legal heir, then its significance to other contexts is easier to discern. As a Pinwheel master explained:

Everything is out of your sincerity. For example, if you ask for help when you worship Wong Tai Sin, you must be sincere. Then your wish will come true. Your belief must not be based on what you want, on the thought of gaining something. When you worship god, you must be sincere.

Worshippers' attitude of "no offerings" is even further removed from that of materialism and conspicuous consumption. Where the right practice may be to do something (burn offerings), it can also be to do nothing at all (not burn offerings). The respondents who made such statements were neither Buddhists nor Christians, who are not required to give offerings, but it is possible that they had been influenced by the thinking of these two great religious traditions. In any case, they were expressing a sentiment which runs like a thread within the fabric of Hong Kong's current popular religious beliefs. How many people ascribe to this way of thinking is difficult to know, but it is likely a significant number; in the June 2003 survey, 64.3 percent of respondents agreed that sincerity was more important than the amount or the quality of paper offerings given to gods or to ancestors. While the main fabric of giving paper offerings shows no sign of dying out in the near future, within it runs parallel this internal thread of "beyond paper offerings," or of "no paper offerings at all."

Notes

Introduction

1. For example, in 2001, the second year of the Hong Kong Heritage Museum in Tai Wai, attendance figures had already reached 306,615 (Leisure and Cultural Services Department, June, 2001).

2. Research for the doctoral degree in anthropology at Cornell University was conducted during 1976–8 in Kowloon. The thesis, "Action and Meaning: Women's Participation in the Mutual Aid Committees of Kowloon," was supported by a National Science Foundation Doctoral Dissertation Research Grant (#7612234), an N.D.F.L awarded through Cornell University, and a grant from the Cornell Center for International Studies. The author is grateful for such generous support.

3. Many China scholars working in Hong Kong during the 1970s were given offices in the Universities Service Center, then at 155 Argyle Street in Kowloon. I owe a great debt indeed to the Director, Mr John Dolfin, and to all his staff, notably Ms

Stella Wong and Ms Moni Tai. Without their generously shared knowledge and support, research of any kind would have been much more difficult.

4. Items were numbered and set into computer files with their names in English or romanization and Chinese characters, with details of the shop where purchased and on what date, the price, and a brief description. The Golden Flowers and Pinwheels were also photographed. The materials were then packed into boxes according to the holiday, or the occasion, or the ethnic group, to which they referred. All of these took a considerable amount of time and attention to detail, for which I am grateful for a background in archaeology.

5. The "superstitious prints" to which Dore referred are the subject of a later examination of a special form of ritual paper. In 1940, Clarence Day published the results of his studies of prints of paper gods, or *ma-chang* (馬張) that he collected in the 1930s in northern Zhejiang Province. Day's dual purpose for collecting these prints was: "to learn something of the religious background of the Chinese people, as well as to stimulate in Chinese students an appreciation of their own religious heritage . . ." By the time his book appeared, he had collected nearly two thousand "original, coloured wood-cuts, lithographs, machine prints and hand paintings" (1940a: ix). Many of the gods represented in these prints and paintings were extensively discussed in the text, including their domestic or village context and the religious values (such as protection of life and property and salvation from Hell) that accompanied their worship. Hong Kong's retail paper shops stock only glossy factory-produced images of the door gods put up at the New Year. Some local bookstores once sold a few images of deities as part of their New Year's wood-block prints, but such prints were not available in the quantities that Day encountered in the 1930s. These bookstores have long ceased selling such prints, and the only places to find them are in antique or craft shops, and the prints for sale at these shops usually depict only the Kitchen God, the gods of the family, or the door gods. Alexeiev (1928) and Goodrich (1991) also made studies of prints of deities. Other references may be found in publications about wood-block prints or New Year prints.

6. The six examples of paper offerings that Hunter selected were, as he termed them: "ceremonial paper" or "joss paper" (today's Gold and Silver Paper), "money for the hereafter" (today's Money to Live), "mock money" (today's White Money), "bamboo ceremonial paper" (today's Longevity Gold), and "hua pao-fu" (Hunter 1937: 34–43). The last includes two versions of today's Fu Jian Bags; one is the version used by worshippers of Shanghai origin).

Chapter 1

1. For some descriptions of general paper offerings, see, for Malaysia, Marjorie Topley, "Paper Charms and Prayer Sheets as Adjuncts to Chinese Worship," *Journal of the Malayan Branch of the Royal Asiatic Society* 26 (1953): 63–81. For the rural New Territories of Hong Kong, see Masahisa Segawa, "Paper Money, Paper Clothing, and Others," *Material Culture* Number 46 (1986) (in Japanese). For urban Hong Kong, see Janet Lee Scott, "Traditional Values and Modern Meanings in the Paper Offering Industry of Hong Kong," in *Hong Kong: The Anthropology of a Chinese Metropolis*, ed. Grant Evans and Maria Tam (Richmond: Curzon, 1997a). See also Marjorie Topley, "Chinese Occasional Rites in Hong Kong: Some Traditional Chinese Ideas and Conceptions in Hong Kong Social Life Today," Symposium Paper, *Journal of the Hong Kong Branch of the Royal Asiatic Society* (1966). See also Naomi Yin-yin Szeto, "Some Chinese Religious Concepts as Reflected in 'Paper Horses'," *Hong Kong Museum of History Newsletter*, October–December (1993). Some reference to paper offerings may also be found in publications devoted to general paper arts or folk arts. See, for example, *Chinese Folk Prints* (Exhibition Catalogue) (Hong Kong: Regional Council, 1994); Wang Shucun, *A Pictorial Album of Chinese Folk Art* (Hangzhou: Zhejiang Literature and Art Publishing House, 1992); Nancy Zeng Berliner, *Chinese Folk Art: The Small Skills of Carving Insects* (Boston: Little, Brown and Company, 1986).

2. Arthur Wolf's classic discussion, "Gods, Ghosts and Ancestors," which detailed the tripartite division of divinities and spirits, first appeared in *Religion and Ritual in Chinese Society*, ed. Arthur Wolf (Stanford: Stanford University Press, 1974). It was reprinted in *Studies in Chinese Society*, ed. Arthur Wolf (Stanford: Stanford University Press, 1978).

3. This is not because the items pose any spiritual danger to their possessors, for their presence is not harmful; it is simply that they are not meant to remain in this world. Funeral offerings elicit a slightly altered reaction. I had a great number of such items stored in my office, but well packed and not obviously on display. While colleagues and many visitors understand why such items are there, on occasion a suggestion is made that they be put even further out of sight. For example, when two sets of small servants for the dead were temporarily placed just inside the door while packing for them was being arranged, some colleagues suggested that they "looked strange" there.

4. A sizeable number of craftsmen believe that lanterns, while deemed pitched products and sold by numerous paper shops, are unique and should be placed in a category by themselves. This ambiguity was most likely because most lanterns are used as decorations (their appearance at the Mid-Autumn Festival being

the obvious example) and are not burned as religious offerings. Still, other shopkeepers felt that Lucky Basins, which are purchased for strictly human concerns, were distinct items, while others deemed Pinwheels a special category (Pinwheels, except in a few situations, are not available in retail paper offerings shops, but only at temples). A minority of shopkeepers preferred yet another design. While agreeing that pitched items should be separated from printed, they preferred to create individual subcategories for lanterns, Pinwheels, and Golden Flowers, and some set the funeral objects within a separate group.

5. The everyday, non-pitched offerings are packed mostly in small stacks, some (like the Gold and Silver Paper and the Longevity Gold) tied with strings or vinyl twine; originally, twisted vegetable fibers were used. Some items purchased years ago were bound with strips of red painted paper for added auspiciousness.

6. In Taiwan, the use of Gold and Silver Paper is considerably more complicated (Seaman 1982: 87; Li 1985: 83).

7. The many kinds of spirit money has been documented for Taiwan, in which the category of gold paper alone has been noted as consisting of no fewer than eight (Li 1985) or nine denominations (So 1939, quoted in Seaman 1982: 87). Studies on offerings of money include: Gary Seaman, "Spirit Money: An Interpretation," *Journal of Chinese Religions* 10 (1982): 80–91; Hill Gates, "Money for the Gods," *Modern China* 13 (1987): 259–77; John McCreery, "Why Don't We See Some Real Money Here? Offerings in Chinese Religion," *Journal of Chinese Religions* 18 (1990): 1–24.

8. Recent observations of worship at the Wong Tai Sin Temple in Kowloon showed that worshippers buying the largest variety of Longevity Gold do not attempt to fold it into classical ingot shapes, but loop each sheet over on itself, then stack the sheets one by one. The result looks much like an Elizabethan ruff.

9. Clarence Day is one author who paid special attention to the First Treasure, an interesting and heavily used item ignored by other observers. When he recorded his observations in 1927, First Treasure was considered a form of protective paper, enfolding completed Buddhist prayer sheets. These sheets, when completed by the worshipper, then became a form of paper money with which to purchase merit in the Western Paradise (Day 1927: 280). In a later publication, Day lists First Treasure as among the paper monies (along with "Hell Money," which he defined as *ming yang*, 冥洋) offered to the Kitchen God at the New Year (Day 1929: 7). In his other writings, it appeared as a sheet on which to record completed prayers for merit (1940a: 21), as an item created when a completed prayer sheet was folded with a silvered sheet (1940b: 8), or as an item hung on strings, in the manner of genuine coins (1928: 291). What Day described as "yuan bo" is not quite the same as that usually identified under this term today, for at one point he describes it as "silvered sheets of metallic

paper onto a coarse grade of brown paper" (1940a: 30). In Hong Kong, the Chaozhou (潮州) shops sell a version of First Treasure in finer cream-colored paper, two sheets together with a separate item resembling a long life charm and gold triangles on the upper corners.

10. Some shopkeepers believe that this "new" version, which few sell, actually more closely resembles an earlier form of Honorable People, one in which the honorable people were cut as individual figures and burned one by one.

11. Cave has described the roundels as mandalas. In Singapore, the central holes are burned "by elderly women in homes funded by the temples" (Cave 1998: 52, figure 4.1). In 1937, Hunter discussed the same item, which he termed "money for the hereafter." It was burned frequently on the night of the New Year before the portraits of the ancestors; the New Year's ritual and burnt roundels assured "affluence and contentment for the deceased persons depicted by the family portraits" (1937: 40–41).

12. Some shops offer this Seven Voice Incantation in a smaller size with six roundels and a hand, but still burned in all places. In other versions, each sheet of the six roundel version is folded into a flattened ingot shape and stacked, one shape inserted into another. Also available are six roundel varieties with no holes burned in them. This form is much less auspicious.

13. Five Colored Paper and Seven Colored Paper are very popular materials used to fashion many other common items, including the clothing in the packages for the ancestors, Closed [gate] Money (關錢), and small clothing for ghosts.

14. Respondents referred to these tigers as being white tigers, yellow tigers, and green tigers but in fact, all appeared to be nearly the same tint of yellow. White tigers are also associated with the rituals of Beating the Small People (Chiao 1983), and are prominent features of the sacrificial rituals before opera performances (S. Y. Chan 1991: 54–56). White tigers made of stone, paper, or wood also appear in temples, in the under altars; a good description may be found in Stevens (1977).

15. Observations at any major temple make clear the great variety in the ways that worshippers handle the paper offerings.

16. These individual honorable people cut-outs bear a striking resemblance to items recorded in 1944 for the Sierra Norte of Puebla, Mexico. These items of paper were used in various ceremonies of witchcraft. See Bodil Christensen, "Notas sobre la fabricacion del papel indigena y su empleo para 'brujerias' en la Sierra Norte de Puebla," *Revista Mexicana de Estudios Antropologicos*, Number 1–2 (1944): 109–23.

17. Another version of Red Money and White Mountain, that some shopkeepers call the "lai see chin" (利是錢), or Lucky Money (named for the red packets given out at the New Year), is used during the Qing Ming festival and also

affixed to the tomb, but with one sheet on the front and one sheet on the back (Hong Kong style), representing the hope that the ancestors will send good luck to the worshipper. It is crafted of one sheet of Red Money (the kind with thirteen rows of lunar-shaped perforations) on a beige backing sheet. Most shops would call this Mountain Money. Similar offerings, likely to be these very items, were recorded by Lewis Hodous: "sheets of perforated paper representing money, are placed upon different parts of the grave and weighted down with stones to prevent them from flying away" (1915: 60).

18. An early account of the popular use of charms during what the author termed the "summer festival," Dragon Boat, is given in an issue of the *Journal of the North China Branch of the Royal Asiatic Society*.

> On the lintel of the door the people paste very powerful charms . . . These charms are made of paper four inches wide and eight inches long. They are printed from blocks and are sold on the streets for two cash a piece . . . Many householders paste five colored slips of paper with charms on them above the lintel. These strips are about three inches wide and five inches long. The dark color is for the north, the white for the south, the red for the east, the blue for the west, and the yellow for the middle direction. According to popular tradition the five spirits of poison descend to earth on the first day of the fifth moon and scatter destructive vapors abroad and these charms on the doors keep them out. (Hodous 1912: 70)

19. Despite the difficulties of consuming plastic components by fire, certain funeral offerings in Macau, such as the latest model sports cars, are crafted with the under frame and the revolving wheels (set on an axel of bamboo) of fine cardboard, but the body of plastic. The author is grateful to Dr William Guthrie of the University of Macau for this information, and for the gift of many of these distinctive offerings.

20. Hunter recorded eight different varieties of bamboo-based paper as suitable for making ceremonial offerings (Hunter 1937: 16).

21. Available in three standard sizes and prices, these ovens have become necessary items for domestic rituals, and are affordable by most families. In November of 2000, for example, the largest sizes were approximately HK$65, the middle sizes HK$60 and the smallest, HK$55.

22. According to officials of the Hong Kong Housing Department, there are no comprehensive regulations for burning paper offerings within public housing estates. Rather, each estate manager and/or management company determines its own policy. For example, in Po Lam Estate (寶林邨) in Tseung Kwan O

(將軍澳), paper burning is tolerated during the Festival of the Hungry Ghosts, when special arrangements are announced to residents.

One proprietor of a very popular shop in a busy public housing estate explained:

> People can go to the street as there is a big bin provided for them. However, there is none in the old housing estate, so the worshippers always make the street dirty after burning the paper. You are not allowed to burn the paper outside your flat or in the street in those new and grand housing estates. If you want to burn paper, you need to go somewhere else, maybe to nearby [public] housing estates instead.

23. The volume of worshippers and accompanying offerings to the Wong Tai Sin Temple is so large that squads of workers, wearing distinctive yellow sweatshirts, continually sweep away the leftover food offerings (not many, as most worshippers take the food home to eat) and the newspapers used as mats. They also clear away the incense sticks from the holders, even if the sticks have not fully burned away.

24. For a look at the Chaozhou community in Hong Kong, see Sparks (1976a and 1976b).

25. An earlier reference to an assemblage of paper ritual materials, this time sets of New Year's prints of the gods, were described by Clarence Day in 1926 (reprinted in 1975).

> An extremely interesting form in which paper gods are put up for sale by enterprising firms came to my notice in February of 1925. My class in comparative religion had been requested to observe the customs of their localities during the China New Year vacation. On his return to college, Yu Erh-chang brought from Chang-an a long yellow cloth bag, about nine-by-twenty-four inches, having a flap tied with cloth strings and a heavy red carrying-cord at the top. In this bag were six sheets of smooth red cardboard printed in black figures . . . What a convenient way in which to procure the household's lares and penates! Just pay cash and carry them home in the handy yellow bag! (1975: 24–25)

26. Many of these assemblages also bear the character for prosperity (福), and a variety of other auspicious phrases. In very traditional shops, such phrases might have once been hand-brushed, although nowadays this is rarely, if ever, seen. Quite acceptable versions are neatly printed in good quality golden paint, and very small shops may do away with such title slips altogether, simply

writing the name of the deity in ink on the outside of the package and omitting the auspicious phrases.

27. These assemblages generally do not include wax candles or incense, which could damage the enclosed paper items. The wax candles, if part of assemblages stored at higher temperatures, could melt or spontaneously combust.

28. The same informant explained the items in assemblages for the Sky Gods in this way. First, two pieces of white First Treasure were placed in a cross shape, then ten pieces of coarser First Treasure, two pieces of circular Honorable People Papers, one sheet of Lucky Basin Paper, one sheet of the Solving of 100 Problems, a few sheets of Longevity Gold, two pieces of the Five Treasures Document, two more rectangular Honorable People Papers, a quantity of Longevity Gold, and the whole topped with a set of paper clothing.

29. Pre-packed assemblages of paper offerings, produced locally or in Chinese factories, are also available on the China Mainland. In November of 1995, the author collected some examples of these assemblages outside the Nan Hua Monastery at Ru Yuan in northern Guangdong. Similar packages were also collected in Tainan, southern Taiwan, in March of 1995.

30. For a review of Hong Kong's temples, see *This Is Hong Kong: Temples* by Joyce Savidge (Hong Kong: Hong Kong Government Information Services, 1977). A more detailed account may also be found in Keith Stevens, "Chinese Monasteries, Temples, Shrines and Altars in Hong Kong and Macau," *Journal of the Hong Kong Branch of the Royal Asiatic Society*, 20 (1980): 1–33. Descriptions of area temples may be found in various Hong Kong official publications such as those printed by the District Boards; for example, *History of the Culture of the Southern District*, published by the Southern District Board in 1996.

31. The practice of the Yu Lan Festival is described in Stephen Teiser, *The Ghost Festival in Medieval China* (Princeton: Princeton University Press, 1988). See also, Stephen Teiser, "Ghosts and Ancestors in Medieval Chinese Religion: The Yu-lan-p'en Festival as Mortuary Ritual," *History of Religions*, 26 (1986): 47–67. Stephen Teiser, "The Ritual behind the Opera: A Fragmentary Ethnography of the Ghost Festival, a. d. 400–1900," in *Ritual Opera, Operatic Ritual*, ed. David Johnson (Berkeley: University of California Institute of East Asian Studies, 1989). See also Choi Chi-cheung, "The Chinese 'Yue Lan' Ghost Festival in Japan: A Kobe Case Study," *Journal of the Hong Kong Branch of the Royal Asiatic Society* 24 (1984): 230–63.

32. Recent events have thrust the good fortune tree of Lam Tsuen village, which has grown into a major attraction for tourists as well as local worshippers, into the news in yet another fashion. Worshippers offering incense and prayers, and then gifts flung onto its branches, were shocked by the breaking off of a huge limb during the Lunar New Year festivities. The limb, which broke

the leg of a sixty-two-year-old male worshipper and slightly injured a child, was said to have been weakened by the large numbers of apple and orange bearing paper wishes it was carrying. To prevent further problems, the Tai Po District Office installed a sign asking worshippers not to throw paper offerings onto the tree, and further underscoring its concern, kept worshippers at a safe distance through the installation of a metal barrier and the employment of police officers (Lam 2005a, 2005b; see also Bradsher 2005, Cheng 2005).

Chapter 2

1. Sources for the events and festivals of the lunar year include: C. Bone (1889a; 1889b); Juliet Bredon, *Chinese New Year Festivals: A Picturesque Monograph of the Rites, Ceremonies, and Observances in Relation Thereto* (Shanghai: Kelly and Walsh, 1930); Juliet Bredon and Igor Mitrophanow, *The Moon Year: A Record of Chinese Customs and Festivals* (Shanghai: Kelly and Walsh, 1927; reprinted by Oxford University Press, Hong Kong, 1982); Derk Bodde, *Annual Customs and Festivals in Peking, as Recorded in the Yen-Ching Sui-Shih-Chi by Tun Li-Ch'en* (Peiping, 1936; Hong Kong: Hong Kong University Press, 1965, second edition); Valentine R. Burkhardt, *Chinese Creeds and Customs, Vols. 1 and 2* (Hong Kong: South China Morning Post, 1953; 1955); Wolfram Eberhard, *Chinese Festivals* (London: Abelard-Shuman, 1958). For Taiwan, see Michael Saso, *Chinese Feasts and Customs: A Handbook of the Principal Feasts and Customs of the Lunar Calendar on Taiwan* (Hsinchu: Fu Jen University Language School Press, 1965). Other accounts include Huang Shaorong, "Chinese Traditional Festivals," *Journal of Popular Culture* 25 (1991): 163–80. For Hong Kong, see Barbara E. Ward and Joan Law, *Chinese Festivals in Hong Kong* (Hong Kong: The Guidebook Company, 1993). The Rev. C. Bone's are among the earliest accounts that describe the religious festivals of the Cantonese. As such, his writings may be usefully partnered with Ward and Law's beautifully illustrated account, covering both Hong Kong's ritual events and the modern ways of celebrating them.
2. Although no specific name is recorded by paper masters, this title likely refers to Zhang Daoling, founder of the Daoist Way of Celestial Masters (Teiser 1996: 9).
3. Some shops sell these four papers as three items, because the Yin Separation and the Yang Separation sheets are combined into one item, the Yin and Yang Separation (陰陽隔). Most, but not all, customers also purchase the two document papers at the same time. These four (or three) papers may be used independently or added to any regular *Bai Fan* assemblage if the customer has been seriously ill.

4. Many of these dates are determined by the *Tung Shing* or almanac. Chiao lists significant dates as the sixth, sixteenth, and twenty-sixth days of each lunar month (Chiao 1983: 140).

5. These ladies are usually quite elderly, retired and have taken up the ritual as a way to earn some income. Most learned the procedure by watching others perform it (a common method in the absence of formal learning), although it is unclear who the original practitioner was. As a rule, these ladies do not teach others how to do it. The fee was approximately HK$40 in the fall of 2000. Chiao records the amount as "three or four Hong Kong dollars" in 1983 (Chiao 1983: 140).

6. An account of this ritual, complete with photographs illustrating the crowds of worshippers seeking assistance, appeared in Hong Kong's *Apple Daily* of March 6, 2001. The larger of the accompanying photos clearly illustrated the procedure of beating the paper replicas of the small people, as well as many of the accompanying paper offerings. It also illustrated a very large ceramic figure of a tiger, used no doubt by the practitioner (a rather young woman) to attract customers.

7. I am grateful for the work of two student assistants, Ms Emily Bales and Ms Yeung Yuk Man, who visited the sites and made observations.

8. Popular lucky phrases for Pinwheels include: To follow the desires of the heart (從心所欲); the desires of the heart come true (心想事成); everything happens as you wish (萬事如意); get a return of 10,000 times on original investment [make a good profit] (一本萬利); business is brisk (生意興隆); gain financial resources in many ways (財源廣進); long life, riches and honor (長命富貴); may your family be prosperous (家宅興隆); one sails with the wind smoothly [everything goes well] (一帆風順); be prosperous all through the year (週年旺財); may Wong Tai Sin bless you (大仙保佑); and, both men and wealth are flourishing (人財兩旺).

9. References to *qian* reading may be found, for example, in Doolittle (1865b); Dennys (1876); Dore (1917); Berkowitz, Brandauer and Reed (1969); Jordan (1972); and Smith (1991). C. K. Yang (1994) also describes such a procedure, which he identifies as "sortilege" (1994: 262). Hayes in 1924 described this method of divination: "On the altar before the image and beside the incense burner usually stands a bamboo receptacle full of sticks of the same material. Each of these strips of weed is numbered. A tube will commonly contain thirty-six, seventy-two, or one hundred. The numbers on these strips correspond to numbers on narrow sheets of printed paper in the keeping of a priest or temple attendant. After a worshipper has lighted his candles and incense, the usual procedure is for him to take the tube from the altar. He first waves this receptacle three or four times over the burning incense and then retires to the mat in front

of the altar. After performing the usual number of obeisances he begins slowly to revolve the bamboo tube. The sticks within push each other from side to side until one is forced out and drops to the floor. Let us suppose the worshipper is concerned over a lawsuit. He picks up the stick, looks at the number and then goes over to the attendant and buys, for a cent, the correspondingly numbered piece of paper. On that paper he will undoubtedly find a reference to lawsuits. There will be a statement such as 'lawsuit successful,' 'lawsuit indeterminate,' or 'lawsuit a failure.' He takes this to be the answer of the god and leaves the temples happy or sad as the case may be" (Hayes 1924: 96–97). A full description of Hong Kong practices may be found in Lang and Ragvald, *The Rise of a Refugee God: Hong Kong's Wong Tai Sin* (1993: 106), or in Anderson's account of Hong Kong's fishermen (1970: 172–3).

10. Fate Changers sold in Macau's temples have a somewhat different appearance. Some are made of six sheets of colored paper (violet, green, yellow, white, blue and brown) which have been folded in half lengthwise, then cut from one end into diamond shapes that reach nearly to the opposite end. Further cuts allow the two sides of this central diamond cut to be opened up in the form of ribbons that hang down along either side. These are hung in clusters to be used in the rituals.

Chapter 3

1. Philip C. Baity's studies in Taiwan clarify how gods are ranked. In his account, three factors must be distinguished: the efficacy of the god, the absolute chronological age of the deity or the temple, and the relative age of the deity compared to other deities (1977: 79). Of these, efficacy appears to be most important.

2. Duyvendak noted that after her death (which some myths attribute to suicide) the goddess appeared in a red dress (1939: 344). See also Watson's explanation of Tian Hou's appearance (1985: 297).

3. In 1935 Williams recorded another very detailed history of the worship of a patron god, this time Lei Tsu, the patron goddess of silk weaving and silk workers (see also Stevens 1997: 129). It included a detailed account of the Qing ceremonies conducted by the Empress. While an elaborate banquet was prepared in the goddess's honor, and complicated preparations made for orchestral music and singing (Williams 1935: 8–9), paper offerings were not mentioned as part of this imperial celebration.

4. For a more detailed explanation of the Lu Pan-inspired carpentry manual, see Ruitenbeek (1993).

5. These red banners or ribbons are generally referred to as Spirit Reds (神紅), but

are also commonly termed Red Cloths (紅布), Flower Reds (花紅), or Hanging Reds (掛紅). The central red rosette, itself centered with a silver toned convex circle, may be termed a Red Ball (紅球) or a Red Head (紅頭). While most of the red ribbons are made of a rather coarse but bright cotton fabric, the handmade varieties are made with fine red silk brocade.

6. The *South China Morning Post* edition of November 16, 2000, contained an article entitled "Roadside joss-sticks gave alleged killers away." Police were alerted to the possible crime when they saw five men burning joss-sticks and paper money by the roadside site late at night a day after the killing. The killers were afraid of the victim's ghost, and had sought to appease his spirit by burning offerings at the site where they had dumped his body. A later article in the May 24, 2003 edition of the *Post* explained the reluctance of Hong Kong residents to purchase, or even rent, flats in which violent deaths had occurred. These flats are termed "dirty," which is a general euphemism for flats that are haunted by victims of murder, suicide or other tragedies. Those still willing to rent or to buy such units could expect sizeable discounts from established market prices, perhaps as much as eighty percent, although one renter of such a "dirty" flat kept a mini-altar inside the door (Western and Chan 2003). In addition, Halloween celebrations and advertisements sometimes fall afoul of local sentiments, as evidenced by complaints made to the Hong Kong Broadcasting Authority concerning two television advertisements commissioned by the Ocean Park amusement park for Halloween of 2003. Some viewers were offended by depictions sessions with mediums, in which the dead appear; Ocean Park managers requested that the advertisements be screened after 9.30 p.m. (Cheung 2003).

7. During my time at the Chinese University of Hong Kong in the early 1980s, my anthropology students would tell me stories of the ghosts of murdered individuals reputed to be lurking about the campus, especially in the wooded lanes and walkways leading up from Chung Chi College. While declaring themselves immune from such beliefs, it was clear that they avoided walking in such places when alone or at night. For more detail on such ghosts and their meanings, see Bosco (2001).

8. The recent epidemic of Severe Acute Respiratory Syndrome, or SARS, in Hong Kong has left a number of families in anguish over not being able to bury their loved ones with the customary rites. Such deceased individuals, some have suggested, may also become unhappy ghosts due to their losing their lives far too early and not being with loved ones at the time of death (see Geoffrey A. Fowler, "Dying Alone," *Far Eastern Economic Review*, June 5, 2003).

9. Shopkeepers explained that customers of Dongguan ancestry especially favor White Money for the ancestors.

10. The discrepancy between the name and the actual number of colored papers does not matter to worshippers, nor do they pay much attention to the variations in color.

Chapter 4

1. For descriptions of the Chinese Hell, see Wolfram Eberhard, *Guilt and Sin in Traditional China* (1967a), Chapter 2, and "The Yu-Li or Precious Records," trans. George W. Clarke, *Journal of the China Branch of the Royal Asiatic Society* 28 (1898): 233–399. A general overview of the differing visions of Hell may be found in Thompson (1989), and an analysis of the growth in visions of the afterlife may be found in Teiser (1993). Further depictions of Chinese conceptions of Hell may be found in Campany (1990) and Pas (1989).

2. For comments on the use of replicas in ancient China, see Berger (1998), Lau (1991) and Rawson (1996a, 1996b). Berger's article provides an interesting discussion of sculptured body doubles.

3. An excellent description of the classic mutual savings societies may be found in Gamble (1954). In Ting Hsien, these societies were formed to assist in meeting expenses for businesses, family matters, and debt repayment. These societies, whatever their form, were accompanied by formal contracts and regulations. Even earlier, Arthur Smith described the operation of village cooperative loan societies in his book, *Village Life in China* (1899: 152–60). Various kinds of formal and informal money lending or financial assistance clubs were discussed in Gallin's *Hsin Hsing, Taiwan* (1966). The money lending clubs provide "a large sum of money for some special purpose such as building a new house, buying some land, or paying for engagement gifts or dowry" (Gallin 1966: 75). Also discussed are the "Father-Mother Societies" which are organized to assist with funeral costs. "The members of a father-mother society stand ready to handle the many tasks which must be carried out for the funeral ritual and burial, and each contributes a sum of money to the family of the deceased" (Gallin 1966: 222). Other accounts of credit societies may be found in Doolittle (1865b), Fei (1939), and Yang (1945).

4. That there may be attempts to deal more openly with the subject of death may be seen in recent conferences in which elderly met to discuss the matter. These discussion sessions, sponsored by the Society for the Promotion of Hospice Care, hope to educate people in how to face losses in life, serious illness, and hospice care. The Society also invites professionals such as lawyers and social workers to discuss practical matters such as will preparation and funeral arrangements. See "Life's final lesson — the facts of death," *South*

China Morning Post, September 3, 2001. A survey conducted by the Society in 2004 found that Hong Kong people were more open to discussing death and related issues, and wanted to learn how to cope positively with death (Chan 2004). In addition, the St. James Settlement has begun a photo-taking service for the elderly who wish to have a portrait taken in advance of the funeral rites. The initiative has received an overwhelming response. As one elderly lady who signed up for the service explained, "I have no taboos in my life. Death is a path that no one can avoid, so why shouldn't we face it bravely?" *South China Morning Post,* June 21, 2002. Other workshop initiatives, this time to help family members and professionals better understand the complexities of quality of life and care for the elderly, have been arranged by local NGOs and advertised via email.

5. In his depiction of the manufacture of paper offerings, Cave included the following account from Singapore:

> As part of the Singapore National Archives' oral history programme a celebrated Singapore maker of paper-works recorded how a paper house was damaged while being taken to the place where it was to be burned. Some days after the ceremony, the man who had commissioned the model dreamed that his ancestor visited him to complain that the roof of the house leaked badly. He went to the paperworks-maker for advice on what to do. The need was clear: the roofing of the paper house had to be repaired, but as it had already been burned, how could this be done? The solution proved simple and effective: at another ceremony, the family burned a paper image of a builder, complete with his tools and a supply of paper tiles. (Cave 1998: 50)

6. While these appear as "dolls" to observers, they are certainly not viewed as such by the worshippers.

7. The cost of a basic set varies according to the level of quality, the materials used, and the amount of labor and time spent on special designs. In 1989, a basic set could be purchased from HK$1,000 to $2,000, with as much as HK$10,000 or more for very elaborate sets. In 1992, the price of a basic set of thirteen items had risen to "a few thousand dollars" as one master put it, meaning, HK$4,000 to $5,000. Prices for 1995 remained roughly the same. (Costs in US dollars can be calculated on a basis of eight to one.) Other aspects of funerals raise the total cost. In the November 26, 1995, edition of the *Sunday Morning Post Magazine* (of the *South China Morning Post*), an article on modern Hong Kong funerals lists one funeral parlor as selling custom-built Chinese-style caskets for HK$800,000 (more than US$100,000). Most families, more

often favoring cremation now, are content with simple models retailing for somewhat less than HK$20,000 (or US$2,500). Cremation and the storage of ashes are somewhat cheaper, although still costly. In April of 2001, the costs for cremation and storage of ashes in a government columbarium cost HK$3,000 for a standard niche, or HK$4,000 for a large niche. Jade urns ranged in price from HK$2,500 to HK$5,000 and a small memorial stone cost HK$3,800 (*Sunday South China Morning Post*, April 1, 2001). When added to the costs of other elements of the funeral ceremonies, a large bill can be expected.

8. Retail paper shops in Hong Kong have recently begun to sell small, portable models of these popular houses for the dead. While some are quite compact and square-shaped, others are two or three-storied and come complete with servants, family dog, furniture, lighting, and a swimming pool on the roof.

9. According to those living in Macau, paper shops sell all manner of guns, from submachines, to AK-47s, rifles, and handguns. Every kind of gun found in the real world may be reproduced as desired, and are often startling in their accuracy of design. While shopkeepers have been vague as to who purchases them and why, many may be made up to burn at the funerals of gang members. I am grateful to Dr William Guthrie of the University of Macau for this information (personal communication, 2002).

10. These new ready-made paper models (first appearing in 2001) include all the most-loved *dian xin* selections, each one packaged in a neat replica of an individual small brown bamboo steamer, complete with "metal" back plate to prevent sticking. Those selections that contain sauce or fluid are set within individual plates or saucers. A partial list of current selections includes *ma lai go* (a kind of sweet steamed sponge cake, 馬拉糕), spring rolls (春卷), chicken feet (鳳爪), *siu mei* (燒賣), *fen go* (粉果), *lo mai gai* (a kind of rice cake, but wrapped in a genuine lotus leaf, 糯米雞), *nai wong bau* (奶皇包), and *gai bau* (buns stuffed with chicken meat, 雞包).

11. As reported in the *Far Eastern Economic Review*, these newly designed air tickets have caused a stir, designed as they are with the logo for Malaysia Airlines but with the name of "Hell Airlines" (Nury Vittachi, *Far Eastern Economic Review*, April 18, 2002).

12. An article in the *South China Morning Post* of November 22, 2000, "Mobile ownership up 50pc in past two years," indicated that seventy-one percent of Hong Kong people aged from 15 to 64 now owned their own mobile phones, with Nokia the most popular brand. Taiwan, with seventy percent ownership, was second.

13. In 1938, Cornelius Osgood recorded the burning of paper clothing for the "Receiving Ancestors Festival" on the fifteenth day of the seventh month. This clothing, which was only of red and green paper, was cut in the shape of a modern Chemex coffee-maker (Osgood 1963: 338–9). Despite this capacity for keeping up to date, so far no copies of the latest in European haute couture

have appeared in the shops; no Armani or Chanel inspired suits, no Missoni knits. It may be only a matter of time.

14. Young children were often disposed of after death in a much less formal manner than adults. "When a young baby dies, the body is not deeply buried and is easily dug up by wild dogs or wolves. When an old woman asks the name of a neighbor's child and is told that the child is ten years old, she will say, 'Good, the child is out of the reach of dogs!' — meaning that the danger of death is past" (Yang 1945: 11). Even earlier (1892), De Groot recorded that, "the disposal of the dead is almost exclusively based upon the doctrine of implicit devotion to husband and parents, it is quite natural that boys and girls, and in general people who leave neither wife nor offspring behind, should be buried with a minimum of ceremony and pomp" (1892: 240). A moving depiction of disposal of a child, as practiced by Hong Kong's fishermen, is given in Anderson (1970: 182–3). For other accounts of the treatment of dead children, see Bryson (1885), Coltman (1891), Cormack (1935), and Wolf (1978).

15. However, those ancestors who are not known are not likely to receive elaborate replicas of anything. In actual practice, most such small pitched items of technology are burned mostly to those recently deceased, who *did* use them while alive.

16. The exception may be the clothing, for if the ancestors are distant, and no one knows them, or even their gender, packages called Ancestor's Clothing (祖先衣) are used.

17. I am indebted to Ms Cindy Wong Shuet Ying for this observation.

18. This photo has been reproduced in Jonathan Spence and Annping Chin's *The Chinese Century* (New York: Harper Collins, 1996, p. 4).

Chapter 5

1. Some shopkeepers, recognizing the potential of tourists, have made efforts to learn basic English terms and descriptions for many items. During one interview in the Yau Ma Tei District in 1992, for example, the shopkeeper asked me to write down the English names of some paper items tourists had asked about. He was interested in the possibility of increasing his sales.

2. A few retail shops also sell other wooden items such as domestic altars and plaques of the eight trigrams (八卦), but customers seeking such items usually patronize specialty crafters in the few remaining workshops that carve wooden figures of deities and ancestors (the latter for Hong Kong's fishermen), ancestral tablets, family altars, and Buddhist accoutrements. Retail shops specializing in the carving of wooden religious artifacts, such as ancestral tablets and statues of the gods, for both Cantonese and Hoklo, still survive in western Kowloon's Canton and Reclamation Streets. An interesting account of the

carving craft may be found in Keith Stevens, "The Craft of God Carving in Singapore," *Journal of the Hong Kong Branch of the Royal Asiatic Society* 14 (1974): 68–75. See also Margaret Sullivan, *Can Survive, La: Cottage Industries in High-Rise Singapore* (Singapore: Graham Brash, 1993).

3. These couplets (揮春, 春聯, 對聯), still very popular among Hong Kong residents, are pasted on scrolls to be hung on gate posts or on each side of the door, expressing the family's desires for the New Year ahead. Those wishing to decorate their homes with this very traditional item (see, for example, Hsieh and Chou 1981) have a great variety to choose from, as contemporary examples are printed up in fine quality paper in very eye-catching colors. Retail paper shops and market hawkers sell large quantities of these couplets, and often, so do retail establishments of other kinds. Much rarer now are the hand-painted varieties as they are prepared by elderly men as a pastime. An interesting account of such itinerant calligraphers was provided by Lowe (1983 [1941]: 145) who explained, "It requires a certain cultural foundation to conduct such a business successfully and it falls to the lot of poor scholars and youthful students to meet this literary demand. Yearly the god-forgotten literati and wayside poets who try to make a little money and the school boys who wish to take advantage of the new year holidays to demonstrate their calligraphical achievement put up temporary stands along down-town streets and hang out these paper strips, properly executed, for sale."

    At the end of the 1980s, if lucky, one could still see elderly gentlemen setting up stalls on busy streets, where they would paint such couplets according to customer order, in gold or black paint on red. The author noted one such individual hard at work using the wall of the Mong Kok Wet Market as a display wall. Although it has been difficult in recent years to find such fine examples, at least one political party has attempted to fill the space; during the Lunar New Year of 2001, four members of the Democratic Alliance for the Betterment of Hong Kong (the DAB) set up a stall within the market street near the Mong Kok Wet Market and did a brisk business painting couplets for their constituents.

4. Eight paper offerings wholesalers were interviewed for this study.

5. One famous lantern maker still works out of his shop in the Mid-Levels of Victoria. So well-designed are these creations, of silk and elegantly painted, that he sells large numbers to overseas markets. He is well respected in Hong Kong, with some paper masters referring to him as "The Star of Paper Pitching" (紮作明星).

6. If handcrafted in red silk, they are made to resemble popular flowers such as the rose or the chrysanthemum, the differences being the style of the elaborate tufting, still done by hand, of the silk.

7. The current arcade within the outer edge of the Wong Tai Sin Temple is a

lively place, with numerous stalls selling materials for worship. These items include miniature drums, metal swords, slips for *kauh chim* and guidebooks for reading them, red plastic firecrackers, silk purses, silk replicas of lucky bananas and peppers, gourds, old coins, images of deities, miniature lion heads, shell ornaments and wind chimes, lanterns, postcards bearing images of Wong Tai Sin, bracelets of semi-precious stones, wooden animal toys, tassel-trimmed key chains, many varieties of paper offerings (Longevity Gold, First Treasure, White Money, Big Bright Treasure, Gold and Silver Paper, paper clothing, Paper for Gods in the Sky, Hell Money), Pinwheels, small vases, various kinds of bells, candles, wine cups, cigarette lighters, incense, Good Fortune Chickens of papiermache, wooden plaques carved with the eight trigrams, and oil for lamps.

8. In 1984, the Sik Sik Yuen (嗇色園), the private organization which has administered the Wong Tai Sin Temple since 1921 (Lang and Ragvald 1993: 3), decided to begin clearance of the stalls that had for so long lined the older entrance to the temple. In this, it cooperated with the Housing Authority, the Wong Tai Sin Administration Department, and the Tung Wah Hospital. The clearance was completed in early 1991 (Yeung 1991). The organization's name may be translated roughly as "leave behind your worldly desires [when you enter this] garden" (Lang and Ragvald 1993: 169, n. 6).

9. Shopkeepers explained that items from Mainland China can come from as far away as Jiangsu (江蘇) Province (varieties of Hell Money) and Tianjin (天津), but most materials come from over the border in neighboring Guangdong (廣東) Province. Certain counties were famous for particular offerings, although individual shopkeepers held different opinions on which produced the finest examples. For example, Shunde (順德) and Panyu (番禺) were famed for high quality Gold and Silver Paper, but some retailers declared that the same papers manufactured in Shantou (汕頭) were even finer. Candles and incense came from Dongguan (東莞), although some retailers asserted that Shuikou (水口) produced items of higher quality. Xinhui (新會) and Xiamen (廈門) also manufacture paper items. Despite individual preferences, there was general agreement that Foshan (佛山) was now the most famous center for the manufacture of paper offerings, and the Golden Flowers made there were the best, second in quality only to the finest handmade examples once crafted in Hong Kong.

10. Other shops take a somewhat disdainful view of this. During a recent visit to a new shop in Phoenix New Village in Kowloon, the owners replied to queries about their resident cat by saying that their shop "was clean, and so didn't need to keep a cat!" Shops keeping cats are by no means dirty, however.

11. References to Mutual Aid Committee offices serving as informal gathering places for the elderly have been explained in Scott (1980; 1997c: 315–7).

12. Shopkeepers responding to questions directed to possible sources of pollution agreed that there was no way in which paper offerings could be dirtied by any occurrence in the shop or in the home. Their ritual efficacy was not affected by being dropped on the floor, by being placed near toilets, by being handled by menstruating women, by being in close proximity to animals, or even by being sat upon (granted, an unlikely occurrence).

13. Both Hunter (1937) and Cave (1998: 31–35) explain the process of crafting the gold and silver content of everyday offerings.

Chapter 6

1. These attachments imitate the characteristic hand-concealing white cloth sleeve extensions of Chinese opera gowns. "Simply a piece of white silk no more than a foot long attached to the sleeve, it helps to portray more rhythmical movements, especially in the dancing of female parts. Its Chinese name is *shuixiu*, literally, the water-like sleeve and its origin can be traced to the long sleeve prevalent in the Ming Dynasty (1368–1644) and has come to the opera stage in an exaggerated form" (Pan 1995: 128).

2. Such items are very rare, for paper offerings long ago supplanted those of real cloth, and few now know how to cut the items. The shopkeeper, while highly talented and skilled in her own right when crafting paper offerings, referred this special task to old ladies who could still make them.

3. Currently, all matters relating to apprenticeship in modern Hong Kong fall under the jurisdiction of the Office of the Director of Apprenticeship, under regulations set out in the Apprenticeship Ordinance and Regulations of 1976. Designated trades are those covered by the Ordinance and include many of the construction or construction-related industries, but very few traditional crafts are listed (wood furniture makers and goldsmiths being the exceptions) and the paper offerings trade is not mentioned. The modern Apprenticeship Ordinance stresses the importance of training the apprentice, and the need for employers to take their responsibilities seriously: those employers whose training programs were deemed inadequate could be "required to improve that training within a specified time" (1976: 6). In addition, the Ordinance provides for the apprentice to attend complementary technical education classes, and prohibits the employer, who must pay the fees for such courses, from deducting such costs from the apprentice's pay (1976: 6).

4. For many years, these Wong Tai Sin shops were the exceptions to the established custom of purchasing Pinwheels at temples; their proximity to the temple grounds allowed such sales, although some shopkeepers asserted that

this "tradition" was nothing more than a simple lack of space in most retail shops. As one explained, "Anyone could sell Pinwheels if they wanted to, it is all a matter of inventory."

5. Once when I was conducting an interview at a funeral offerings workshop in Sai Ying Poon in the late 1980s, the young owner suggested that I come and work in the shop, thereby learning how to make the paper offerings we were discussing. He saw nothing incongruous in having a foreign woman working in the shop, although Cooper has remarked that, "The reluctance of Hong Kong craftsmen to teach their skills to a foreigner was a serious obstacle in my previous unsuccessful efforts to secure an apprenticeship" (1980: 25).

6. Pomelo leaves are also floated in the bath water at the Lunar New Year, as a way to protect against evil.

7. In 1997, the Hong Kong Branch of the Royal Asiatic Society, with the Joint Publishing Company of Hong Kong, produced a volume of essays on life in old and new Yau Ma Tei, *In the Heart of the Metropolis: Yaumatei and Its People*, edited by Patrick H. Hase.

Chapter 7

1. Classic references on empowerment include Strathern and Strathern (1971), Tambiah (1968), and Ball and Smith (1992).

2. During the Festival of the Hungry Ghosts, very large gowns, over six feet in height, are offered to the King of Hell. Organizers of the festival declared that the small individual "dolls" adorning many of these gowns were themselves replicas of gods.

3. Another less charming version of word play, this time referring to anti-foreign sentiments towards Christianity after the Opium War, may be found in Pfister's discussion of "propagandistic caricatures of Christian teachings and institutions . . . word-plays replete with pejorative derision." These included the term "foreign religion" (*yangjiao* 洋教) rendered into the "teachings of goats" (*yangjiao* 羊教), and the common phrase for Catholicism (Tianzhu jiao 天主教) becoming "grunting of the heavenly pig" (*tianzhu jiao* 天豬叫) (Pfister 2001: 11). A more detailed discussion of the use of animals as caricatures of foreigners in China, under the term teratology, may be found in Dikotter's *The Discourse of Race in Modern China* (1992), while an account of animal terms of abuse may be found in Eberhard (1968).

Chapter 8

1. This is also the well-recorded style of worship in Taiwan. As Gallin (1966) noted for Hsin Hsing, "Ancestor worship, as it generally takes place, is on a small scale, is private, and tends to be rather informal. As a result, the women, in the presence of their children, usually take the main part in carrying out ancestor worship. As some of the villagers noted, 'The men are busy, and the women are more religious anyway' " (1966: 148). This accords with Freedman (1958): "The rites performed in the [ancestral] halls [of the *tsu*] were conducted by and in the presence of men; their daughters and wives played no direct part in the proceedings. In the home, in contrast, it is clear that, whatever the theoretical inferiority of women in the sphere of ancestor worship, they occupied a central position in its performance" (p.85).

2. This interpretation has been challenged by Cammann (1968).

3. That there is some truth to informants' perceptions of the antiquity of paper offerings may be found in museum examples of paper offerings originally taken out of China as souvenirs or as parts of paper collections. For example, the collections of the Peabody Museum of Cambridge contain an example of a Fate Changer (in cream colored paper), pieces of Gold and Silver Paper, an example of a silver coin (bearing the image of Yuan Shikai), and Longevity Gold. All resemble modern examples, but date to (probably) the late nineteenth century. One piece of White Money and a piece of Silver Paper were placed in an envelope bearing the following inscription: "Charms thrown overboard, by the thousand, from steamer 'City of Peking' in Yokohama Harbor September 26, 1881, after trip from San Francisco. To keep the 'devil' so busy, in his curiosity [the word underlined in the original] to pick them up and see what they are that the Chinese would have time to get safely ashore." The envelope was dated 1884. The Peabody Museum also holds a large collection of paper charms and *qian* reading slips, collected in the 1920s and 1930s in Sichuan Province. The author is grateful to the Peabody Museum for permission to examine these items, and for the assistance given by Ms Kathleen Skelly. Dore's drawings of selected items, namely the White Money, are also helpful in establishing some temporal context for the items.

4. For variations on this theme, see also Cohen (1977: 4) and McCreery (1990: 2).

5. Lang and Ragvald also noted the presence of a few Christians (around 4 percent) in their Wong Tai Sin study (1993).

6. This habit was also noticed by Lang and Ragvald when asking informants about the history of Wong Tai Sin. Not clear on the details, informants crafted their own: "this general lack of detailed knowledge leaves gaps which people will sometimes fill with their own constructions, borrowing details from other local stories" (1993: 91).

7. While Chaozhou worshippers can use the same paper offerings as do other Cantonese, they prefer to substitute their own items, which are unique in their size and decoration. For example, they will use Peaceful Money (平安錢) instead of Honorable People Charms and circular Honorable People Papers. Or, they burn Big Gold (大金) to the deities while others use Longevity Gold. They also use a special form of First Treasure paper, and assemble a sub-set of materials to use only at the New Year (including the Cake Money or Bamboo Carrying Pole Money, 竿錢). A partial list of items used by the Chaozhou includes Cake Money (糕錢, also termed Bamboo Carrying Pole Money, 竿錢), Heart of Money (錢心), Peaceful Money (平安錢), Heaven Head Money (天頭錢), Family Money (家門錢), Kung Money (公錢), Big Gold (大金), Four Seasons Money (四季錢), Invitation Card (請怡), Money to Escape from Difficulties (脫難錢), Clothing for the Good Brothers (好兄弟衣), Ko Money (哥錢), the Prosperous/Green Horse (貴人, 祿／綠馬), and Yellow and White Paper (黃白紙).

Chapter 9

1. Robert J. Smith has noted for Japan: "It is a society whose members will generally tell you that the Japanese way of doing a thing is thus and so, often with considerable specificity. When confronted with evidence of contrary behavior, the response is likely to be 'Well, that's not the Japanese way,' but with absolutely no implication that it should therefore be stopped. A man's religious convictions and practices are, in short, no one else's business; his observance of social obligation, on the other hand, is everyone's business" (Smith 1974: 347).
2. Accounts of Hong Kong's fisherfolk may be found in Akers-Jones (1975), Anderson (1967, 1969, 1970, and 1979), Hayes (1987) and Ward (1954, 1965, 1966, and 1985b).
3. In 2000, bookstores in Cambridge, Massachusetts, carried greeting cards bearing glued-on pieces of Gold and Silver Paper, and one specialty housewares shop also stocked Money to Live, to use as coasters or cocktail napkins. Much earlier in Hong Kong, a shop selling popular household ceramics made on the Mainland in the 1950s decorated its walls with hand-painted gowns for the gods. More recently, an April 2004 exhibition was held at the Hong Kong Arts Centre featuring a Japanese photographer who fabricated paper models of Japanese street scenes, complete with individual buildings, for his photo essays (*Hong Kong Standard*, April 4, 2004). Whether or not he burned them afterwards was not mentioned.
4. The opposite has been suggested for Singapore (Tong 1993: 149).

5. While it has been reported for Taiwan that some, on discovering unidentified bones or remains, might worship these in the hopes of persuading the attached wandering soul to cause harm to an enemy or gaining evil benefits (Wang 1974), this seems not the practice in Hong Kong.

Glossary

"A long time" 長時間
"All things come to pass in accordance with the heart's desires" 心想事成
Almanac (Tung Shing) 通勝
Ancestors' Clothing 祖先衣
Ask Rice Woman 問米婆
[To] Assemble Offerings 疊, 疊出來
Assembling Treasure Basin 聚寶盤
Auspicious Paper 吉紙
Bamboo Carrying Pole Money 竿錢
Bank of Hell Notes 冥錢
Basin Meal 食盆
Beating the Small People Ritual 打小人
Big Boat 大船
Big Bright Treasure 大光寶
Big God 大神
Big Gold [Chaozhou] 大金

Big Red and Green 大紅大綠

Black Small People 黑小人

Blackwood 酸枝

Bo Lin Temple 寶蓮寺

Boat Close 船關

Boat Gate 船閘

Boat Tablet 船牌

Breaking out of Prison [Hell] Spirit 破獄神

Brook Money [White Money] 溪錢

Buddha's Hand [citron] 佛手

Burning First Treasure 燒元寶

Burning Gold and Silver Paper 燒金銀衣紙

Burning Paper Bound Offerings 燒紙紮祭品

Burning Paper Sacrificial Offerings 燒紙祭品

Cai Lun 蔡倫

Cai Shen 財神

Cake Money 糕錢

Catholicism 天主教

Chaoyang people 潮陽人

Chaozhou people 潮州人

Chaozhou Paper Offerings [additional items listed separately]

    Clothing for the Good Brothers 好兄弟衣

    Family Money 家門錢

    Four Seasons Money 四季錢

    Heaven Head Money 天頭錢

    Invitation Card 請怡

    Ko Money 哥錢

    Kung Money 公錢

    Money to Escape from Difficulties 脫難錢

    Yellow and White Paper 黃白紙

Charm [*fu*] 符

Charm of Cheung and Lau (willow) 張柳符

Che Gong 車公

Check/Worship the Foot of the Day 查 / 拜日腳

Chi (Qi) 氣

Chief Dragon Tablet 正龍牌

Chinese Paper Merchants Association 中華紙業商會

Chong Yang 重陽

Civil Sedan Chair 文明轎

Circular Honorable People Paper 圓貴人紙

Closed [Gate] Money 關錢

Closed [Gate] Paper 關紙

Closed Separation Paper 關疏紙

Clothing Burned at the Street 燒街衣

Clothing for All the Gods 通神衣

Clothing for Boat Head 船頭衣

Clothing for Gods in the Sky/Clothing for Big Gods 天神衣 / 大神衣

Clothing for the Monkey God 大聖衣

Clothing for the Spirits 孤衣

Clothing Package 衣包

Clothing Paper 衣紙

Compassionate Heart Document 慈心牒

Contract 契

Cow Ghosts and Snake Gods 牛鬼蛇神

Crown for Monkey 金剛圈

Da Jiao Ritual 打醮

Desires of the Heart Come True 心想事成

Di Zhu 地主

Dian Xin 點心

    Paper Varieties of Dian Xin

    Fen Go 粉果

    Fung Jiao 鳳爪

    Gai Bau 雞包

    Lo Mai Gai 糯米雞

    Ma Lai Go 馬拉糕

    Siu Mai 燒賣

Dirty Things [ghosts] 污糟邋遢嘢

Disgraceful Affair Paper 醜事紙

Divination Blocks [bei] 杯

Door Gods 門神

Dongguan 東莞

Double Happiness 囍

"Dragon and Horse Spirit" 龍馬精神

Dragon Boat Festival 端午節

Dragon Tablet 龍牌

Earth Contract 地契

Earth Cow Charm 土牛符

Earth God [Tudi] 土地

Eight Characters 八字

Eight Immortals 八仙

Eight Trigrams 八卦

Eight Trigrams Charm 八卦符

"Everything as You Wish" 如意

Fairy Rat [Bat] 仙鼠

Fate 命

Fate Changers [Lucky Money, Lucky Paper] 運錢, 運紙

[To] "feel at ease and justified" 心安理得

Festival of the Hungry Ghosts [Yu Lan] 盂蘭

First and Fifteenth Days of the Month 初一初十五

First Treasure [yuan bo] 元寶

Fish Gate 魚門

Fishermen 水上人

Five/Seven Color Paper 五 / 七色紙

"Five blessings knocking on the door" 五福臨門

"Five generations have a good performance" 五世其昌

Five Ghosts Charm 五鬼符

Five Star Card 五星東

Five Treasures Document 五寶牒

Flower Basket (for Monkey) 花籃

Flower Boat 花艇

Flower Cannon 花炮

Flower of the Number One Scholar [zhuang yuan] 壯元花

Flower Red 花紅

Flower to Thank God 還神花

[To] Fold (Up) 疊出來

Fo Tan 火炭

Foot of the Day 日腳

Foreign Religion [yangjiao] 洋教

Foshan 佛山

Four Corners and the Center 五方土地

Flying Rat [bat] 飛鼠

Forgiving Book 赦書

Frighten Festival / Feast of Excited Insects 驚蟄 / 節

Fu Jian 附薦

Fu Jian Bag 附薦袋

Fu Jian Cabinet 附薦槓

Gate Passing 過關

Ghost [gui] 鬼

"Go to Fairyland" 仙遊

"Go to San Francisco to sell Salted Duck Eggs" 去舊金山賣鹹鴨蛋

God of Wealth 財神

[When] Going out, Encounter Honorable People 出路遇貴人

Gold and Silver Paper 金銀紙

Gold and Silver Mountain 金山銀山

Gold Boy 金童

Gold Crown worn by Monkey 金剛圈

Gold First Treasure 金元寶

Gold Flower/Silver Hands 金花銀掌

Gold Ingot 金錠

Gold Lotus 金蓮花

Gold Money Pinwheel 金錢車

Gold Pineapple 金菠蘿

Gold Tripod 金鼎

Golden Flower [*jin hua*] 金花

Good Luck Couplet 揮春, 春聯, 對聯

"Good Luck in Dog and Horse Racing" 狗馬亨通

Good Meaning [for pinwheels] 好意頭

Great Auspiciousness 大吉

Great Luck Document 鴻運牒

Great Sage Equal to Heaven 齊天大聖

Great Sage Huang Da Xian 大聖黄大仙

Grooms 馬夫

Grunting of the Heavenly Pig [*tianzhu jiao*] 天豬叫

Guan Di 關帝

Guan Gong 關公

Guan Yin 觀音

Guangdong Province 廣東

Hakka 客家

Han Jing 喊驚

Hanging Red 掛紅

Happy Event and Disgraceful Affair Paper 喜事紙, 醜事紙

Heart of Money 錢心

Heavenly Jockey Club 天堂賽馬會

Heavenly Teacher [*tianshi*] Charm 天師符

Heavenly Rat [bat] 天鼠

Hell Money 冥錢, 陰司紙, 假銀紙, 銀紙, 冥洋

Hell Restaurant 冥通酒樓

Ho Ti (He Di) 和帝

Hold the Peach of Longevity 手執壽桃

Hong Sheng 洪聖

Hong Xian 洪仙

Honorable People Paper 貴人紙

Honorable People Charm 貴人符

Honorable People and Prosperous/Green Horse 貴人, 祿 / 綠馬

Horoscope 八字

Immortal Twins [He He Er Xian] 和合二仙

Incantation of Great Sorrow 大悲咒

"Invite [ask] to Leave" 請走

Jade Fastening Paper 玉扣紙

Jade Girl 玉女

Jiangsu Province 江蘇

King of Hell 東獄大帝

Kitchen God [Zao Jun] 灶君

Label [sealing strip, for the Fu Jian Bag] 封條

Lam Tsuen 林村

Lantau Island 大嶼山

Large First Treasure 大元寶

Large Hell 大幽

Large Red and Green 大紅大綠

Lei Zu 雷祖

Li Bo 李伯

Life 生

Listening to the Scriptures 聽經

Long Life 壽

Long Money [White Money] 長錢

Long Pennant 長旛

Longevity Gold 壽金

Longevity Money Packet 壽錢封

Lotus Flower Basin 蓮花盤

Low Value Currency 散錢

Lu Ban 魯班

Lucky Basin 運盤

Lucky Basin Paper 運盤紙

Lucky Money/Paper [Fate Changers] 運錢, 運紙

Lucky Phrases/Couplets 揮春, 對聯

Machine Made Paper 機器紙

Made by Binding [pitched] 紮作

Mailing Bag [Fu Jian Bag] 郵包

[To] "Make a Profit" 一本萬利

[To] "Make Lives Smooth" 順景

Meaning/Wish Head 意頭
  Popular Meaning Head Phrases for Pinwheels:
  Both men and wealth are flourishing. 人財兩旺
  Business is brisk. 生意興隆
  [The] desires of the heart come true. 心想事成
  Everything happens as you wish. 萬事如意
  Gain financial resources in many ways. 財源廣進
  Get a 10,000 return on original investment. 一本萬利
  Long life, riches, and honor. 長命富貴
  May Wong Tai Sin bless you. 大仙保佑
  May your family be prosperous. 家宅興隆
  Prosperous all through the year. 週年旺財
  Sail through the wind smoothly. 一帆風順
Medicine for Regulating the Heart 正心藥
Men Kou 門口
Ming Yang [Hell Money] 冥洋
Model Paper Pitching 模型紮作
Money Ingot 錢錠
Money to Escape From Difficulties 脫難錢
Money to Live [Towards Life Money, Towards Life Spirit Incantation] 往生錢
Money to Pass the Road 買路錢
Monkey 孫悟空, 齊天大聖
Mountain Money 紅錢山帛
Mutual Aid Committee 互助委員會
Net of Sky and Earth 天羅地網
"Never Ending Luck" 好運不停
"Not Here" 不在, 唔喺度
Number One Scholar 壯元
Panyu 番禺
Paper Cuts 剪紙
Paper of Five Ghosts 五鬼紙
Paper Pitching 紮作
Paper Shop [Retail] 衣紙舖
Paper to Buy a Passage [White Money] 買路錢
"Passed Away" 過身
Passport 通行證, 拜景
"Peaceful Family, Honorable People Seek and Assist" 家門平安, 貴人求助
Peaceful Money 平安錢
Pear 梨
"Pin Flowers [in the hair], Hang up the Red" 參花掛紅

Pinwheel [*feng che*] 風車

[To] Pitch 紮作

Platform for Observing One's Home Village 望鄉台

Po Lam Estate 寶林邨

Private Worship at Home 拜神

Prosperity 福

Prosperous/Green Horse 祿, 綠馬

Qing Ming 清明

Qiu Qian [*kauh chim*] 求籤

Rectangular Honorable People Paper 長貴人紙

Red Affairs 紅事

Red and White Banner 紅白旛

Red Ball 紅球

Red Cloths 紅布

Red Head 紅頭

Red Money 紅錢

Red Money and White Mountain [Laisee Money] 紅錢白山

Red Paper Envelopes [for Money] 利是

Restful Heart Document 息心牒

Rice Color 米色

Sai Ying Pun 西營盤

San Bei [divination] 三杯

Sau Mau Ping Estate 秀茂坪邨

Scapegoat 代人, 替身

Scattering Money [White Money] 散錢

Scepter 如意

Second and Sixteenth Days of the Month 初二初十六

Sedan Chair 轎

Sending Treasuries 寄庫

Seven Color Money 七色錢

Seven Month Fu Jian 七月附薦

Seven Voice Incantation 七言咒

Sha Tin 沙田

Shanghai 上海

Shantou 汕頭

Shui Kou 水口

Shunde 順德

Sik Sik Yuen 嗇色園

Silver Coins 洋銀

Silver Paper (Hell Money) 銀紙

Sincerity 誠
Small Clothing 衣仔
Small First Treasure 細元寶
Small People [*xiao ren*] 小人
Small People Fan 小人扇
Small People Paper 小人紙
Small Solving of 100 Problems 細百解
Small Temples 小廟
Small Water Clothing 水衣仔
Solving of 100 Problems 百解
Song Dynasty 宋代
Soul Pursuing Charm 追魂符
Spirit Flower 神花
Spirit Red 神紅
Spirit Soul License 神魂執照
Star of Paper Pitching 紮作明星
Steel Headband worn by Monkey 頭筋圈
Stock Mailing 寄庫
Street of the Dead 陰州街
Superstition 迷信
Tai Wai 大圍
Tan Gong 譚公
Tang Dynasty 唐代
Tang lou 唐樓
Tang Tai Zong 唐太宗
Tangerine 桔
Teaching of Goats [*yangjiao*] 羊教
Temple of the Ten Thousand Buddhas 萬佛寺
"Ten Fingers are not the same length" 十隻手指沒有一樣長
Ten Treasures 十寶
[To] Thank God 還神
"Thirty-six Roads" 三十六道
Thirty-six [Secluded] Hell Clothing 三十六幽衣
Thirty-six Hell Clothes Hell Green 三十六幽衣幽綠
Three Kingdoms 三國
Three Number Ones Reach [Home] 三元及第
Three Star Card 三星卡
Three Star Gods 三星 (福祿壽)
Three Strands of Popular Belief 三教合一
Tian Gong 天公

Tian Guan 天官

Tian Hou 天后

Tianjin 天津

Towards Life Money [Money to Live] 往生錢

Towards Life Spirit Incantation [Money to Live] 往生神咒

Treasure Heart [White Money] 寶心

Tsuen Wan 荃灣

Tseung Kwan O 將軍澳

Two First Treasure 二元寶

Tze Wan Shan Estate 慈雲山邨

Unreal Money [Hell Money] 假銀紙

"Vast Prosperity all the Days" 鴻福齊天

Vice Dragon Tablet 副龍牌

Village House 鄉村屋

Wandering Souls 遊魂

Water Bucket (for Monkey) 水桶

Water Duck 水鴨

Water Gate 水閘

Water Ladder 水梯

"When going out, encounter honorable people" 出路遇貴人

Wheeled Sedan Chair 轎

White Affairs 白事

White Money [Brook Money] 溪錢

Willow Banner 柳旛

"With the beginning and the ending" 有頭有尾

Wong Tai Sin 黃大仙

Worship Against a Violation 拜犯

[To] Worship the Ancestors 拜祖先

[To] Worship the Four Corners 拜四角

[To] Worship the Gods 拜神

Worship the Street 拜街

Written Accusation 狀詞

Wu Pei Fu 吳佩孚

Xiamen 廈門

Xinhui 新會

Yang Separation 陽隔

Yau Ma Tei 油蔴地

Yin Administered Paper [Hell Money] 陰司紙

Yin and Yang Separation 陰陽隔

Yin Contract 陰契

Yin Separation 陰隔
Young Workers 童工
Yu Lan [Festival of the Hungry Ghosts] 盂蘭
Yuan Shikai 袁世凱
Zao Jun 灶君
Zhang Tianshi 張天師

References Cited

Ahern, Emily Martin. 1973. *The Cult of the Dead in a Chinese Village*. Stanford: Stanford University Press.

——. 1975. The Power and Pollution of Chinese Women. In Women in Chinese Society, edited by Margery Wolf and Roxane Witke. Stanford: Stanford University Press.

Akers-Jones, David. 1975. Boat People's Ceremonies Observed from Island House, Tai Po. *Journal of the Hong Kong Branch of the Royal Asiatic Society* 15: 300–2.

Alexeiev, Basil M. 1928. *The Chinese Gods of Wealth*. Hertford: Stephen Austin and Sons, Ltd.

Anderson, E. N. 1967. The Folk Songs of the Hong Kong Boat People. *Journal of American Folklore* 80 (317): 285–96.

——. 1969. Sacred Fish. *Man* 4: 33–39.

——. 1970. *The Floating World of Castle Peak Bay*. Washington: American Anthropological Association.

——. 1977. The Changing Tastes of the Gods: Chinese Temple Fairs in Malaysia. *Asian Folklore Studies* 36 (1): 19–30.

——. 1979. A Social History of Hong Kong Boat-Folk Songs. In *Legend, Lore and*

Religion in China, edited by Sarah Allen and Alvin P. Cohen. San Francisco: Chinese Materials Center, Inc.

——. 1988. *The Floating World of Castle Peak Bay*. University Microfilm International.

Baber, E. Colborne. 1882. *Travels and Researches in Western China*. Royal Geographical Society, Supplementary Papers, Vol. 1. London: John Murray.

Baity, Philip C. 1977. The Ranking of Gods in Chinese Folk Religion. *Asian Folklore Studies* 36 (2): 75–84.

Baker, Hugh D. 1964. Burial, Geomancy and Ancestor Worship. In *Aspects of Social Organization in the New Territories*. Week-end Symposium, The Hong Kong Branch of the Royal Asiatic Society. Hong Kong: Cathay Press.

——. 1983. Life in the Cities: The Emergence of Hong Kong Man. *China Quarterly* 95: 469–80.

——. 1993. Social Life in Hong Kong: Hong Kong Man in Search of Majority. *China Quarterly* 136: 864–77.

Ball, J. Dyer. 1926. *Things Chinese*. Fifth edition. London: John Murray.
Ball, Michael and Gregory W. H. Smith. 1992. *Analyzing Visual Data*. London: Sage.

Bell, Catherine. 1989. Religion and Chinese Culture: Toward an Assessment of "Popular Religion." *History of Religions* 28: 35–57.

Berger, Patricia. 1998. Body Doubles: Sculpture for the Afterlife. *Orientations* 29 (2): 46–53.

Berkowitz, M. I. 1975. *The Tenacity of Chinese Folk Tradition – Two Studies of Hong Kong Chinese*. Occasional Paper No. 33. Singapore: Institute of Southeast Asian Studies.

Berkowitz, M. I., Frederick P. Brandauer, and John H. Reed. 1969. *Folk Religion in an Urban Setting: A Study of Hakka Villages in Transition*. Hong Kong: Christian Study Centre on Chinese Religion and Culture.

Berliner, Nancy Zeng. 1986. *Chinese Folk Art: The Small Skills of Carving Insects*. Boston: Little, Brown and Company.

Bird, Isabella. [1899] 1985. *The Yangtze Valley and Beyond*. Bury St. Edmonds: Virago Press.

Black, Alison H. 1986. Gender and Cosmology in Chinese Correlative Thinking. In *Gender and Religion: On the Complexity of Symbols*, edited by Caroline Walker Bynum, Stevan Harrell, and Paula Richman. Boston: Beacon Press.

Bodde, Derk. [1936] 1965. *Annual Customs and Festivals in Peking, as Recorded in the Yen-Ching Sui-Shih-Chi by Tun Li-Ch'en*. Hong Kong: Oxford University Press.

Boltz, Judith Magee. 1986. In Homage to T'ien-fei. *Journal of the American Oriental Society* 106(1): 211–32.

Bonavia, David. 1995. *China's Warlords*. Hong Kong: Oxford University Press.

Bone, C. 1889a. The Religious Festivals of the Cantonese. *The Chinese Recorder and Missionary Journal* 20(8): 367–71.

——. 1889b. The Religious Festivals of the Cantonese. *The Chinese Recorder and Missionary Journal* 20(9): 391–402.

Bosco, Joseph. 2001. The Ghosts of the Chinese University of Hong Kong and What They Mean. Lecture delivered to the Hong Kong Anthropological Society, October 29.

Bradsher, Keith. 2005. "Hong Kong's Official Tree of Good Fortune Runs out of Luck." *International Herald Tribune*. February 16.

Bredon, Juliet. 1930. *Chinese New Year Festivals: A Picturesque Monograph of the Rites, Ceremonies, and Observances in Relation Thereto*. Shanghai: Kelly and Walsh, Ltd.

Bredon, Juliet and Igor Mitrophanow. 1927. *The Moon Year: A Record of Chinese Customs and Festivals*. Shanghai: Kelly and Walsh, Ltd. Reprint, Hong Kong: Oxford University Press, 1982.

Bryson, Mary Isabella. 1885. *Child Life in Chinese Homes*. London: Religious Tract Society.

Burgess, J. S. 1928. *The Guilds of Peking*. New York: Columbia University Press.

Burkhardt, V. R. 1953. *Chinese Creeds and Customs*, Vol. 1. Hong Kong: South China Morning Post.

——. 1955. *Chinese Creeds and Customs*, Vol. II. Hong Kong: South China Morning Post.

——. 1958. *Chinese Creeds and Customs*, Vol. III. Hong Kong: South China Morning Post.

Cammann, Schulyer. 1968. On the Decoration of Modern Temples in Taiwan and Hong Kong. *Journal of the American Oriental Society* 88: 785–90.

Campany, Robert F. 1990. Return from Death Narratives in Early Medieval China. *Journal of Chinese Religions* 18: 92–125.

Carter, Dagny. 1948. *Four Thousand Years of China's Art*. New York: The Ronald Press Company.

Cave, Roderick. 1988. Chinese Paper Offerings. Hong Kong: Oxford University Press.

Chan, Anita, Richard Madsen and Jonathan Unger. 1984. *Chen Village*. Berkeley: University of California Press.

Chan, David K. K. 1986. The Culture of Hong Kong: A Myth or Reality. In *Hong Kong Society: A Reader*, edited by Alex Y. H. Kwan and David K. K. Chan. Hong Kong: Writers and Publishers' Cooperative.

Chan Hoi-man. 1994. Culture and Identity. In *The Other Hong Kong Report*, edited by Donald H. McMillen and Man Si-wai. Hong Kong: The Chinese University Press.

Chan, K. Y. 1991. Joss Stick Manufacturing: A Study of a Traditional Industry in Hong Kong. *Journal of the Hong Kong Branch of the Royal Asiatic Society* 29: 94–120.

Chan, May. 2004 Strong Family Ties Pave Way for "Good Death." *South China Morning Post.* September 3.

Chan, Sau Y. 1991. *Improvisation in a Ritual Context: The Music of Cantonese Opera.* Hong Kong: The Chinese University Press.

Chaney, David. 1971. Job Satisfaction and Unionization. In *Hong Kong: The Industrial Colony,* edited by Keith Hopkins. Hong Kong: Oxford University Press.

Chao, Paul. 1983. *Chinese Kinship.* Boston: K. Paul International.

Ch'en Hsiang-ch'un. 1942. Examples of Charm against Epidemics with Short Explanations. *Asian Folklore Studies* 1: 37–54.

Cheng, Andy. 2005. Root of Famed Tree's Ills Lies in Soil. *South China Morning Post.* February 15.

Cheng, May M. and Wong Siu-lun. 1997. Religious Convictions and Sentiments. In *Indicators of Social Development,* edited by Lau Siu-kai, Lee Ming-kwan, Wan Po-san and Wong Siu-lun. Hong Kong Institute of Asian Pacific Studies Research Monograph No. 33. Hong Kong: The Chinese University Press.

Cheng Sea Ling. 1997. Back to the Future: Herbal Tea Shops in Hong Kong. In *Hong Kong: The Anthropology of a Chinese Metropolis,* edited by Grant Evans and Maria Tam. Richmond: Curzon.

Cheng, Y. K. L. 1967. *A Study of Patron Gods.* Taipei: Chinese Books Company.

Cheung Chi-fai. 2003. Scary Ads for Halloween Draw Complaints from TV Viewers. *South China Morning Post.* October 8.

———. 2004. Two Golden Paper Primates Sent to Join Monkey Man. *South China Morning Post.* July 27.

Chiao Chien. 1983. Cognitive Play: Some Minor Rituals among Hong Kong Cantonese. *East Asian Civilizations* 2: 138–44.

Chiao Chien and Chor-on Leung. 1982. "Beating the Small Person" Ritual in Hong Kong. *Bulletin of the Institute of Ethnology of the Academia Sinica* 54: 115–28 (in Chinese).

Choi Chi-cheung. 1984. The Chinese "Yue Lan" Ghost Festival in Japan: A Kobe Case Study. *Journal of the Hong Kong Branch of the Royal Asiatic Society* 24: 230–63.

———. 1995. Reinforcing Ethnicity: The Jiao Festival in Cheung Chau. In *Down to Earth: The Territorial Bond in South China,* edited by David Faure and Helen Siu. Stanford: Stanford University Press.

Chow, Vivienne. 2005. Offerings Keep Ancestors up with the Joneses. *South China Morning Post.* April 5.

Christensen, Bodil. 1944. Notas sobre la fabricacion del papel indigena y su empleo para "brujerias" en la Sierra Norte de Puebla. *Revista Mexicana de Estudios Antropologicos*: 1–2: 109–23.

Chu, C. C. and T. Blaisdell. 1924. Peking Rugs and Peking Boys: A Study of the Rug Industry in Peking. *The Chinese Social and Political Science Review* [Supplement] 8: 1–47.

Ch'u T'ung-tsu. 1961. *Law and Society in Traditional China*. Paris: Mouton.

Clarke, George, trans. 1898. The Yu-Li or Precious Records. *Journal of the China Branch of the Royal Asiatic Society* 28: 233–399.

Cohen, Alvin P. 1977. A Chinese Temple Keeper Talks about Chinese Folk Religion. *Asian Folklore Studies* 36 (1): 1–17.

Cohen, Myron L. 1991. Being Chinese: The Peripheralization of Traditional Identity. *Daedalus* 120 (2): 113–34.

Cooper, Eugene. 1980. *The Wood Carvers of Hong Kong*. Cambridge: Cambridge University Press.

Coltman, Robert. 1891. *The Chinese, Their Present and Future: Medical, Political, and Social*. Philadelphia: F.A. Davis.

Cormack, Annie. 1935. *Everyday Customs in China*. Edinburgh: The Moray Press.

Couling, Samuel. 1917. *The Encyclopedia Sinica*. Shanghai: Kelly and Walsh.

Coy, Michael W., ed. 1989. *Apprenticeship: From Theory to Method and Back Again*. Albany: State University of New York Press.

David, Bernice. 2000. Oral Exchange between the Living and the Dead: The Ritual Function of the Cantonese Manmaipo. *Archives de Sciences Sociales des Religions* 111: 135–48 (in French).

Day, Clarence Burton. 1927. Paper Gods for Sale. *The China Journal* 7 (6): 277–84.

——. 1928. Shanghai Invites the God of Wealth. *The China Journal* 8 (6): 289–94.

——. 1929. The Cult of the Hearth. *The China Journal* 10 (1): 6–11.

——. 1940a. *Chinese Peasant Cults: Being a Study of Paper Gods*. Shanghai: Kelly and Walsh.

——. 1940b. The New Year Ceremonials of Chou Wang-Miao. *The China Journal* 32 (1): 6–12.

——. 1975. *Popular Religion in Pre-Communist China*. San Francisco: Chinese Materials Center, Inc.

Dean, S. M. 1924. Industrial Education in China. *The Chinese Social and Political Science Review* 8: 115–21.

Dennys, N. B. 1876. *The Folklore of China*. London: Trubner.

Dikotter, Frank. 1992. *The Discourse of Race in Modern China*. Hong Kong: Hong Kong University Press.

Doolittle, Rev. Justus. 1865a. *Social Life of the Chinese*. Vol. I. New York: Harper and Brothers.

——. 1865b. *Social Life of the Chinese*. Vol. II. New York: Harper and Brothers.

Dore, Henry S. J. 1914. *Researches into Chinese Superstitions*, translated by M. Kennelly. Shanghai: T'usewei Printing Press.

Duyvendak, J. J. L. 1939. The True Dates of the Chinese Maritime Expeditions in the Early Fifteenth Century. *T'oung Pao* 34: 341–412.

Eberhard, Wolfram. 1958. *Chinese Festivals*. London: Abelard-Shuman.

——. 1967a. *Guilt and Sin in Traditional China*. Berkeley: University of California Press.

——. 1967b. Topics and Moral Values in Chinese Temple Decorations. *Journal of the American Oriental Society* 87: 22–33.

——. 1968. On Some Chinese Terms of Abuse (Collected by Frank Huang). *Asian Folklore Studies* 27 (1): 25–40.

——. 1986. *A Dictionary of Chinese Symbols*. London: Routledge and Kegan Paul.

Ebrey, Patricia Buckley. 1991. *Chu Hsi's Family Rituals*. Princeton: Princeton University Press.

Endacott, G. B. 1964. *Government and People in Hong Kong, 1841–1962: A Constitutional History*. Hong Kong: Hong Kong University Press.

Endacott, G. B. and A. Hinton. 1962. *Fragrant Harbour: A Short History of Hong Kong*. Westport: Greenwood Press.

Evans, Grant and Maria Tam. 1997. Introduction. In *Hong Kong: The Anthropology of a Chinese Metropolis*. Richmond: Curzon.

Fang Jing Pei and Juwen Zhang. 2000. *The Interpretation of Dreams in Chinese Culture*. Trumbull: Weatherhill.

Fei Hsiao-tung. 1939. *Peasant Life in China: A Field Study of Country Life in the Yangtze Valley*. London: Routledge and Kegan Paul.

Feuchtwang, Stephan. 1986. Religious Revival, or How to Succeed in Business? *China Now* 118: 17–20.

Feuchtwang, Stephan and Wang Ming-ming. 1991. The Politics of Culture or a Contest of Histories: Representations of Chinese Popular Religion. *Dialectical Anthropology* 16: 251–72.

Fowler, Geoffrey. 2003. Dying Alone. *Far Eastern Economic Review*. June 5.

Freedman, Maurice. 1958. *Lineage Organization in Southeastern China*. London: Athlone Press.

——. 1967. Ancestor Worship: Two Facets of the Chinese Case. In *Social Organization: Essays Presented to Raymond Firth*, edited by M. Freedman. Chicago: University of Chicago Press.

——. 1973. On the Sociological Study of Chinese Religion. In *Religion and Ritual in Chinese Society*, edited by Arthur Wolf. Stanford: Stanford University Press.

Gallin, Bernard. 1966. *Hsin Hsing, Taiwan*. Berkeley: University of California Press.

Gamble, Sidney. 1954. *Ting Hsien: A North China Rural Community*. Stanford: Stanford University Press.

Gamble, S. D. and J. S. Burgess. 1921. *Peking: A Social Survey*. London: Oxford University Press.

Gardner, Daniel K. 1995. Ghosts and Spirits in the Sung Neo-Confucian World: Chu Hsi on Kuei-Shen. *Journal of the American Oriental Society* 115 (4): 598–611.

Garrett, Valery M. 1994. *Chinese Clothing*. Hong Kong: Oxford University Press.

Gates, Hill. 1987. Money for the Gods. *Modern China* 13: 259–77.

Gennep, Arnold L. Van. 1960. *The Rites of Passage*. Chicago: University of Chicago Press.

Golas, P. J. 1977. Early Ch'ing Guilds. In *The City in Late Imperial China*, edited by G. William Skinner. Stanford: Stanford University Press.

Goodrich, Anne Swann. 1961. *Folk Religion in Southwest China*. Washington, DC: Smithsonian Press.

———. 1964. *The Peking Temple of the Eastern Peak*. Nagoya: Nippon Oyo Printing Company.

———. 1981. *Chinese Hells*. St. Augustin: Monumenta Serica.

———. 1991. *Peking Paper Gods: A Look at Home Worship*. Nettetal: Steyler Verlag.

Graham, David Crockett. 1961. *Folk Religion in Southwest China*. Washington, DC: Smithsonian Press.

Groot, J. J. M. de 1892. *The Religious System of China*, Vol. I. Leiden: E. J. Brill.

———. 1894. *The Religious System of China*, Vol. II. Leiden: E. J. Brill.

———. 1910. *The Religious System of China*, Vol. VI. Leiden: E. J. Brill.

———. 1912. *The Religion of the Chinese*. New York: The Macmillan Company.

Guldin, Gregory. 1977. "Little Fujian": Sub-Neighborhood and Community in North Point, Hong Kong. *Journal of the Hong Kong Branch of the Royal Asiatic Society* 17: 112–9.

———. 1982. Whose Neighborhood Is This? Ethnicity and Community in Hong Kong. *Urban Anthropology* 9 (2): 243–63.

———. 1997. Hong Kong Ethnicity: of Folk Models and Change. In *Hong Kong: The Anthropology of a Chinese Metropolis*, edited by Grant Evans and Maria Tam. Richmond: Curzon.

Guthrie, William. 2002. Personal Communication.

Gutzlaff, Charles. 1834. Temple of Teen-how at Mei-chow. *Chinese Repository* 2: 563–5.

Harrell, Stevan. 1986. Men, Women and Ghosts in Taiwanese Folk Religion. In *Gender and Religion: On the Complexity of Symbols*, edited by Caroline Walker Bynum, Stevan Harrell, and Paula Rickman. Boston: Beacon.

Hase, Patrick. 1981. Traditional Funerals. *Journal of the Hong Kong Branch of the Royal Asiatic Society* 21: 192–6.

———. 1984. Observations at a Village Funeral. In *From Village to City*, edited by David Faure, James Hayes, and Alan Burch. Hong Kong: Hong Kong University Press.

———. 2000. Village in the Wood. Manuscript.

———. n.d. The New Territories. Manuscript.

——. n.d. Dajiao. Manuscript.

Hase, Patrick, ed. 1997. *In the Heart of the Metropolis: Yaumatei and Its People*. Hong Kong: Joint Publishing Company and Hong Kong Branch of the Royal Asiatic Society.

Hayes, James. 1975. A Tale of Two Cities. In *Hong Kong: The Interaction of Tradition and Life in the Towns*, edited by Marjorie Topley. Hong Kong: Hong Kong Branch of the Royal Asiatic Society.

——. 1987. Hong Kong's Own Boat People. *Journal of the Hong Kong Branch of the Royal Asiatic Society* 27: 280–2.

——. 2001. *South China Village Culture*. New York: Oxford University Press.

Hayes, L. Newton. 1924. The Gods of the Chinese. *Journal of the North China Branch of the Royal Asiatic Society* 55: 84–104.

Heintz, Ruth Inge. 1981. The Nine Imperial Gods of Singapore. *Asian Folklore Studies* 40: 151–71.

Hodous, Lewis. 1912. The Great Summer Festival of China as Observed in Foochow: A Study in Popular Religion. *Journal of the North China Branch of the Royal Asiatic Society* 43: 69–80.

——. 1915. The Ch'ing Ming Festival. *Journal of the North China Branch of the Royal Asiatic Society* 46: 58–60.

——. 1929. *Folkways in China*. London: Arthur Probsthain.

Hong Kong Government, Leisure and Cultural Services Department. 2001. Attendance Record of the Museums under Hong Kong Heritage Museum. Office of the Chief Curator.

Hong Kong Government, Office of the Director of Apprenticeship. 1976. A Guide to the Apprenticeship Ordinance and the Apprenticeship Regulations. Hong Kong: Office of the Director of Apprenticeship.

Hong Kong Standard. 2004. Cut out for the city. April 14.

Hou Ching-Lang. 1975. *Monnaies d'Offrande et la Notion de Tresorerie dans la Religion Chinoise*. Paris: Press Universitaires de France.

Hsieh, Jiann and Ying-Hsiung Chou. 1981. Public Aspirations in the New Year Couplets. *Asian Folklore Studies* 40(2): 125–49.

Hsieh Yu Wei. 1967. Filial Piety and Chinese Society. In *The Chinese Mind: Essentials of Chinese Philosophy and Culture*, edited by Charles A. Moore. Honolulu: University of Hawaii Press.

Hsu, Francis. 1948. *Under the Ancestors Shadow: Chinese Culture and Personality*. New York: Columbia University Press.

Huang Shaorong. 1991. Chinese Traditional Festivals. *Journal of Popular Culture* 25: 163–80.

Hui, C. Harry. 1991. Religious and Supernaturalistic Beliefs. In *Indicators of Social Development*, edited by Lau Siu-kai, Lee Ming-kwan, Wan Po-san, and Wong

Siu-lun. Hong Kong Institute of Asia-Pacific Studies Research Monograph No. 2. Hong Kong: The Chinese University Press.

Hunter, Dard. 1937. *Chinese Ceremonial Paper*. Chillicothe: Mountain House Press.

———. 1943. *Papermaking: The History and Technique of an Ancient Craft*. New York: Alfred A. Knopf.

Ikels, Charlotte. 1996. *The Return of the God of Wealth*. Stanford: Stanford University Press.

———. 2004. *Filial Piety*. Stanford: Stanford University Press.

Ingrams, Harold. 1952. *Hong Kong*. London: Her Majesty's Stationary Office.

Irwin, Lee. 1990. Divinity and Salvation: The Great Goddesses of China. *Asian Folklore Studies* 49: 53–68.

Johnson, David. 1986. Actions Speak Louder than Words – the Cultural Significance of Opera in Late Imperial China. Paper Presented at the Conference of U.S.–Japanese Historians. Occidental College and the Huntington Library.

Johnson, Graham E. 1971. From Rural Committee to Spirit Medium Cult: Voluntary Associations in the Development of a Chinese Town. *Contributions to Asian Studies* 1–2: 123–43.

———. 1997. Links to and Through South China: Local, Regional, and Global Connections. In *Hong Kong's Reunion with China: The Global Dimensions*, edited by Gerard A Postiglione and James T. H. Tang. Armonk: M. E. Sharpe.

Johnston, R. F. 1910. *Lion and Dragon in North China*. New York: Dutton.

Jordan, David K. 1972. *Gods, Ghosts, and Ancestors: The Folk Religion of a Taiwanese Village*. Berkeley: University of California Press.

Kani, Hiroaki. 1982. The Control of Temples and Festivals in Hong Kong. In *Research on Chinese Traditional Entertainments in Southeast Asia, Part I*, edited by Kanehide Onoe. The Institute of Oriental Culture. Tokyo: University of Tokyo.

Katz, Paul. 1986. Demons or Deities? – The Wangye of Taiwan. *Asian Folklore Studies* 46: 197–215.

Knapp, Ronald. 1986. *China's Traditional Rural Architecture*. Honolulu: University of Hawaii Press.

Laing, Ellen Johnston. 1989. The Persistence of Propriety in the 1980s. In *Unofficial China*, edited by Perry Link, Richard Madsen, and Paul G. Pickowicz. Boulder: Westview Press.

Lam, Agnes. 2005a. Wishes Banned to Save Ailing Tree. *South China Morning Post*. February 15.

———. 2005b. Blockade Protects Besieged Wishing Tree. *South China Morning Post*. February 16.

Lang, Graeme. 1997. Sacred Power in the Metropolis: Shrines and Temples in Hong Kong. In *Hong Kong: The Anthropology of a Chinese Metropolis*, edited by Grant Evans and Maria Tam. Richmond: Curzon.

Lang, Graeme and Lars Ragvald. 1987. Official and Oral Traditions about Hong

Kong's Newest God. *Journal of the Hong Kong Branch of the Royal Asiatic Society* 27: 93–100.

——. 1993. *The Rise of a Refugee God: Hong Kong's Wong Tai Sin.* Hong Kong: Oxford University Press.

Lau, Aileen, ed. 1991. *Spirit of Han.* Singapore: Southeast Asian Ceramic Society/ Sun Tree Publishing.

Lau, Angel. 2000. Roadside Joss Sticks Gave Alleged Killers Away. *South China Morning Post.* November 16.

Lau Siu-kai. 1982. *Society and Politics in Hong Kong. Hong Kong*: The Chinese University Press.

Lau Siu-kai and Kuan Hsin-chi. 1988. *The Ethos of the Hong Kong Chinese.* Hong Kong: The Chinese University Press.

Laufer, Berthold. 1989. *Jade: Its History and Symbolism in China.* Mineola: Dover.

Lee, Ella. 2001. Life's Final Lesson – The Facts of Death. *South China Morning Post.* September 3.

Lee Ming-kwan. 1992. Family and Gender Issues. In *Indicators of Social Development: Hong Kong,* edited by Lau Siu-kai, Lee Ming-kwan, Wan Po-san, and Wong Siu-lun. Hong Kong: Hong Kong Institute of Asia-Pacific Studies, The Chinese University of Hong Kong.

Lee, Rance, Cheung Tak-sing and Cheung Yuet-wah, 1979. Material and Non-Material Conditions and Life-Satisfaction of Urban Residents in Hong Kong. In *Hong Kong: Economic, Social, and Political Studies in Development,* edited by Tzong-biau Lin, Rance P. L. Lee, and Udo-Ernst Simonis. White Plains: M. L. Sharpe.

Lee Wai Yee and Leung Wai Kei. 1994. Taboos in Paper Offering Shops. *The Hong Kong Anthropologist* 7: 40–48.

Legge, James. 1960. *The Chinese Classics.* Vol. One. Hong Kong: Hong Kong University Press.

Li Chi Si, ed. 1985. *A View on the Customs of Taiwan.* Vol. 2. Taipei: Da Wai Publications Ltd.

Li Chien. 1990. *Research on the Patron Gods of China.* Beijing: China Overseas Publishing Company.

Liao, T. C. 1948. The Apprentices in Ch'eng Tu During and after the War. *Yenching Journal of Social Studies* 4: 89–106.

Liu Tik-sang. 2003. A Nameless but Active Religion: An Anthropologist's View of Local Religion in Hong Kong and Macau. *The China Quarterly* 174: 373–94.

Loehr, Max. 1961. The Question of Individualism in Chinese Art. *Journal of the History of Ideas* 22: 147–58.

Lopez, Donald S. Jr., ed. 1996. *Religions of China in Practice.* Princeton: Princeton University Press.

Lowe, H.Y. [1940–41] 1983. *The Adventures of Wu: The Life Cycle of a Peking Man.* Princeton: Princeton University Press.

Lubar, Steven and W. David Kingery. 1993. *History from Things: Essays on Material Culture.* Washington: The Smithsonian Institution.

Macgowan, D. J. 1886. Chinese Guilds or Chambers of Commerce and Trade Unions. *Journal of the North China Branch of the Royal Asiatic Society* [New Series] 21: 133–92.

———. 1908. *Sidelights on Chinese Life.* Philadelphia: J. B. Lippincott Company.

MacInnis, Donald E. 1989. *Religion in China Today: Policy and Practice.* Maryknoll: Orbis Books.

Mark, Lindy Li. 1979. Orthography Riddles, Divination, and Word Magic: An Exploration in Folklore and Culture. In *Legend, Lore and Religion in China,* edited by Sarah Allan and Alvin P. Cohen. San Francisco: Chinese Materials Center, Inc.

Mathews, Gordon. 2000. *Global Culture/ Individual Identity.* London: Routledge.

May, Patsy. 2002. Photo Offer Shatters Funeral Taboo. *South China Morning Post.* June 21.

McClure, Floyd Alonzo. 1986. *Chinese Handmade Paper.* Newtown: Bird and Bull Press.

McCracken, Grant. 1988. *Culture and Consumption: New Approaches to the Symbolic Character of Consumer Goods and Activities.* Bloomington: Indiana University Press.

McCreery, John. 1990. Why Don't We See Some Real Money Here? Offerings in Chinese Religion. *Journal of Chinese Religions* 18: 1–24.

Medley, Margaret. 1964. *A Handbook of Chinese Art.* London: G. Bell and Sons Ltd.

Meyers, William Frederick. 1869. On Wen-Ch'ang, the God of Literature: His History and Worship. *Journal of the North China Branch of the Royal Asiatic Society* [New Series] 6: 31–44.

Migot, Andre. 1956 *Tibetan Marches.* London: Readers Union/Rupert Hart-Davis.

Mitchell, Robert E. 1969. *Levels of Emotional Strain in Southeast Asian Cities.* Hong Kong: A Project of the Urban Family Life Survey.

Morgan, Harry T. 1942. *Chinese Symbols and Superstitions.* South Pasadena: P. D. and Ione Perkins.

Morgan, W. P. 1960. *Triad Societies in Hong Kong.* Hong Kong: Hong Kong Government Press.

Munsterberg, Hugo. 1972. *Dragons in Chinese Art.* New York: Hacker.

———. 1986. *Symbolism in Ancient Chinese Art.* New York: Hacker Art Books.

Myers, John T. 1981. Traditional Chinese Religious Practices in an Urban-Industrial Setting: The Example of Kwun Tong. In *Social Life and Development in Hong Kong,* edited by Ambrose Y. C. King and Rance P. L. Lee. Hong Kong: The Chinese University Press.

Naquin, Susan. 1988. Funerals in North China: Uniformity and Variation. In *Death*

Ritual in Late Imperial and Modern China, edited by James L. Watson and Evelyn S. Rawski. Berkeley: University of California Press.

Newell, William H. 1976. *Ancestors*. The Hague: Mouton.

Ng, Pedro. 1975. *The People of Kwun Tong Survey* — Data Book. Hong Kong: Social Research Centre, The Chinese University of Hong Kong.

Niida, N. 1950. The Industrial and Commercial Guilds of Peking and Religion and Fellowcountrymanship as Elements of their Coherence. *Folklore Studies* 9: 179–206.

Osgood, Cornelius. 1963. *Village Life in Old China*. New York: The Ronald Press.

——. 1975 *The Chinese*. Vol. II. Tucson: The University of Arizona Press.

Paludan, Anne. 1998. *Chronicle of the Chinese Emperors*. London: Thames and Hudson.

Pan Xiafeng. 1995. *The Stagecraft of Peking Opera*. Beijing: New World Press.

Pas, Julian F. 1989. A New Report of Shamanistic Travel to the Courts of Hell. *Journal of Chinese Religions* 17: 43–60.

Pfister, Lauren F. 2001. Reconsidering Three Faces of the "Revived One" from Mid-19th Century China. Unpublished paper.

Phillips, Heike. 2000. Mobile Ownership up 50pc in Past Two Years. *South China Morning Post*. November 22.

Po Sung Nien and David Johnson. 1992. *Domesticated Deities and Auspicious Emblems*. Publications of the Chinese Popular Culture Project 2. Berkeley: Arcata Graphics Company.

Poon Shuk Wah. 2004. Refashioning Festivals in Republican Guangzhou. *Modern China* 30 (2): 199–227.

Potter, Jack M. 1969. The Structure of Rural Chinese Society in the New Territories. In *Hong Kong: A Society in Transition*, edited by I. C. Jarvie. London: Routledge and Kegan Paul.

——. 1974. Cantonese Shamanism. In *Religion and Ritual in Chinese Society*, edited by Arthur Wolf. Stanford: Stanford University Press.

Qin Ling Yun. 1958. *Minjian Huagong shiliao*. Beijing: Zhongguo gudian yishu chupanshe.

Ragvald, Lars and Graeme Lang. 1987. Confused Gods: Huang Daxian (Wong Tai Sin) and Huang Yeren at Mt. Luofu. *Journal of the Hong Kong Branch of the Royal Asiatic Society* 27: 74–92.

Rawski, Evelyn S. 1979. *Education and Popular Literacy in Ch'ing China*. Ann Arbor: University of Michigan Press.

Rawson, Jessica. 1996a. *Mysteries of Ancient China*. London: British Museum Press.

——. 1996b. From Ritual Vessels to Pottery Tomb Figures: Changes in Ancient Chinese Burial Practice. *Orientations* 27 (9): 42–49.

Regional Council. 1994. *Chinese Folk Prints*. Exhibition Catalogue. Hong Kong: Regional Council.

Reynolds, Michael. 1999. *Hemingway: The Paris Years*. New York: W. W. Norton and Company.

Roberts, Glenn and Valerie Steele. 1997. The Three Inch Golden Lotus. *Arts of Asia* 27: 69–86.

Ruitenbeek, Klaas. 1992. *Carpentry and Building in Late Imperial China*. Leiden: E. J. Brill.

Sangren, P. Steven. 1986. *History and Magical Power in a Chinese Community*. Stanford: Stanford University Press.

———. 1992. Power and Transcendence in the Ma Tsu Pilgrimages of Taiwan. *American Ethnologist* 20(3): 564–82.

Saso, Michael. 1965. *Chinese Feasts and Customs: A Handbook of the Principal Feasts and Customs of the Lunar Calendar on Taiwan*. Hsinchu: Fu Jen University Language School Press.

———. 1997. Chinese Religions. In *A New Handbook of Living Religions*, edited by John Hinnells. Oxford: Blackwell.

Savidge, Joyce. 1977. *This Is Hong Kong: Temples*. Hong Kong: Government Information Services.

Schoppa, R. Keith. 2000. *The Columbia Guide to Modern Chinese History*. New York: Columbia University Press.

Schwartz, Benjamin I. 1985. *The World of Thought in Ancient China*. Cambridge: The Belknap Press of Harvard University Press.

Scott, Janet Lee. 1980. Action and Meaning: Women's Participation in the Mutual Aid Committees. Unpublished PhD dissertation, Cornell University.

———. 1992. Ritual Paper Products in Contemporary Hong Kong. Paper delivered to the Fairbank Center for East Asian Research, Harvard University, December 11.

———. 1997a. Traditional Values and Modern Meanings in the Paper Offering Industry in Hong Kong. In *Hong Kong: The Anthropology of a Chinese Metropolis*, edited by Grant Evans and Maria Tam. Richmond: Curzon.

———. 1997b. Paper Offerings for the Worship of Tin Hau. Paper presented to the Conference, The Tianhou/Mazu Temple. Chinese University of Hong Kong, Hong Kong, January 3–4.

———. 1997c. Mutual Aid Committee Offices. In *A Documentary History of Hong Kong Society*, edited by David Faure. Hong Kong: Hong Kong University Press.

———. 1999. Good Fortune and Fate Changing: The Fung Che of Hong Kong. Paper presented to the Conference, Tradition and Change: Identity, Gender, and Culture in South China. The Chinese University of Hong Kong, June 3–6.

———. 2002. The Experience of Apprenticeship in the Paper Offering Industry of Hong Kong. Working Paper #5. David C. Lam Institute for East-West Studies. Hong Kong Baptist University.

———. 2004. Sustaining the Dead: Real and replica in food offerings. Paper presented to the Conference, The Production of Food and Foodways in Asia. The Hong Kong Heritage Museum, March 18–20.

Seaman, Gary. 1982. Spirit Money: An Interpretation. *Journal of Chinese Religions* 10: 80–91.

Segawa, Mashisa. 1986. Paper Money, Paper Clothing, and Others. *Material Culture* Number 46 (in Japanese).

Serebrennikov, J. J. 1933. Funeral Money in China. *The China Journal* 18 (4): 191–3.

Shahar, Meir and Robert P. Weller, eds. 1996. Unruly Gods: Divinity and Society in China. Honolulu: University of Hawai'i Press.

Siu, Anthony K. K. 1987. Tam Kung: His Legend and Worship. *Journal of the Hong Kong Branch of the Royal Asiatic Society* 27: 278–9.

Siu, Helen. 1989. Recyling Rituals: Politics and Popular Culture in Contemporary Rural China. In *Unofficial China: Popular Culture and Thought in the People's Republic*, edited by Perry Link, Richard Madsen, and Paul Pickowicz. Boulder: Westview Press.

——. 1996. Remade in Hong Kong: Weaving into the Chinese Cultural Tapestry. In *Unity and Diversity: Local Customs and Identities in China*, edited by Tao Tao Liu and David Faure. Hong Kong: Hong Kong University Press.

Smith, Arthur H. 1894. *Chinese Characteristics*. New York: Fleming H. Revel Company.

——. 1899. *Village Life in China*. New York: Fleming H. Revel Company.

Smith, D. Howard. 1986. Chinese Religions. New York: Holt, Rinehart and Winston.

Smith, Richard J. 1991. *Fortune-Tellers and Philosophers: Divination in Traditional Chinese Society*. Boulder: Westview Press.

——. 1992. *Chinese Almanacs*. New York: Oxford University Press.

——. 1994. *China's Cultural Heritage. The Qing Dynasty, 1644–1912*. Second edition. Boulder: Westview Press.

Smith, Robert J. 1974. Afterword. In *Religion and Ritual in Chinese Society*, edited by Arthur P. Wolf. Stanford: Stanford University Press.

So Kei-rai. 1939. Taiwan Shukyo to Meishin Roshu. Taihoku. Taipei: Shukyo Kenkyukai.

South China Morning Post. 2001. Life's Final Lesson — the Facts of Death. September 3.

South China Morning Post Sunday Post Magazine. 2001. You Only Die Twice. April 1.

Southern District Board. 1996. *History of the Culture of the Southern District*. Hong Kong: Southern District Board (in Chinese).

Sowerby, Arthur de Carle. 1940. *Nature in Chinese Art*. New York: The John Day Company.

Sparks, Douglas. 1976a. The Teochiu: Ethnicity in Urban Hong Kong. *Journal of the Hong Branch of the Royal Asiatic Society* 16: 25–56.

——. 1976b. Interethnic Interaction – a Matter of Definition: Ethnicity in a

Housing Estate in Hong Kong. *Journal of the Hong Kong Branch of the Royal Asiatic Society* 16: 57–80.

Spence, Jonathan. 1990. *The Search for Modern China*. London: Century Hutchison, Ltd.

Spence, Jonathan and Annping Chin. 1996. *The Chinese Century*. New York: Harper Collins.

Stahlberg, R. H. and Ruth Nesi. 1980. *China's Crafts*. New York: Eurasia Press.

Stevens, Keith G. 1972. Three Chinese Deities: Variations on a Theme. *Journal of the Hong Kong Branch of the Royal Asiatic Society* 12: 169–96.

——. 1974. The Craft of God Carving in Singapore. *Journal of the Hong Kong Branch of the Royal Asiatic Society* 14: 68–75.

——. 1977. Under Altars. *Journal of the Hong Kong Branch of the Royal Asiatic Society*. 17: 85–101.

——. 1980. Chinese monasteries, temples, shrines and altars in Hong Kong and Macau. *Journal of the Hong Kong Branch of the Royal Asiatic Society* 20: 1–33.

——. 1997. *Chinese Gods: The Unseen World of Spirits and Demons*. London: Collins and Brown.

——. 2001. *Chinese Mythological Gods*. New York: Oxford University Press.

Strathern, Andrew and Marilyn Strathern. 1971. *Self Decoration in Mount Hagen*. Toronto: University of Toronto Press.

Sullivan, Margaret. 1993. *Can Survive, La: Cottage Industries in High-Rise Singapore*. Singapore: Graham Brash.

Szeto, Naomi Yin Yin. 1993. *Some Chinese Religious Concepts as Reflected in Paper Horses*. Newsletter, Hong Kong Museum of History, October to December, 1993.

——. 1996. *Of Hearts and Hands: Hong Kong's Traditional Trades and Crafts*. Hong Kong: The Urban Council.

Tambiah, S. J. 1968. The Magical Power of Words. *Man*, New Series 3: 175–208.

Tapp, Nicholas. 2001. The Barbara Ward Lecture. Post-Colonial Anthropology: Local Identities and Virtual Nationality in the Hong Kong–China Region. *Journal of the Hong Kong Branch of the Royal Asiatic Society* 39: 165–94.

Teiser, Stephen F. 1986. Ghosts and Ancestors in Medieval Chinese Religion: The Yu-lan-p'en Festival as Mortuary Ritual. *History of Religions* 26: 47–67.

——. 1988. *The Ghost Festival in Medieval China*. Princeton: Princeton University Press.

——. 1989. The Ritual behind the Opera: A Fragmentary Ethnography of the Ghost Festival, a.d. 400–1900. In *Ritual Opera, Operatic Ritual*, edited by David Johnson. Berkeley: University of California Institute of East Asian Studies.

——. 1993. The Growth of Purgatory. In *Religion and Society in T'ang and Sung China*, edited by Patricia Buckley Ebrey and Peter N. Gregory. Honolulu: University of Hawaii Press.

———. 1996. Introduction. In *Religions of China in Practice*, edited by Donald S. Lopez. Princeton: Princeton University Press.

Thompson, Laurence G. 1988. Dream Divination and Chinese Popular Religion. *Journal of Chinese Religions* 16: 73–82.

———. 1989. On the Prehistory of Hell in China. *Journal of Chinese Religions* 17: 27–41.

Thompson, Stuart E. 1988. Death, Food, and Fertility. In *Death Ritual in Late Imperial and Modern China*, edited by James L. Watson and Evelyn S. Rawski. Berkeley: University of California Press.

Tong Chee Kiong. 1993. The Inheritance of the Dead: Mortuary Rituals among the Chinese in Singapore. *Southeast Asian Journal of Social Science* 21: 130–58.

Topley, Marjorie. 1953. Paper Charms and Prayer Sheets as Adjuncts to Chinese Worship. *Journal of the Malayan Branch of the Royal Asiatic Society* 26: 63–81.

———. 1954. Chinese Women's Vegetarian Houses in Singapore. *Journal of the Malayan Branch of the Royal Asiatic Society* 27 (1): 51–67.

———. 1963. The Great Way of Former Heaven: A Group of Chinese Secret Religious Sects. *Bulletin of the School of Oriental and African Studies* 26: 362–92.

———. 1966. Chinese Occasional Rites in Hong Kong. In *Some Traditional Chinese Ideas and Conceptions in Hong Kong Social Life Today*. Hong Kong: The Hong Kong Branch of the Royal Asiatic Society.

———. 1970. Chinese Traditional Ideas and the Treatment of Disease: Two Examples from Hong Kong. *Man* (N.S.) 5: 421–37.

———. 1974. Cosmic Antagonisms: A Mother-Child Syndrome. In *Religion and Ritual in Chinese Society*, edited by Arthur Wolf. Stanford: Stanford University Press.

———. 1976. Chinese Traditional Etiology and Methods of Cure in Hong Kong. In *Asian Medical Systems: A Comparative Study*, edited by Charles Leslie. Berkeley: University of California Press.

Townsend, William John. 1890. *Robert Morrison, the Pioneer of Chinese Missions*. London: Partridge.

Tseng Yu-ho. 1977. *Chinese Folk Art II*. Honolulu: University of Hawaii Press.

Turner, Victor. 1970. Betwixt and Between: The Liminal Period in Rites of Passage. In *Man Makes Sense: A Reader in Modern Cultural Anthropology*, edited by Eugene A. Hammel and William S. Simmons. Boston: Little, Brown and Company.

Vittachi, Nury. 2002. Travelers' Tales. *Far Eastern Economic Review*, April 18.

Waltner, Anne. 1990. *Getting an Heir*. Honolulu: University of Hawaii Press.

Wang Shucun. 1992. *A Pictorial Album of Chinese Folk Art*. Hangzhou: Zhejiang Literature and Art Publishing House (in Chinese).

Wang Sung-hsing. 1974. Taiwanese Architecture and the Supernatural. In *Religion and Ritual in Chinese Society*, edited by Arthur Wolf. Stanford: Stanford University Press.

Ward, Barbara. 1954. A Hong Kong Fishing Village. *Journal of Oriental Studies* 1 (1): 195–214.

———. 1965. Varieties of the Conscious Model: The Fishermen of South China. In *The Relevance of Models for Social Anthropology*, edited by Michael Banton. London: Tavistock Publications.

———. 1966. Sociological Self-Awareness: Some Uses of the Conscious Models. *Man* 1 (2): 201–15.

———. 1967. Chinese Fishermen in Hong Kong: Their Post-Peasant Economy. In *Social Organization: Essays Presented to Raymond Firth*, edited by Maurice Freedman. London: Frank Cass and Co.

———. 1979. Not Merely Players: Drama, Art and Ritual in Traditional China. *Man* 14: 18–39.

———. 1983. Rediscovering Our Social and Cultural Heritage in the New Territories. *Journal of the Hong Kong Branch of the Royal Asiatic Society* 20: 116–24.

———. 1985a. Regional Operas and Their Audiences: Evidence from Hong Kong. In *Popular Culture in Late Imperial China*, edited by David Johnson, Andrew Nathan, and Evelyn S. Rawski. Berkeley: University of California Press.

———. 1985b. *Through Other Eyes*. Hong Kong: The Chinese University Press.

Ward, Barbara and Joan Law. 1993. *Chinese Festivals in Hong Kong*. Hong Kong: The Guidebook Company Ltd.

Waters, Daniel D. 1991. Chinese Funerals: A Case Study. *Journal of the Hong Kong Branch of the Royal Asiatic Society* 31: 104–34.

Watson, James L. 1976. Anthropological Analyses of Chinese Religion. *The China Quarterly* 66: 355–64.

———. 1985. Standardizing the Gods: The Promotion of T'ien Hau ("Empress of Heaven") Along the South China Coast, 960–1960. In *Popular Culture in Late Imperial China*, edited by David Johnson, Andrew J. Nathan, and Evelyn Rawski. Berkeley: University of California Press.

———. 1987. From the Common Pot: Feasting with Equals in Chinese Society. *Anthropos* 82: 389–401.

———. 1988a. The Structure of Chinese Funerary Rites: Elementary Forms, Ritual Sequence, and the Primacy of Performance. In *Death Ritual in Late Imperial and Modern China*, edited by James L. Watson and Evelyn S. Rawski. Berkeley: University of California Press.

———. 1988b. Funeral Specialists in Cantonese Society: Pollution, Performance, and Social Hierarchy. In *Death Ritual in Late Imperial and Modern China*, edited by James L. Watson and Evelyn S. Rawski. Berkeley: University of California Press.

——. 1991. The Renegotiation of Cultural Identity in the Post-Mao Era: An Anthropological Perspective. In *Perspectives on China: Four Anniversaries*. Edited by Kenneth Lieberthal. Armonk: M.E. Sharpe, Inc.

——. 1993. Rites or Beliefs? The Construction of a Unified Culture in Late Imperial China. In *China's Quest for National Identity*, edited by Lowell Dittmer and Samuel S. Kim. Ithaca: Cornell University Press.

——. 1996. Fighting with Operas: Processionals, Politics, and the Spectre of Violence in Rural Hong Kong. In *The Politics of Cultural Performance: Essays in Honor of Abner Cohen*, edited by David Parkin, Lionel Caplan, and Humphrey Fisher. London: Berghahn Books.

Watson, James L. and Rubie S. Watson. 2004. *Village Life in Hong Kong: Politics, Gender, and Ritual in the New Territories*. Hong Kong: The Chinese University Press.

Webb, Richard. 1994. Earth God and Village Shrine in the New Territories. *Journal of the Hong Kong Branch of the Royal Asiatic Society* 34: 183–93.

Weller, Robert P. 1987. *Unities and Diversities in Chinese Religion*. Seattle: University of Washington Press.

Western, Neil and Carrie Chan. 2003. The Dispossessed. *South China Morning Post*, May 24.

Whyte, Martin King. 1988. Death in the PRC. In *Death Ritual in Late Imperial and Modern China*, edited by James L. Watson and Evelyn S. Rawski. Berkeley: University of California Press.

Whyte, Martin King and William Parish. 1984. *Urban Life in Contemporary China*. Chicago: University of Chicago Press.

Wieger, L. 1913. *Moral Tenets and Customs in China*. Ho Kien Fu: Catholic Mission Press.

——. 1927. *A History of the Religious Beliefs and Philosophical Opinions in China from the Beginning to the Present Time*. New York: Arno Press. Reprint, Paragon Book, 1969.

Williams, C. A. S. [1941] 1976 *Outlines of Chinese Symbolism and Art Motives*. New York: Dover Publications.

Williams, Edward. 1935. The Worship of Lei Tsu, Patron Saint of Silk Workers. *Journal of the North China Branch of the Royal Asiatic Society* 66: 1–14.

Wolf, Arthur. 1970. Chinese Kinship and Mourning Dress. In *Family and Kinship in Chinese Society*, edited by Maurice Freedman. Stanford: Stanford University Press.

——. 1974. Gods, Ghosts and Ancestors. In *Religion and Ritual in Chinese Society*. Stanford: Stanford University Press.

——. ed. 1978. *Studies in Chinese Society*. Stanford: Stanford University Press.

Wong Siu-lun. 1986. Modernization and Chinese Culture in Hong Kong. *The China* Quarterly 106: 306–25.

Wu, David and Sidney Cheung. 2002. *The Globalism of Chinese Food.* Honolulu: University of Hawaii Press.

Yang, C. K. 1994. *Religion in Chinese Society.* Taipei: SMC Publishing Inc.

Yang, Martin. 1945. *A Chinese Village.* New York: Columbia University Press.

Yetts, Percival. 1941. Notes on Flower Symbolism in China. *Journal of the Royal Asiatic Society* 1: 1–21.

Yeung, A. 1991. *Sik Sik Yuen.* Hong Kong: America Advertising Limited.

Zhang Li-hua. 1997. Aspects of the Apprenticeship System of Craft and Trade Guilds in Beijing during the late Qing Dynasty and early Republican Era. In *Guild-hall and Government: An Exploration of Power, Control and Resistance in Britain and England,* edited by Brian A. Ranson. David C. Lam Institute for East-West Studies Occasional Paper. Hong Kong: Hong Kong Baptist University.

Zhu Shing Leung, ed. 1997. *Old Photos: A Series of Picture Albums.* Nanjing: Jiangsu Art Publishing.

INDEX